T0340381

"Customer loyalty is the golden fleece of retailing. Great efforts are required to obtain it but once gained it gives authority and advantage for the owner. Cristina Ziliani and Marco Ieva provide us with insights based on sound theory and evidence on how to capture and use this golden fleece. They point out that the development of tools to … manage loyalty is not new in retail management, but importantly, now, there are new tools and concepts based on new data sources that change the ways to generate and exploit customer loyalty. The book proves an excellent guide through these new approaches, examining the why and how of their use, and their benefits and problems."

— Professor John Dawson, Emeritus Professor
at the University of Edinburgh and the
University of Stirling

"A book that is really worth reading for at least three reasons. First, it takes the reader on a one hundred year long journey through the evolution of loyalty marketing, from the Green Stamps to the digital (branded) wallets. Second, the book is a very interesting and involving reading thanks to a balanced mix of theory and practice, in which the richness of details (a great value added) does never sacrifice the whole picture. Third, Cristina Ziliani's expertise on loyalty marketing is a guarantee."

— Professor Chiara Mauri, Professor of Marketing at
LIUC and SDA Bocconi

"Ziliani and Ieva, through a deep analysis of the evolving loyalty practices worldwide, give us precious food for thought. A book to be kept on every marketer desk for years to come."

— Stefano Piazzolla, Marketing Information Manager, Esselunga

"This is a welcome and very timely contribution to a fast-moving subject in an omnichannel world. The insights build on extensive experience from twenty years' research and engagement through the Università di Parma's Loyalty Observatory and the team led by Professor Ziliani."

— Professor Jonathan Reynolds, Academic Director,
Oxford Institute of Retail Management,
Oxford University

"The book presents an intriguing and wide analysis of loyalty management challenges in the digital age. The authors drive the reader along a longitudinal path: from the first reward programs proposed by the supermarket chains to the last AI-based CRM approaches. They show that in this journey – even if the relational tools used by companies are constantly changing over time – the increase of customer loyalty constantly remains the main goal for brands and retailers. The contents of the book are very insightful for researchers, but also for managers and professionals, who intend to discover in a nutshell 'the roots and the frontiers of loyalty management'."

— Prof. Sandro Castaldo, Professor of Marketing, Bocconi University

LOYALTY MANAGEMENT

In this insightful new text, Cristina Ziliani and Marco Ieva trace the evolution of thinking and practice in loyalty management. From trading stamps to Amazon Prime and Alibaba 88 Membership, they present a fresh take on the tools, strategies and skills that underpin its key significance in marketing today.

Loyalty management is increasingly identified with the design and management of a quality customer experience in the journey across the many touchpoints that connect the customer with the brand. Evaluating the research on best practice and offering concrete examples from industry, the authors argue that existing schemes and systems are not just things of the past but should be the optimal starting point for companies needing to foster customer loyalty in an omnichannel world.

Drawing on 20 years of experience in research, consulting and teaching, the authors have compiled a unique research-based practice-oriented text. It will guide marketers, business leaders and students through the changes in marketing thought and practice on loyalty management as well as offering practical guidance on the skills and capabilities that companies need if they want to be successful at delivering essential loyalty-driving customer experiences.

Cristina Ziliani is Professor of Marketing at the University of Parma, Italy. She lectures on loyalty management at leading universities and business events around the world, including Japan, USA, UK, France, Spain and Thailand. She is also the scientific director of the Osservatorio Fedeltà UniPR (Loyalty Observatory).

Marco Ieva is a postdoctoral research fellow in marketing at the University of Parma, Italy, where he lectures in customer relationship management and customer analytics. He is also a senior researcher at the Osservatorio Fedeltà UniPR (Loyalty Observatory).

LOYALTY MANAGEMENT

From Loyalty Programs to Omnichannel Customer Experiences

Cristina Ziliani and Marco Ieva

Routledge
Taylor & Francis Group

LONDON AND NEW YORK

First published 2020
by Routledge
2 Park Square, Milton Park, Abingdon, Oxon OX14 4RN

and by Routledge
52 Vanderbilt Avenue, New York, NY 10017

Routledge is an imprint of the Taylor & Francis Group, an informa business

© 2020 Cristina Ziliani and Marco Ieva

The right of Cristina Ziliani and Marco Ieva to be identified as authors of this work has been asserted by them in accordance with sections 77 and 78 of the Copyright, Designs and Patents Act 1988.

British Library Cataloguing in Publication Data
A catalogue record for this book is available from the British Library

Library of Congress Cataloging-in-Publication Data
A catalog record has been requested for this book

ISBN: 978-0-367-07762-4 (hbk)
ISBN: 978-0-367-21072-4 (pbk)
ISBN: 978-0-429-02266-1 (ebk)

Typeset in Bembo
by Taylor & Francis Books

CONTENTS

ILLUSTRATIONS

Figures

Tables

INTRODUCTION

A central proposition frames the rationale and content of the book currently in your hands: securing customer loyalty is a priority for businesses. In today's world, marketing is largely based on the goal of earning long-term loyal customers, and long-standing loyalty tools – transformed by the information revolution into data-rich, interactive touchpoints – have become the enablers of loyalty-oriented and customer-centred omnichannel strategies that are shaping the consumer world. This book discusses the changes in society and markets that have made the goal of loyalty so central and examines how this has been reflected in the evolution of marketing paradigms and business practices throughout the world.

In both the academic and business worlds, loyalty management has grown in stature. What makes and how to make customers loyal has been debated in lecture halls, discussed at conferences, designed in boardrooms and played out on shop floors. The rise of digital has added a new online dynamic and along with it, inevitable challenges and opportunities. Over more than a century, a variety of loyalty tools and practices have arisen and diffused across industries and countries. The paraphernalia of loyalty management has taken manifold forms from tickets, tokens and stamps to plastic cards, vouchers and coupons to digital wallets, wish lists and personalized journeys. And it's not only aimed at customers – ensuring the loyalty of channel partners and strengthening business-to-business (B2B) relationships is just as essential in today's interconnected business environment. The journey of loyalty management traces a path that leads from Green Stamps to the Tesco Clubcard to Amazon Prime and the Starbucks wallet. Managing both customer and partner loyalty has shifted from running programmes to managing relationships to curating experiences.

Over the past three decades loyalty management has undergone three phases. From 1980 to the end of the twentieth century, it meant running a loyalty programme. Since 2000, companies have shifted their focus towards harnessing the 'invisible' advantages of such programmes: the insight they offer into the world of their customers, the opportunity this gives them to develop and manage positive relationships with those customers, and the value created by being able to use scheme data to inform decision-making and shape targeted marketing efforts to retain, upsell, cross-sell or reactivate their customer base. Today, in 2019, we are entering a new phase. Loyalty management is increasingly now being identified with the design and management of a quality customer experience across the various touchpoints that connect the customer and the brand and through which the customer journey evolves.

Overall, loyalty management is, and has always been, a continuous effort to create and expand a space of *free circulation* for the customer, in which she is identified as an individual with unique characteristics derived from data collected at various touchpoints, and to provide superior value based on individual preferences and needs in doing so. The advances made in recent years in technology have only accelerated and expanded this trend. Tools and methods derived from data science and artificial intelligence have improved the ways in which customers can be identified and tracked across an ever-increasing variety of touchpoints and have given brands the means to reach new heights of sophistication in the personalizing of interactions, offers, conversations and environments. The information revolution made it possible for companies to collect, analyse and use vast amounts of individual customer data upon which more accurate marketing decisions could be made, thus helping to bring about the shift in emphasis towards customer relationship management (CRM) techniques. Customer-centric measures of success, such as share of wallet, retention rates and customer lifetime value, soon entered the boardroom and are today valued very highly by business leaders and investors, as the chapter by dunnhumby on customer-based decision-making illustrates.

The rise of ubiquitous digital technology was profound. Not only is print media, such as coupons, flyers, cards and direct mail, increasingly delivered to your mobile phone screen, traditional one-size-fits-all price cuts and special offers are now personalized to individuals and sequenced to nudge the customer towards brand and store loyalty. New business models have emerged centred on price or loyalty promotion: daily deals platforms, promotion aggregators, mobile rewards platforms, curated subscription models, loyalty currency exchanges and wallets, to mention but a few. The environments in which we consume products, services and experiences have become intelligent, mixed realities, simultaneously operating offline and online, where identified customers can move freely. New digital services such as click and collect, persistent shopping baskets, wish lists and in-store virtual catalogues interweave touchpoints and bridge channels, providing the customer with a unified and seamless experience with the end goal of retaining them, making them loyal. We now live in an omnichannel environment.

The customer experience management (CEM) and omnichannel management frameworks that have emerged in this environment aim to help managers eliminate barriers across channels so that customers might have a seamless experience in which they are recognized and served based on their individual preferences, needs and loyalties. Central to this is understanding and managing how they perceive their interaction with all the different touchpoints they encounter in offline and online channels. The two frameworks share a common goal: achieving customer loyalty. Companies are now wrestling with how to organize resources to provide such loyalty-building omnichannel experiences. This book provides some empirical responses to this challenge and demonstrates that the means actually already exist within most companies. Companies that already have loyalty programmes and CRM models, and thus the people and skills required to execute them, already have in place the building blocks of omnichannel CEM. They may also already believe in the principles and philosophy that drives it. In any case, an overhaul is not generally necessary – existing loyalty programmes and CRM systems are optimal starting points.

The aims of this book are twofold. First, to assist the reader in navigating the changes that have shaped marketing thought and practice on loyalty management. Second, to offer guidance on the skills and capabilities that companies will require if they want to be successful at delivering omnichannel customer experiences that drive loyalty. We believe there is something here for everyone, whether you are a marketer, business leader or student, or simply someone curious about how loyalty works in a consumer setting. We draw on 20 years of scientific research, consultancy and education to try to bring a fresh take on concepts seen by some as buzzwords and by others as irrelevant outside of a marketing department. We believe they are neither. Rather, loyalty programme, CRM, CEM and omnichannel are steps in the evolutionary process of any successful, value-creating organization. They are lived by every customer and business partner. And each provides the foundation for the next. Nothing is lost, but everything is transformed: to take the first steps towards omnichannel transformation, companies need to look no further than their 'old' loyalty scheme. It starts from there.

THE LOYALTY OBSERVATORY

The Osservatorio Fedeltà (Loyalty Observatory) was created in 1999 at the University of Parma with the goal of studying the adoption of loyalty management and the use of customer data in European retailing and overseas. Tracking of the loyalty practices of over 130 retail groups began in 1997 and provided the foundation for our understanding of the loyalty management phenomenon between 1980 and 2000, when we expanded the monitoring to loyalty activities in other industries.

The Loyalty Observatory is based within the Department of Economics and Management, where it draws on over 30 years of research in the fields of marketing, retail management, channel relationships and trade marketing. From the beginning, our goal has always been to contribute to the development of a customer loyalty culture among Italian managers across all industries and support managers, researchers and students interested in developing research projects or training or simply knowing more about loyalty management and customer relationship management (CRM). At our annual workshop, where more than 400 managers, marketing practitioners and academics gather together in Parma, the Observatory's research is disseminated among companies in the consumer goods manufacturing, retailing and services sectors.

The Observatory develops research and training projects for companies on loyalty, CRM and customer experience management. We also promote theses and dissertations that result from close cooperation between firms and students. In 2015 we celebrated 15 years of our annual workshop and its related activities and by 2019, our reach had grown significantly. As this book goes to press, the workshop's record makes for impressive reading: nearly 3,000 delegates (representing 1,400 companies), over 150 speakers, 24 sponsors, and more than 500 student workshop organizers. We are proud of the work that has been achieved: over 100 master's theses on loyalty, more than 60 academic papers and five books.

Our partners and sponsors

The Observatory Steering Committee is formed of managers from companies that aim to support the Observatory in its research and dissemination activity. Dialogue is established with the Observatory team to exchange ideas, develop projects, create events and recruit talented graduates and professionals in the fields of loyalty and CRM. Our partners help shape the Observatory research agenda and are visible at our events, on our website and in our publications. Over the years, we have partnered with distinguished players in the fields of marketing intelligence, customer data, loyalty, CRM, promotion platforms, consulting and services. dunnhumby, which contributes a chapter to this book, has been a sponsor and close partner for several years. We continue to enjoy long-time partnerships with Amilon, Brand Loyalty, Catalina, Comarch, *Promotion Magazine*, Kettydo+ and SINT, and Nielsen has partnered with us on consumer studies for over a decade.

The annual workshop

Since 1999 the Observatory has showcased its research at its annual workshop in Parma. The format has been established over the years as a full day of research presentations, successful case histories, industry roundtable discussions and a networking lunch. The theme of the workshop differs each year:

2018 Loyalty in the Age of Experience
2017 Loyalty Marketing Evolution: International Stories and Leaders
2016 Loyalty Disruption? Emotions, Big Data and New Players
2015 15 Years of Loyalty Marketing: What's Next?
2014 From Print to Digital: What Happens to Loyalty?
2013 Growing Through loyalty in Times of Economic Crisis
2012 Brand Loyalty Strategies: From Macro to Micro Approaches
2011 The Value of Loyalty in the Choice Overload Age
2010 The Future of Loyalty Marketing: New Models and Technologies
2009 Ten Years of Loyalty Marketing in European Retailing
2008 Channel Loyalty: Making Channel Partners Loyal
2007 Innovation in Promotions
2006 Partnerships for Value Creation
2005 Creating Value with Customer Information
2004 Measuring Promotion Effectiveness
2003 Data Mining for Value Creation and Loyalty
2001 Creating Relationships in the Internet Age
1999 Value from Customer Relationships

Our research projects

2018 The Market for Loyalty Services and Products
2017 Omnichannel Loyalty Management

ACKNOWLEDGEMENTS

This book is testament to two decades of work conducted at the Loyalty Observatory and we would like to thank the people and organizations that have supported, advised, worked with and inspired us throughout this period. Our first thought goes to Jonathan Reynolds and Richard Cuthbertson at the Saïd Business School, University of Oxford. It was there in 1998, while Cristina was completing her doctorate, that she first became interested in research on loyalty programmes. Back in Parma, Professor Gianpiero Lugli saw how promising this research stream was, especially for retailers, and pushed her to delve into it. In the same year, John Dawson at University of Edinburgh started supporting Cristina in her research efforts, providing advice, contacts and research opportunities. John has become a very dear friend.

We thank Oracle, WincorNixdorf, ICTeam and Buongiorno, who supported the early editions of the Observatory Conference and our first website www.partnership4loyalty.com, and Seri Group for creating the CRM Award, which was assigned to distinguished CRM campaigns during the Observatory Conference from 2005 to 2008. We'd also like to acknowledge our current partners (Amilon, Brand Loyalty, Catalina Marketing, Comarch, Kettydo+, *Promotion Magazine* and SINT) and former partners of the last three years (Doveconviene, Epipoli, EYC, Klikkapromo-Pazzi per le offerte, Payback, T-Frutta and Valassis) for sponsoring the Observatory and enriching our work through precious dialogue. A special mention goes to Filippo Genzini whose advice and friendship continues to be as indispensable to us as his work on coordinating sponsors and partnerships.

Special thanks go to our many friends working in the field of market research who are always ready to collaborate and share their expertise: Maria Grazia Bolognesi, Christian Centonze, Debora Costi, Chiara De Maio, Lorenzo Facchinotti, Gabriella Bergaglio and Cristina Colombo, Roberto Borghini, Enrico Billi and Stefano Di Palma.

We have benefited from the contribution of over 150 speakers at conferences held by the Loyalty Observatory and at lectures on loyalty marketing and CRM hosted by the University of Parma. The conference has seen over 2,900 attendees from almost 1,400 companies, some of whom have been with us since the first iteration in 1999. Their input has been immensely helpful, as have the hundreds of managers and experts who responded to our surveys, dedicated their time and shared their ideas with us.

Special thoughts go to: Bruno Aceto, Maurizio Alberti, Odoardo Ambroso, Augusta Angelino, Nicola Antonelli, Stefano Araldi, Filippo Arroni, Massimo Baggi, Enrico Barboglio, Lorenza Bassetti, Stephane Baizeau, Marc Battailler, Elena Bernardelli, Chiara Bignazzi, Maurizio Bonfante, Graham Bradley, Alessandro Bucich, Giuseppe Calabrini, Furio Camillo, Fausto Caprini, Carlo Caranza, Rosa Carbone, Alessandra Carnelli, Valentina Carnevali, Sergio Cassingena, Roberto Catanzaro, Luciano Cavazzana, Daniele Cazzani, Andrea Cerioli, Manuel Chinchio, David Ciancio, Ruggero Colombo, Davide Cozzarolo, Donnino Dalla Turca, Marta Dall'Arche, Francesco Daveri, John Dawson, Romolo De Camillis, Gianfranco Delfini, Antonio De Martini, Andrea Demodena, Barbara Del Neri, Anna Del Piccolo, Francesco Del Porto, Pietro De Nardis, Matteo De Tomasi, Gabriele Dorfmann, Andrea Duilio, Roberto Falcinelli, Claudia Filippini, Marco Filipponi, Stefano Fiorentino, Michele Fioroni, Maura Franchi, Valeria Freschi, Marco Formisano, Valentina Francot, Alberto Frau, Fulvio Furbatto, Monica Gagliardi, Ludovico Galimberti, Marco Gandolfi, Michela Giacomini, Gaetano Giannetto, Sharon Glass, Claudia Golinelli, Enzo Grassi, Angelo Grisolia, Alberto Gualtieri, Michele Guerra, Paolo Iabichino, Laura Lavizzari, Luca Leoni, Edoardo Loasses, Paolo Lucci, Luca Luminoso, Irene Lunelli, Valeria Maniscalco, Luigi Mansani, Giovanna Manzi, Michele Marchigiani, Stefano Masi, Stefano Mazza, Patrizia Meneghini, Marco Metti, Paolo Michelis, Roberta Mincione, Sara Molteni, Valentina Motta, Sergio Müller, Federico Mussetto, Bianca Mutti, Anja Nachtwey, Kamila Niekraszewicz, Paolo Palomba, Mara Panajia, Silvio Panetta, Miriam Panico, Federica Paterno, Giles Pavey, Ambra Pazzagli, Simone Pescatore, Davide Pellegrini, Alessandro Petazzi, Giuliano Pezzano, Ferruccio Piazzoni, Enrico Piccirilli, Jeroen Pietryga, Marco Pisani, Mauro Poli, Stefano Poli, Osvaldo Ponchia, Stefano Portu, Stefano Quartullo, Massimo Rabuffo, Eleonora Radici, Stefania Ranieri, Umberto Rapetto, Marco Ravagnan, Ornella Raveane, Fabio Regazzoni, Jonathan Reynolds, Alexander Rittweger, Federico Rocco, Valentina Rocco, Samuele Ronchin, Diego Rosso, Luigi Rubinelli, Giorgio Santambrogio, Marco Santambrogio, Massimo Schembri, Ansgar Schneider, Joan Schwoerer, Henry Sichel, Vincenzo Sinibaldi, Giuseppe Staglianò, Roberto Stanco, Bart Steenken, Davide Surace, Tiziano Tassi, Christoph Teller, Daniele Tirelli, Susi Tondini, Alessandra Tosi, Melissa Tosi, Angelo Tosoni, Davide Vegetti, Andrea Verri, Marino Vignati, Barbara Vignola, Lucio Volponi, Antonio Votino, Alvise Zanardi, Sergio Zani, Matteo Zenoni, Filippo Zuffada, Giuseppe 'Pino' Zuliani, and to all fellow members of the scientific committees of *Promotion Magazine*, the DMA Italia Awards and the Promotion Awards. We would also like to specifically thank Andrea Demodena for his ongoing support and valuable advice throughout the years.

Thank you to our friends and colleagues at the Academy of Marketing Science, the EAERCD, the NBPL and the CERR conferences, and of the Italian SIM and SIMA, for consistently stimulating our thoughts about loyalty over the years. We are grateful to the Hartman Center for Sales, Advertising and Marketing at the Duke University in North Carolina for seeing the value in the study of sales promotions and awarding Cristina with a research grant to work on B2B loyalty programmes. We are grateful too to Professor Dirk Van den Poel at the University of Ghent for his availability and support throughout the years. Marco gained invaluable knowledge and experience during his time there, where he had the opportunity to learn state-of-the-art techniques in customer relationship management (CRM) and market research from Prof. Van den Poel, Prof. Michael Ballings, Prof. Dauwe Vercamer, Prof. Andrey Volkov, Prof. Mario Pandelaere and Prof. Jeroen D'Haen. We thank them all. We also thank our colleagues at the Department of Economics and Management at the University of Parma, with whom we share a passion for research and teaching. We are especially grateful to our friends and colleagues, Maura Franchi and Alberto Guenzi, with whom Cristina shares a love for sociology and the history of marketing.

We also acknowledge the hard work of the junior researchers who spent periods with the Observatory, long and short: Chiara D'Onofrio, Annalisa Guarnieri, Francesco Termite, Elena Mosca, Alberto Frau, Chiara Bonaretti Alessandri, Virginia Bonaretti, Nicola Pizzolato, Roberto Boniburini, Davide Bessi, Elisabetta Mariano, Rita Giulia Rizzitello, Jessica Borsi, Greta Pescarossa, Marcello Fantuzzi, Fabio Fichera, Gabriele Longo, Valentina Spinozzi, and indeed our students, who make the Loyalty Observatory annual workshop possible every year, organizing each and every aspect of it with ceaseless commitment and enthusiasm. Special thanks must go to those who work more closely with us on loyalty and marketing research: Silvia Bellini, Maria Grazia Cardinali, Ida D'attoma, Marta Frasquet, Juan Carlos Gàzquez-Abad and Chieko Minami. As teachers, our students help make our work meaningful and Cristina has been the proud director of the Trade and Consumer Marketing master's course at the University of Parma since 2012. More than a hundred of you have graduated with theses on aspects of loyalty, CRM and customer experience and for many of you it was the beginning of a sparkling career. We are very proud of you.

In bringing this book to the world, we are indebted to Jacqueline Curthoys and her team at Routledge who took on our proposal and helped see it into print. We'd also like to thank Jon Wilcox who worked with us on our original pitch and the early drafts of this book, helping us to clarify our ideas and improve our expression. His efforts have been invaluable and we could not have accomplished this book without his expertise, acumen and patience. Several anonymous reviewers helped us fine-tune our thesis and we are grateful for all the feedback we received in preparing the manuscript for publication. We reserve a special thanks to Michela Giacomini and Miriam Panico of dunnhumby for contributing a chapter to this book and we are grateful to dunnhumby for continuing to share ideas and give their time and effort to collaborating with us on developing an understanding of loyalty. Genuine progress is made when academia and business work together and common efforts are made to advance both theoretical insight and practical application.

Our final thanks go to our families and partners whose encouragement and patience gave us the time and the strength to accomplish this book.

Cristina Ziliani and Marco Ieva

ABBREVIATIONS

ACORN	A Classification of Residential Neighborhoods
AI	Artificial intelligence
AMA	American Marketing Association
B2B	Business-to-business
B2C	Business-to-consumer
CHAID	Chi-square automatic interaction detector
CEM	Customer experience management
CRM	Customer relationship management
DEM	Direct emailing
DLT	Distributed ledger technology
EDLP	Everyday low price
EDV	Everyday value
EPOS	Electronic point-of-sale
EXQ	Customer experience quality
FMCG	Fast-moving consumer goods
GDPR	General Data Protection Regulation
IAT	Intelligent agent technology
KPI	Key performance indicator
LMPS	Loyalty management products and services
LP	Loyalty programme
LMUK	Loyalty Management UK
MSR	My Starbucks Rewards
NDL	National Demographics & Lifestyles
POP	Point-of-purchase
RFM	Recency, frequency, monetary

ROI	Return on investment
SERVQUAL	Service quality measure
SKU	Stock keeping unit
WER	Word error rate

AUTHOR BIOGRAPHIES

Cristina Ziliani, PhD, is full professor of marketing at the University of Parma. She lectures on loyalty management at leading universities and business events around the world, including Japan, US, UK, France, Spain and Thailand. Her research focuses on loyalty marketing, customer relationship management, promotions and customer experience. She is the author of several books and numerous publications and is the scientific director of the Osservatorio Fedeltà UniPR (Loyalty Observatory) since 1999.

Marco Ieva, PhD, is a postdoctoral research fellow in marketing at the University of Parma where he lectures in customer relationship management and customer analytics. He is also a senior researcher at the Loyalty Observatory. He has been a visiting scholar at the University of Ghent, where he worked on analytical customer relationship management and marketing models. His research spans media effectiveness, retailing, customer relationship management, loyalty marketing and customer experience.

Contributors

Michela Giacomini has 20 years of experience in the customer data world, having worked for 10 years with dunnhumby and 10 years with SAS before that. Michela leads a team of client managers who runs projects with all new dunnhumby partners in Europe. Her objective is to deliver recognizable value to retailers and to dunnhumby, through the company's vision of using data and science to delight customers, earn loyalty and grow partners' sales. She runs strategic pricing, category management, CRM and loyalty projects. Michela has a solid statistical and analytical background, having previously worked as an insight director and analytical consultant.

Miriam Panico is a Customer Engagement Manager EMEA at dunnhumby. With over 10 years of loyalty and CRM experience in the retail business, she consults and supports the launch and transformation of loyalty programmes, as well as on the definition of lifecycle marketing strategies leveraged by customer insights. She has worked with European clients such as Tesco, Gruppo Pam, CRAI and other European retailers, as well as FMCG companies. She previously worked as a communications manager at ENIT, the Agenzia Nazionale del Turismo (Italian Government Tourist Board).

1

LOYALTY AND MARKETING

Cristina Ziliani

Amazon and Alibaba: loyalty-centred strategies

The concept of customer loyalty has long been at the heart of marketing. But its centrality, as well as understandings of what precisely it is have varied and evolved as much as the tools, strategies and technologies that companies have employed to achieve it have. It can seem like the Holy Grail: something to do with the customer's attitude or revealed behaviour, something shaped by an individual's context and circumstances, something that manifests in repeat buying and recommendation – ultimately something that can help a company keep existing customers and acquire new ones. But although it may seem complex and multifaceted to some, and downright elusive to others, it has increasingly dawned on the business world that pursuing customer loyalty as a strategic objective is worth doing. And as more and more companies adopt loyalty-centred strategies, the results are paying off. We need look no further than two companies who are currently leading the way: Amazon and Alibaba.

Amazon Prime and customer insight

In October 2018 Amazon opened its first 4-star store in New York City. This is relevant for several reasons. First, it is a testimony to the need for retailers to operate multiple channels, and specifically for purely e-commerce players to develop a physical presence and weave it with their online operations in ways that are more and more integrated or 'omnichannel'. Second, the new store mirrors two of Amazon's greatest strengths online: its star-rating system and customer reviews. Customers visiting the 4-star store discover that merchandise is displayed according to rating (all are rated four stars and above, hence the store's name) or by other categories such as 'Frequently Bought Together', 'Most-Wished-For' or 'Trending Around NYC' (Howland, 2018).

Since the emergence of e-commerce in the 1980s and 1990s, the online shopping process has been refined and shaped around features that customers today find familiar, such as wish lists, reviews, rankings and recommendations based on previous purchases or derived from similar customers' shopping histories. All this has been applied to the store layout and product displays in the Amazon 4-star store. Amazon has thus applied the insight gained from analysing customer shopping behaviour in one channel (online) to the design of the customer experience in another (in-store), creating a consistent look and feel of the brand across channels. The third reason why Amazon's new store is relevant to our purposes has to do with loyalty. Every item in the store is accompanied by an electronic shelf label, a kind of digital price tag. The label gives the name of the product, its star rating and number of customer reviews. Beneath that, two prices are given: the regular price and the discounted price for Amazon Prime customers. Non-members can register there and then in the store for a 30-day free trial subscription. Thus the launch of the 4-star store is yet another move by Amazon to acquire new members to its Prime loyalty scheme.

Amazon Prime was launched in 2005 and grew to over 100 million members by 2019, attracting interest in the now flourishing subscription model and demonstrating its pivotal role in sustaining Amazon's growth. Users gain access to free two-hour, one-day or two-day delivery of over 100 million items, streaming of thousands of movies and TV episodes, Alexa voice shopping, free access to thousands of Kindle books and other content. The annual charge in the US increased from $99 to $119 in May 2018. The subscription model incentivizes users to make additional purchases in order to achieve a return on their investment. From 2015 to 2018 the programme boomed. The penetration of Prime among US households grew from 23% in 2015 to 51% in 2018 (Columbus, 2018). With 63% of Amazon online shoppers also being Prime members, according to Columbus, attracting more members from the existing online user base has started to slow down compared to other areas of Prime that are experiencing double-digit growth. Amazon has been adding services and devices to get more consumers into their Prime ecosystem. In early 2018, revenue for online subscriptions to services like its Amazon Prime, Prime Video, and Prime Music Unlimited was up 49% year over year, more than twice the growth of Amazon's online store revenues (Columbus, 2018).

In 2017, soon after the Federal Trade Commission approved the $13.7 billion merger of Amazon and Whole Foods Market, the two companies announced their joint vision of 'making Whole Foods Market's high-quality, natural and organic food affordable for everyone' (Springer, 2017). Whole Foods' high-quality private label products such as 365 Everyday Value, Whole Foods Market and Whole Paws were made available through Amazon.com, Amazon Fresh, Prime Pantry and Prime Now (Kolodny, 2017) thus increasing the variety and appeal of Amazon's range to fresh products. Amazon Lockers were installed in Whole Foods Market stores so that customers could conveniently pick up or return products purchased from Amazon.com at their local supermarket. With this move, Amazon gained 350 new locations.

Amazon had been developing its online grocery offer through Amazon Pantry and Amazon Fresh. But what consumers purchase online to put in their pantries doesn't drive purchase frequency like fresh perishables and prepared foods do, and although consumers know Amazon for its logistics expertise, they don't think of it for its line in groceries. A deal with Whole Foods Market, then, looked attractive precisely because it would instantly lend Amazon credibility in this category. The merger has since benefited Amazon. In April 2018 it reported a net profit of $1.6 billion and revenues of $51 billion (a 43% increase year over year). A significant slice of that revenue – $4.2 billion – came from Whole Foods (Thakker, 2018). After the acquisition, 2,000 of Whole Foods' 365 private-label products became available via the Amazon website, and almost all sold out, generating sales worth more than $500,000 in the first week (Thakker, 2018). More growth is projected ahead, however, by means of a loyalty-building strategy. Amazon announced that Prime would become Whole Foods Market's customer rewards programme, providing members with special savings and other in-store benefits – which happened six months after the deal. This was not welcome news for everybody else in the grocery industry. Competitors' stocks started dropping the same day of the announcement. In fact, shares in Kroger, Costco and Sprouts all hit their lowest trading prices in months (Huston, 2017; Kilgore, 2017).

Adding new customers to Prime means a lot for current and future growth at Amazon. In fact, Prime members spend an average of $1,400 a year with Amazon as opposed to non-members, who spend only $600, a difference that has been widening over time (Green, 2018). Just under half (46%) of Amazon Prime members make a purchase online by using the benefits of Prime at least once a week. Weekly purchases, by contrast, are made by only 13% of non-Prime customers (Chadha, 2018). As far as the value for the customer is concerned, J.P. Morgan estimates that the compound of Prime service is actually worth $785 a year – that's six times the cost of a year's subscription (Green, 2018). Let's compare this with the original Whole Foods Market loyalty programme that offered 10% discount on purchases. Under Amazon Prime, Whole Foods Market shoppers receive an additional 10% off on already discounted products, free delivery of Whole Foods Market products to Prime members in certain locations, 5% cashback when members use Amazon Visa rewards card at Whole Foods Market stores, and exclusive member deals. Customers who have their groceries delivered through Prime Now will also have access to these discounts online (Thakker, 2018).

Another reason, besides value, that makes Whole Foods Market shoppers likely to be receptive to Prime is their demographic similarity: both customer bases tend to be younger and affluent. Seventy per cent of Americans with incomes of $150,000 or more who shop online have Amazon Prime memberships (Columbus, 2018). Estimates differ on the percentage of Whole Foods' shoppers who are already Prime members. Just after the merger, Morgan Stanley estimated that value at 62% (Sonenshine, 2018), or a 38% acquisition opportunity thanks to the extension of Prime as the stores' loyalty programme (at the same time, just 20% of US Amazon Prime members were Whole Foods Market shoppers). That figure may indeed grow, since the opportunity to enjoy the benefits of Prime on their grocery shopping at Whole Foods and to try Whole Foods products by ordering them online might attract a substantial number of new customers to the stores.

In a nutshell, a value-rich loyalty scheme developed for the online channel will be extended to the physical store and ultimately enriched by new benefits. The possibility of merging data and insight on each customer's behaviour both online and in the store will create a richer, fuller picture and highlight opportunities to exploit that with targeted offers and communication. This will drive enhanced retention of those who are already in the scheme that translates to a higher long-term value for the company. At the same time it will power the acquisition of qualified prospects, who can be selected based on their similarities with Whole Foods' best customers. Last, but not least, Prime, and the wealth of data-driven targeting opportunities that it opens up, is an opportunity for Whole Foods suppliers – manufacturers of local, natural and organic brands – to improve their own retention and acquisition efforts. Most Whole Foods suppliers reach small, niche customer bases that Amazon analytics and recommendations will help identify, target and leverage in order to find similar ones online and retain them over time.

Alibaba 88 Membership and a global loyalty ecosystem

As this was taking place in the Western hemisphere, even bigger developments were underway in China. In 2017, Alibaba Group merged its Tmall and Taobao loyalty programmes into a single membership club (Chou, 2017). The new '88 Membership' programme (88, a number considered lucky in China, is pronounced 'baba') offers members greater discounts and benefits than the preceding loyalty clubs. Over 500 million users will receive a personalized and more convenient experience, rich in offers from domestic and international brands such as L'Oréal, Hugo Boss, Rimowa and Clarks (who were among the first to join), brands eager to connect with Alibaba's top shoppers. AI algorithms power the personalization of offers and communication with members, and the focus is on customer experience. Alibaba's head of the scheme Jiang Fan clarifies: 'We used to place a lot of importance on growth, rapid growth every year … . Today, we are looking beyond growth to experiences' (quoted in Chou, 2017).

The 88 Membership programme rewards customers equally for their purchasing activity on Alibaba's platforms, and for their online engagement. This can take the form of writing product reviews, posting images of product pages on social media, or posting or answering questions in community forums. The fact that engagement is rewarded with points and privileges should drive more activity and engagement in a reinforcing cycle that supports repeat visits and purchases on the platforms as well as referrals. If one considers that Taobao is not simply an e-commerce website but a huge consumer community, the strategy is sensible.

Members accumulate points based on the number and variety of online stores visited, amount spent and types of goods they buy, in addition to the above-mentioned engagement activities. Points are translated into a score, called Taoqizhi.

Based on the score, customers are divided into three groups: Standard Members, Super Members, who have a score of 1,000 or more, and APASS Members (Alibaba Passport), whose score is higher than 2,500. APASS members are customers who spend a minimum of $15,000 per year. They do 90% of their purchases online, and spend an average of $45,000 per year, or eight times the average programme member. The majority were born in the 1980s. There were around 100,000 APASS members in 2017 (Leaver, 2018). They are assigned personal account managers/shopping assistants and are invited to wine tastings and fashion shows.

Alibaba Group held its first 88 Members' festival on 8 August 2017. It was intended as an annual shopping festival to deliver rewards to the club. Super Members were taken to Shanghai for a private concert. They received exclusive discounts in selected stores such as Gap and Old Navy. Online, they received gift cards from a variety of brands entitling them to 12% off the original price. Super Members also received a promotion for Tmall Supermarket and access to an exclusive Super Members' shop on Tmall that offers fresh produce, not open to other customers. The company is constantly working with brands to create non-price rewards for members such as access to limited edition or bespoke products. In turn, brands receive in-depth insights on shopper preferences and behaviours (Chou, 2017).

In 2018 a new tier was added to the 88 Membership programme called '88 VIP'. What is interesting about this move is that 88 VIP resembles Amazon Prime in that it is a subscription service that, for an annual fee of 888 yuan (around $128) entitles members to access content on the video-streaming platform Youku Tudou and Alibaba's music platform Xiami, discounts on food delivery platform Ele.me and a 5% discount on Tmall Supermarket and the flagship stores of 88 local and international brands on Taobao and Tmall (Bluesea Research, 2018). The total value of benefits available to an 88 VIP member across the Alibaba ecosystem is estimated to reach 2,000 yuan. Existing 88 Membership members who have accumulated 1,000 points can upgrade their membership to 88 VIP with an annual payment of 88 yuan (Kwok, 2018).

Alibaba also formed a joint venture with global hospitality company Marriott International. Overall, the move was aimed at profiting from the new behaviours of Chinese consumers, who travel more and combine online and offline more than ever to plan, discover, book, shop and enjoy their holidays. In July 2018 a facial recognition check-in pilot was launched in two Marriott locations in partnership with Fliggy, Alibaba's travel service platform. Fliggy's facial recognition technology will automate and speed up the check-in process from three to one minute, freeing up time for hotel staff to deliver a more personalized service (Hotel Business, 2018). As part of their partnership, the two companies plan to link Marriott's loyalty platform, Marriott Rewards, the Ritz-Carlton Rewards programme and Starwood Preferred Guest status with Alibaba's 88 Membership programme. The initiative will include benefits such as status-tier matching and the possibility to exchange and redeem points between the two programmes for purchases (Brennan, 2017).

But it doesn't stop there. Alibaba also announced a series of smart mobility initiatives in partnership with auto brands and technology service providers (Retail News Asia, 2018a). They focus on the 'connected car' and the opportunity to provide services – information, navigation, ordering, booking, purchasing and paying – on the go. Just as Amazon is striving to own more moments in the customer life by placing smart devices like Echo and the Dash buttons in consumers' homes, Alibaba is concentrating on connecting to customers while they are in their cars – a substantial portion of daily routines for millions. The company sees the idea of connecting different brands' loyalty programmes as another way of delivering seamless experiences. As its CEO Daniel Zhang said in the summer of 2017:

> We see it as our opportunity to build a unique, global brand alliance, where the loyalty schemes of each brand can be connected to Alibaba's membership system … . We want our members to feel like they have a passport to exclusive experiences within the Alibaba ecosystem.
>
> *(Quoted in Chou, 2017)*

This is part of Alibaba's New Retail vision of employing technology, interactivity and a mixture of online and offline commerce to deliver efficiencies and enhanced services in shopping, not only to Alibaba's own businesses but to any business, in China and worldwide. As Alibaba sets out to deliver services to two billion consumers and millions of businesses, not only with its cloud computing, advertising services and logistics, but, thanks to research and development in AI, quantum computing, biometric recognition and more, we may soon see a global loyalty ecosystem (Retail News Asia, 2018b).

The success stories of Amazon and Alibaba demonstrate just how far the concept of loyalty has come. Marketing today is largely based on the goal of earning long-term customer loyalty, and long-standing loyalty tools – transformed by the information revolution in data-rich, interactive touchpoints – have become the enablers of loyalty-oriented and customer-centred omnichannel strategies that will shape the future.

Why loyalty matters today

Thirty years ago, Frederick Reichheld, author of *The Loyalty Effect* and a pioneer in loyalty research, wrote that companies considered loyalty 'a problem for the marketing department' (Reichheld, 1996, p. 2), nothing that top management and investors should be concerned with. However, in recent years financial analysts and authoritative news sources have started signalling that something had changed.

In 2016, in the wake of a change in Starbucks' loyalty programme aimed at rewarding only the high spenders among its customer base, *Fortune* magazine published an article with the headline 'This is why Starbucks might not be the best stock to buy right now', implying a link between delusional customers and a plunge in future returns on the company's stock (Shen, 2016). Around the same time, as Dunkin' Brands (owner of several consumer brands such as Dunkin'

Donuts) announced that it had reached the milestone of eight million members in its loyalty scheme, a special report on the US network CNBC TV pointed out that shares in Dunkin' Brands rose nearly 2% after the company's announcement (Whitten, 2016). To consecrate Wall Street's 'love affair' with customer loyalty, *Forbes* magazine published a global study of retail and publishing executives in September 2016 entitled 'Retentionomics: the path to profitable growth'. Loyalty had finally left the marketing department and taken over the boardroom.

So, what has changed? Why are companies now paying so much attention to a concept that is a century old and has been neglected for so long – at least in mainstream marketing literature? Several factors are at play. Companies today must tackle significant changes in consumer behaviour and the marketplace. In terms of changing consumer behaviour, it is necessary to deal with several things, such as consumers' time scarcity, multitasking, reduced attention spans, the need for convenience, and the growing appetite for products and services to be provided on demand. Consumers are more demanding and expectations are increasing. They have access to information at reduced or no cost and they can share information at the click of a button thanks to advances brought about by Web 2.0 and tools such as social media. As the previous sentence implies, many of these consumer changes are a consequence of the information revolution (see Chapter 4). And the result is a continued threat to or actual reduction of customer loyalty to specific brands and stores.

But there are other factors. Changes in the marketplace have occurred too. Markets have become globalized, competition has increased, substitute products and services are now increasingly available, and it has become increasingly difficult to differentiate products based on intrinsic quality. At the same time, the service industries, and the related centrality and empowerment of the customer, have become increasingly relevant, if not dominant: companies turn to the building of service relationships with customers as key differentiators. The information revolution has enabled the introduction of new channels and touchpoints in the customer journey, thus making company strategies multichannel and omnichannel. It has ushered in a range of new technological tools for customer contact, data collection, analysis and personalization. Decades of direct and database marketing knowledge and, more recently, customer relationship management (CRM) knowledge, and of academic research into the economic effects of customer retention, have provided the conceptual frameworks for adopting both technological and marketing tools, such as loyalty programmes. Imitation, as companies seek not to be left behind in the ever-increasing pace of technological and marketing innovation, has done the rest.

The interplay of these trends in consumer behaviour and the marketplace has led to closer scrutiny of the impact of customer loyalty on company results – that is, sales and profits – and to the adoption of retention approaches in a number of industries, so much so that it is tempting to say that loyalty has 'disrupted' marketing. In this book we argue, however, that with closer scrutiny, the emergence of loyalty at the forefront of marketing and in the boardroom was more an evolution than a disruption. There is no doubt that the increasing emphasis on loyalty has brought about major changes in marketing and business theory and practice. Specifically, we have seen a shift from acquisition orientation to retention orientation, the adoption of customer-based metrics to measure company performance, the systematic collection of individual customers' information and the establishment of interactive, tracking customer databases, the widespread adoption of CRM approaches and large-scale CRM systems, and the diffusion of loyalty programmes. The rest of this chapter is devoted to discussing these changes, starting with the growing relevance of loyalty across marketing paradigms in academic literature and moving to marketing practice, where we will focus on customer-based success measures.

Evolution of marketing paradigms

Marketing is both an activity, or set of activities, performed by organizations in the market, and a field of study and research. The term was first employed in 1910, in universities in the American Midwest, by agricultural economists in their studies of how commodity markets worked. The dominance of the farm sector made it relevant to explore and make sense of how crops were brought to market and prices determined. According to these scholars, marketing was 'a set of social and economic processes', that made it possible for goods to move from production to consumption (Webster, 1992, p. 2). The schools of thought of those early days all tended to be descriptive, rather than normative. In his analysis of the intellectual and pragmatic roots of marketing as a body of knowledge, theory and practice, Frederick Webster (1992, p. 2) identified three schools that evolved within this tradition that 'focused on the *commodities* themselves, on the marketing *institutions* through which products were brought to market, especially brokers, wholesalers, and retailers in their many forms … and finally on the *functions* performed by these institutions'. This last 'functionalist' approach had the most success and became the conceptual framework for the marketing discipline. In their description of the various aspects they privileged, those early approaches shared a view of marketing as a set of social, not only economic, processes.

In 1948 the American Marketing Association (AMA) defined marketing as the 'performance of business activities that direct the flow of goods and services from producers to consumers' (Keefe, 2004, cited in Ringold and Weitz, 2007, p. 256). This marked an important shift in emphasis. Marketing activities were defined as business activities rather than as social or economic processes. The flow of goods and services towards the final users was considered 'manageable', that is, plannable and controllable. During the 1950s and 1960s several textbooks appeared which adopted this marketing management perspective and focused on problem-solving, planning, implementation and control as the essence of marketing.

Marketing was no longer about describing what organizations were doing in the marketplace. These early managerial authors borrowed analytical frameworks from economics, psychology, sociology and statistics. The adoption of the behavioural and quantitative sciences gave important legitimacy to marketing as a separate academic discipline in an era in which rigour in management education was strongly advocated. The main tenets of this marketing management paradigm were:

- Marketing takes the form of scientific solutions to specific decision-making problems.
- Attention is paid to problem-solving, planning and control.
- The company's goal is to maximize profit.
- Success is measured by sales volume.
- The relevant viewpoint is the 'transaction', i.e. the individual sale.

At the root of most of the research literature on marketing in those days was the basic microeconomic paradigm, with its emphasis on profit maximization (Anderson, 1982, cited in Webster, 1992, p. 3). Companies such as Procter & Gamble, Colgate-Palmolive, General Foods, General Mills and Gillette hired specialists who could apply rigorous methods to solve problems in sales, distribution, advertising and promotion and marketing research, and organized them into marketing departments. The new marketing departments were a good fit in the large, hierarchical organization that was the American corporation in the 1950s and 1960s. The companies that were the cornerstone of the US economy were characterized by multiple layers of management and functional specialization. They organized and managed internally all the necessary operations (production, pricing, distribution, sales and advertising) for *taking the goods and the services from the producer to the consumer/user.* In this framework, the tasks of the marketing function were (Webster, 1992, p. 4):

1. to develop an exhaustive understanding of the marketplace to ensure that the firm was producing goods and services required and desired by the consumer
2. to generate demand for these standardized products
3. to create consumer preference through mass and personal communications
4. to manage the channel of distribution through which products flowed to the consumer.

Marketing practice and theory inevitably draws from the historical and social context in which it emerges, and so it was in the 1970s as the world was transformed by the advent of flexible technologies and advances in transport and communication – in a word, globalization. The oil crises of the early 1970s marked the 'end of predictability' and companies realized the world was becoming a global marketplace. What happened in one country directly affected what would happen in others. The inputs of managerial decision-making processes were no longer easy to forecast or predict. Just as the price of crude oil was no longer predictable, so were other costs on the supply side. And neither was the disposable income and growth rates that drive demand.

This new environment was unfavourable to the large, fully integrated US corporations. Their enormous size and carefully planned processes were cumbersome and not easy to change in order to adapt to the new circumstances. For the first time, the structure of the big corporations was questioned: high fixed costs and slow decision-making made them unfit to thrive in the new era of unpredictability. Companies had to look for new ways to be successful. New forms of business organization and relationships developed among companies: partnerships, joint ventures, alliances and networks. These partnerships were characterized by flexibility, specialization and an emphasis on relationship management instead of market transactions. Within these new types of organizations, traditional ways of organizing the marketing function and of thinking about the purpose of marketing activity were re-examined, with a new focus on long-term customer relationships, partnerships and strategic alliances.

Marketers began to see the necessity of moving away from a focus on the individual sale towards an understanding of the need to develop long-term, mutually supportive relationships with their customers. The *keiretsu*, which are a Japanese institution, provided inspiration for this new organizational thinking and turned managers' attention towards the importance of relationships. The *keiretsu* are 'complex groupings of firms with interlinked ownership and trading relationships' (Webster, 1992, p. 8). They are not formal organizations with clearly defined hierarchical structures. Nor are they impersonal, decentralized markets. Rather, they are bound together in long-term relationships based on reciprocity.

National economies all over the world in the late 1970s and 1980s set into recession and stagnation, frequently accompanied by serious deteriorations in labour and social conditions, rising unemployment and insecurity. Yet a few localities stood out as exhibiting a remarkable resilience and even growth: the industrial districts in Italy, England and Germany. These districts were geographically defined, productive systems, characterized by a large number of small firms that are involved at various stages, and in various ways, in the production of a homogeneous product. A characteristic of the industrial district is that it should be conceived as a social and economic whole. That is to say, there are close interrelationships between the different social, political and economic spheres, and the functioning of one is shaped by the functioning and organization of the others. Their success lay not just in the realm of the 'economic': broader social and institutional aspects were just as important. In his review of the literature on districts, Jesús M. Zaratiegui (2004) argued that the essence of a district is that the different members of it trust each other. He cites Bennett Harrison (1991), who pointed out that 'Trust is built up over a period of time, through continual contracting and re-contracting, through informal deal-making, through one firm or group's offering assistance to one another in moments of stress' (cited in Zaratiegui, 2004, p. 91). Another feature of the industrial district is an internal ethical code that limits the temptation of opportunism: 'All district's participants must accept a set of moral values, such as honesty, loyalty and hard work, which identify them as members of the group' (Dardi and Gallegati, 1992, cited in Zaratiegui, 2004, p. 92).

Alfred Marshall (1961) argued that 'districts offer certain advantages when compared to more traditional types of organisation, which are the result of the spatial proximity of producers and the specific atmosphere beneficial to the exchange/emulation of knowledge, to learning effects and trust' (cited in Zaratiegui, 2004, p. 93). In his transaction cost analysis, Oliver Williamson (1975) drew from the same perspective when he argued that the 'atmosphere' of a transaction comprises, on the one hand, the social, legal and technological framework of the transaction and, on the other, factors like trust and the sharing of common values of the involved parties.

In Europe, and specifically in the work of academics active in the Nordic countries in the 1980s, a new view of how companies should operate to be successful was being developed. The economies of these countries were characterized by strong business-to-business (B2B) industries and service sectors: in such contexts, companies pursuing success ought to develop relationships with customers, distributors and suppliers. No wonder that to observers such as local academics the relevance of relationships, trust and loyalty was evident, and reflected in their work.

The importance of establishing, strengthening and developing long-term and enduring customer relations was stressed in a new theory of industrial marketing and purchasing that emerged in the 1980s and 1990s called the network or interaction theory (see Takala and Uusitalo, 1996). In this view, marketing is defined as all the activities of a firm to build, maintain, and develop customer relations. Thus, marketing is not primarily concerned with the manipulation of the 4Ps (product, place, promotion, price) of consumer goods marketing. Rather, it is aimed at reaching a critical mass of relationships with customers, distributors, suppliers, public institutions and individuals (Gummesson, 1987). Grönroos, an advocate of the Nordic view of marketing, stated that:

> Marketing is to establish, maintain and enhance (usually, but not necessarily, long-term) relationships with customers and other partners, at a profit, so that the objectives of the parties involved are met. This is achieved by a mutual exchange and fulfilment of promises.
>
> *(Grönroos, 1990, p. 138)*

Relationship marketing thus differs from traditional marketing since

> it does not seek a temporary increase in sales but attempts to create involvement and product loyalty by building a permanent bond with the customer. While it may be used to facilitate product repositioning, gain competitors' customers or help to launch new products, the ultimate goal is to increase sales in the long term.
>
> *(Takala and Uusitalo, 1996, p. 46)*

The relationship marketing paradigm criticizes the overarching goal of profit maximization, the rigidity of the 'marketing mix', the marketing department and the transactional focus. Instead, its core ideas are that:

1. Marketing is responsible not only for sales and profits but also for making sure that every aspect of the business is focused on delivering superior value to customers in the competitive marketplace
2. The business is likely to be a network of strategic partnerships
3. Marketing as a distinct management function is responsible for being the expert on the customer and for keeping the rest of the network organization informed about the customer
4. Everyone in the organization is a 'part-time marketer'.

The relationship marketing paradigm was pioneering in so far as it foresaw the roles both information technology and loyalty were going to play in marketing.

From around the mid-1990s to the mid-2000s, the marketing discipline in the US started focusing on customer profitability and the use of organizational resources to enhance marketing effectiveness (see Kumar, 2015). Specifically, researchers conducted studies in the following broad areas: identifying the customer value potential for the organization and building an approach to appropriately align marketing resources; maximizing the value of each customer; optimizing marketing resources for customers at the individual and segment levels; developing and implementing resource allocation strategies on the basis of customer profitability. Kumar (2015) traces the reasons primarily to the significant improvements in data processing and data storage which enabled sophisticated empirical studies based on individual customer data of various types collected about massive samples of customers. Analysis could then be performed at the level of the individual customer. This called for scholars to assess the needs and wants of individual customers and to identify appropriate ways and means of communicating with them. Such an approach meant identifying customers' lifetime value, which in turn led managers to allocate marketing resources to the areas that would generate the greatest impact. Managers became empowered to determine the frequency of each of the available marketing and communication strategies so that customer lifetime value was maximized. This line of marketing thought and practice gradually increased the knowledge base in this area and shaped what Kumar (2015) defines as the 'resource-conscious view' of marketing.

Technological progress brought about a range of sophisticated data management applications, including electronic data interchange, spreadsheets, sales forecasting tools, inventory management tools and content management systems. These tools made it possible for managers to access customer and product inventories and market intelligence data. This, in turn, enabled a more tailored response to customers. In B2B industries, account managers focused on creating long-term relationships, rather than increasing sales transactions, and quickly recognized the value of these tools in enabling customer profiling, customer acquisition and retention strategies, customized marketing messages, upsell and cross-sell communications, and marketing promotions. Technological advancements enabled managers to make decisions regarding customer behaviour and company actions more easily. Specifically, marketing resources were directed towards customer acquisition, customer retention and relationship-building efforts according to their value to the firm. Academic studies appeared that heralded the transition from product/brand management to customer management, and from product portfolio management to customer portfolio management (Johnson and Seines, 2004; Sheth, 2005).

In 2005 the *Journal of Marketing*, the world's most influential academic marketing publication, devoted a special section to CRM. The same year, the AMA put forward a definition of marketing as 'an organizational function and a set of processes for creating, communicating and delivering value to customers and for managing customer relationships in ways that benefit the organization and its stakeholders' (Grönroos, 2006, p. 397). It appears from this definition that the paradigms of marketing management (using scientific methods to solve problems; transactional focus) and relationship marketing (retaining customers; relational focus) have been synthesized and coexist today. It is worth noting, however, that the verb 'manage' is still employed when referring to customer relationships, implying that these are under the control of the firm. Certainly, developments in information and communication technologies made the granularity of individual customer behaviours and features visible, and this seems to have instilled an illusion of manageability, at least in American academic and practitioner circles.

Any idea of control would soon to be challenged, in the US and Europe alike. With the advent of Web 2.0 tools, and social media in particular, individuals were now constantly connected with their social groups and interests. Value creation and co-creation could take place anywhere and anytime. The discourse about brands was no longer controlled by those brands or by the traditional media: companies could no longer control what people said about them. The power of the social media revolution has been further amplified by the massive worldwide adoption of portable devices, smartphones in particular. People carry the Internet in their pockets at all times now, and the view of two separate 'times' and 'contexts' – online and offline – has rapidly morphed into a new hybrid, mixed reality that is enriched every day with the latest development in augmented reality.

The Italian scholars Mandelli and Accoto (2014) have suggested that with the emergence of ubiquitous social media, 'social mobile marketing' is a new marketing paradigm. We agree, and argue that loyalty will play a major role in it. Certainly, new media and touchpoints that cannot be controlled by the company – but, at best, listened to – confirm every day that loyalty cannot be bought but must be earned. In the new era of social mobile marketing, managing loyalty for businesses means building customer identification mechanisms for tracking them, analysing their rich data profiles – not only behaviours but attitudes and lifestyles – and deriving insights to create value through a proposition that is delivered across touchpoints in a consistent, responsive and individual way. The opening of channels for individual customer data collection brings with it a responsibility to measure changes in their loyalty (whatever metrics we employ for it) and to listen to what they have to say, take it into account and react accordingly. After all, loyalty management is, in the era of the social, a promise that the company will behave like a human being: talk, listen, reply, remember what was said and proceed from there. And with the advances of big data and AI these are not mere figures of speech; they are reality. Some argue that we are now in the era of another marketing paradigm: that of big data marketing. Following Mandelli (2018) we see instead a continuum in the evolution of marketing stimulated by the information revolution and we discuss the impact of big data and AI on marketing in Chapter 4.

From direct marketing to database marketing to CRM

To support retention efforts, the adoption of CRM approaches and loyalty programmes has become commonplace over the past 30 years. Since we see the adoption of CRM as the first step in the evolution of loyalty management from tactical tool to company strategy (see Chapter 2), it would be useful here to recall the origin of CRM and how it relates to, and stems from, direct marketing, database marketing and relationship marketing.

We start with the history of direct marketing, borrowing from the fascinating account made by Petrison, Blattberg and Wang (1993). In its early days, direct marketing was a synonym of catalogue sales. Commercial catalogues existed in Europe as early as the fifteenth century, when the invention of the printing press made reproducing documents relatively inexpensive. At first, it was books and surgical instruments that were sold through catalogues, followed by luxury goods for the home such as china, furniture and wine. The American colonies expressed high demand for European goods not available domestically and ordered them via mail from overseas manufacturers and traders. From the fifteenth to the nineteenth century, catalogue customers largely belonged to the elite in society – the few who could read, write and purchase luxury goods. The Industrial Revolution opened up mass markets and impacted direct marketing. In Europe, high population density and short distances enabled the proliferation of retail stores. In the US, by contrast, with the frontier constantly pushed westward, people moved to territories where the goods they were used to were not available: to procure them it made more sense to move the goods rather than having people travel long distances.

The first variety merchandise catalogues, Montgomery Ward and Sears, date back to the nineteenth century. These companies developed quickly and in the 1920s were among the largest businesses on American soil. In 1927, Sears mailed 10 million letters, 15 million catalogues and 23 million special catalogues (the catalogue itself had grown in its first ten years from listing 700 products to listing 6,000 by 1897). During the 1920s, catalogue companies were calculating costs, revenues and profits at the level of the individual customer – individual customer records were kept for shipping and for managing payments. They soon managed to reduce costs by saving on those customers who generated higher costs than profits, and invested in retaining profitable ones. Two 'rules' were commonly employed: the '12-month prune rule', which consisted in eliminating from catalogue mailing lists those customers who had not purchased within the previous 12 months, and the RFM – recency, frequency, monetary – rule still widely in use today to assess customer value and probability of repurchase. Up until 1950, direct marketers – that is, catalogue companies – were mainly focused on retention, in that acquisition efforts by means of lists, and list brokers, were still scarce and quality low. The practice of keeping individual customer records in order to contact them at the right time to secure repeat business existed outside of the catalogue business, as the story of Jewel Tea Company (see Chapter 2) illustrates. Jewel Tea employed expensive 'advance premiums' to secure customer loyalty and were very successful in that venture.

During the 1950s a virtuous circle stimulated the expansion of direct marketing, driven by a sharp increase in the demand for goods following the end of World War II and the availability of high-quality lists, such as the Polk & Donnelley, comprising names and addresses of any American who owned a car, driving licence and telephone. At the same time, the US Post Office allowed post to be mailed to the 'Occupant' (i.e. to addresses with no need for names), which created the opportunity for manufacturers of consumer goods of any kind to massively distribute samples – a form of non-price promotion – of their products, further stimulating demand. The 1960s marked the progressive adoption of information technology by direct marketers. This was a watershed in history. From this moment onwards, the costs and possibilities of list management, mailings, segmentation, statistical testing, modelling and customized communication would be determined by the various technologies through which they were executed. The first in the industry to adopt computers were list brokers. Direct marketers then followed in their droves after a federal law was passed making the use of postal codes mandatory in addresses and requiring companies to deliver letters and packages to post offices in homogenous groups by zip code. To contain costs, manual labour was supplanted by computers.

Computer power was soon employed to manage another problem: that of duplications. Merge/purge programmes were the first computer software adopted in the industry, the precursors to the database. De-duplication was crucial in that it improved both the efficiency and effectiveness of direct marketing efforts, and this made it attractive to a wider variety of industries and company sizes. Computers also supported the production of personalized communication. Mass mailings targeting all American citizens with the surname Smith had been pioneered by *Time* magazine since the late 1940s and enjoyed response rates six times as high as untargeted mailings, which made up for higher printing costs. However, with the widespread adoption of direct marketing practices, perceptions of disturbance arose as well as early concerns about privacy. Advances in list segmentation characterized this decade: the need to use them brought attention to postal codes – a 1967 *Harvard Business Review* article called them 'a new tool for marketers' (Baier, 1967) – and compelled marketers to experiment with them, expanding segmentation criteria from internal variables (e.g. RFM) to external ones, and supporting the communication and marketing efforts of all sorts of location-based businesses, such as car dealers and retailers.

It is worth noting that the expression we have used so far – direct marketing – was unheard of until the late 1960s: the business was referred to as 'mail order', 'catalogue business' or 'direct mail'. But with the expansion of the industry, the range of activities and players was no longer confined to distance selling, and even the most authoritative industry publication at the time – the *Reporter of Direct Mail Advertising* – changed its name to *Direct Marketing* in 1968. During the following decade, several factors contributed to the growth and increased scientific vigour of the direct marketing business. To paraphrase Petrison, Blattberg and Wang (1993), they were as follows.

- There was a sharp increase in postage costs, which required mailings to yield higher returns. Efforts multiplied to reduce the cost per response by improving list quality and testing.
- Credit cards changed consumer habits and the perception of the costs and benefits of distance selling. Credit became one of the services offered by direct marketers. Major credit cards had been available since the 1950s but only to a few affluent consumers who were reluctant to disclose details to marketers. Catalogue orders were paid in advance or on delivery well into the 1970s, when credit card companies, thanks to analytics, were able to predict credit risk, and cards spread among less affluent and even low-income consumers.
- Toll-free numbers played the same role and attracted consumer goods manufacturers' attention onto direct marketing tools to get in touch with customers and prospects.
- A reduction in consumers' – especially working women's – time devoted to purchase activities made distance ordering of a wide array of products more attractive.
- Technological developments, growing interest from statisticians and mathematicians in direct marketing issues, and the development of data analysis software packages such as SAS and SPSS enabled direct marketers to tackle the above challenges and seize opportunities. As mentioned above, direct marketers had been able since the 1940s to longitudinally evaluate a customer's worth by totting up her total purchases and calculating her lifetime value. In the 1970s, however, predictive techniques based on regression, CHAID,[1] factor, discriminant and multivariate analysis were developed. Initially it was magazines and non-profit organizations that invested in those pioneering techniques – *Reader's Digest* was the first to use multiple regression to predict response rates – while cataloguers were anchored to RFM to 'milk' loyal customers. By the end of the decade though, any given direct marketing company had its own proprietary models to forecast customer loyalty and determine the maximum allowable spend for acquisition and retention.
- New mail-order companies selling niche products emerged, making the identification of highly targeted prospects crucial.

As the direct marketing industry expanded, government and consumer groups took to attacking it, complaining about the levels of unsolicited and unwanted junk mail and offensive materials. It would not be until 20 years later that a new wave of

---

1 Chi-square automatic interaction detector (CHAID) is a tool created by Gordon Kass in 1980 and used to discover interaction effects between different types of variables.

concerns arose, this time regarding unwanted mailings and companies harnessing and selling information about individuals.

The 1980s saw the consolidation of direct marketing practices and their diffusion to other industries. The new analytical techniques ceased to be experimental and became rules of business. Advances in technology,[2] notably in processing power and decreasing costs of data storage, made it possible to process growing amounts of data for organizations of all sizes. IBM launched DB2, one of the first ever database software programs that, thanks to its SQL operating language, became one of the most successful tools to aggregate and analyse customer data, even from multiple sources. This progress enabled the rise of specialist companies – early 'information intermediaries' – that created and analysed databases of consumer information. Two such databases were ACORN,[3] a segmentation tool which categorizes households into demographic groups, and NDL,[4] which classifies consumers based on their lifestyles and hobbies, data gleaned from product warranties and purchase receipts mailed in by consumers (Harris et al., 2005).

Database marketing practices started to appear in several industries. Airlines were first. Following pricing deregulation, companies had flooded the market with discount coupons to make frequent flyers loyal. To fight fraud related to the birth of an illicit coupon market, airlines built customer databases and began the systematic management of discounts and incentives through mailings and loyalty cards. American Airlines' AAdvantage card launched in 1981, the first 'modern' loyalty programme, using a plastic card to identify its members and match their details on a customer database. Credit card companies followed suit, with American Express a forerunner, then telephone companies, car manufacturers and consumer goods manufacturers – especially cigarette manufacturers, who were denied access to mass advertising on TV. Every direct marketing effort was based on databases: 'direct marketing' started being employed as the label to specifically designate mail order and catalogue sales, while direct marketing practices began to be known as 'database marketing'.

During the 1990s, the market factors mentioned earlier in this chapter (competition, the high cost of customer acquisition and rising cost of mass media, availability of technology, etc.) stimulated the adoption of database marketing approaches across a variety of industries to measure individual customer costs and revenues, and returns on marketing efforts. Customer databases and loyalty programmes were established, transaction records were parsed to model prospective customer behaviours, and customer magazines were printed using selective binding in order to target consumers based on their individual interests. As all this was taking place, a powerful new catalyst emerged that accelerated the spread of database marketing approaches, tools and techniques – the Web.

2   Well-illustrated by Moore's Law (see Chapter 4).
3   A Classification of Residential Neighborhoods, developed by CACI Ltd in London.
4   National Demographics & Lifestyles, the name both of the tool and the Colorado-based company that developed it.

The Internet made it possible for any business to organize and operate as direct marketers. Indeed, nascent e-commerce companies shared with established catalogue companies and direct marketers several traits and practices: (1) direct channels to market (no intermediaries); (2) no physical stores; (3) distribution and delivery as a major cost, when they sold physical goods; (4) evidence of the relevance of customer retention to sustain the business; (5) relevance of technologies both as customer touchpoints and as data collection tools; (6) availability of individual customer data; (7) opportunities to track individual customer costs and revenues, and marketing efforts return on investment (ROI); (8) trial-and-error mindset, based on small-scale testing before the rollout of any activity, to optimize efforts. This is still the case today and the success of e-commerce we are witnessing in the twenty-first century – a trillion-dollar industry worldwide, no less – can rightly be considered a triumph of the principles that have guided the direct marketing industry for a century.

Direct/database marketing was defined by Alan Tapp in 1998 as a way of acquiring and retaining customers by providing a framework for three activities: analysis of individual customer information, the definition of strategies and their implementation in order to obtain a direct response from them (Tapp, 1998). A few years later, Payne and Frow (2005, p. 168) offered the following comprehensive definition of CRM:

> CRM is a strategic approach concerned with creating improved shareholder value through the development of appropriate relationships with key customers and customer segments. CRM unites the potential of relationship marketing strategies and IT to create profitable, long-term relationships with customers and other key stakeholders. CRM provides enhanced opportunities to use data and information to both understand customers and co-create value with them.

When we recall the definition of relationship marketing given earlier in this chapter, it becomes evident that CRM is the fusion of the relational focus on the one hand, and the use of individual information available in databases for marketing purposes on the other.[5]

Neslin argued that 'CRM is about getting things done – developing a relationship, improving marketing productivity, etc.' (Winer and Neslin, 2014, p. 290). Along this line, the history of CRM can be told by looking at the history of its applications. CRM (and its predecessors, database marketing and the early algorithms developed in the era of direct marketing) has seen the emphasis shift from campaign management to customer management to programme management. Campaign management focuses on granting the success of a short-term marketing effort, such as a direct mail or an email campaign. Customer management, on the other hand, is concerned with

---

5   Chapter 4 will explore in more detail how technology has been involved in loyalty becoming the cornerstone of marketing.

managing the value of each customer over the long term. The RFM method to improve the success of direct mailings, and customer management systems that aim to maximize the value of the customer base by defining period-to-period marketing efforts targeted at individual customers by means of econometric predictive models, are both early examples of CRM.

With the diffusion of loyalty programmes (LPs), CRM studies and applications were developed to support their design and management. Such studies flourished in the 2000s and addressed challenges such as cross-selling and upselling, reducing churn, enhancing loyalty and making the best use of multiple channels (Winer and Neslin, 2014). Key metrics in CRM studies and applications have followed the shift from campaign management to customer management, which in turn reflects the general marketing trend from focusing on the short term to focusing on the long term and on relationships. Metrics in fact have moved from immediate-term profit, ROI and response rates of short-term actions such as direct mail campaigns to customer lifetime value and its submetrics such as retention rate, migration probability and more, as shall be discussed in the final section of this chapter.

Advances in technologies have made unprecedented quantities of empirical data available and at the same time provided the means to access, store and process them. There is new interest in the findings of research on artificial intelligence (AI), and what AI may mean for marketing. Of course, the impact of AI goes well beyond marketing applications – one only need think of its impact on healthcare, transportation and industrial production, to name but a few – but we should note that several algorithms, models and approaches that have been developed in this field are having a powerful impact on marketing and CRM. AI applications, such as natural language processing and image recognition, that are already powering recommender systems, conversational commerce robots (chatbots) and automated content creation, give marketers unprecedented power to create unique, personalized experiences for customers. At present, there is more talk than reality in the application of AI to loyalty management, but the authors of this book believe things will change incredibly quickly and, for that reason, devote Chapter 4 to discussing this topic.

A brief history of customer loyalty metrics

The growing attention towards customer relationships in marketing has brought about the adoption of customer-based measures of company success. Among these, a series of loyalty measures have emerged and gained ground in marketing literature and business practice over time.

As far as the marketing literature is concerned, the rich early history of customer loyalty research allowed Jacoby and Chestnut to cite as early as 1978 more than 50 definitions of loyalty. At a recent workshop on customer retention, however, some of the most distinguished scholars in the field (Ascarza et al., 2018) made the point that despite the plethora of contributions, research on loyalty has failed to completely align with managerial needs. We choose therefore to concentrate in this section on the loyalty metrics that have found favour among marketers and become common practice in business. Table 1.1 marks out some key dates in the history of approaches to measuring customer loyalty.

It was in 1923 that a marketer named Melvin Copeland gave the deceptively simple definition that a brand-loyal person was 'anyone in a market who buys your brand 100% of the time' (Copeland, 1923). From then on, a view of the market developed as being composed of 'Loyals' and 'Switchers'. It is easy to understand that such a definition was rooted in the times. This was a period where few substitute products were available and the reassuring role of brands amid unbranded, generic products was evident. As markets and consumer behaviour matured, the degree of a person's loyalty to a brand started to be measured by looking at what 'share' of that person's requirements in a category were fulfilled by that brand. In the 1950s, the concept of 'share of requirements' (known as 'share of wallet' when retail stores, instead of brands, are considered) emerged in marketing literature and practice. The share of requirements is calculated solely among buyers of a specific brand. Within this group it represents the percentage of purchases within the relevant category accounted for by the brand in question.

Identifying who is loyal is then a matter of agreeing on how many times a person should buy a brand to be classified as loyal. If a person buys Levi's seven out of ten times when buying jeans, then Levi's has a 70% share of that person's requirements when it comes to jeans. In many industries it became practical and common to use the standard of 67% share, i.e. two times out of three, as the threshold for considering a customer 'loyal'. But what if a customer buys a brand because it is the only one available? People can buy a brand 'loyally' but still not be attached to it. We cannot deduct how a consumer feels from observing her behaviour: she may be buying the same brand again because she is unaware of alternatives, or because that type of purchase has minimal relevance to her. Thus

TABLE 1.1 Timeline of measuring customer loyalty

Year	Key event
1923	Copeland introduces the concept of brand loyalty
1950s	Relative measures of loyalty emerge (share of requirements and share of wallet)
1969	Day distinguishes between behavioural loyalty and attitudinal loyalty
1988	Parasumaran, Zeithaml and Berry introduce the Servqual model and attract managers' attention to the relevance of customer satisfaction to obtain customer loyalty
1990s	Reichheld introduces the retention rate as the litmus test of a company's value creation capability
2001	Keiningham and Vavra introduce 'customer delight', thus stressing the fact that only high satisfaction turns into loyalty
2003	Reichheld introduces the net promoter score, an easy to compute, highly successful measure of customers' intention to spread positive word of mouth.

a distinction needed to be made. Buying a brand repeatedly without attachment is 'behavioural loyalty'. Buying a brand repeatedly because it is preferred to others is 'attitudinal loyalty'.

Although there is no consensus definition of loyalty, current theories most often delineate attitudinal loyalty and behavioural loyalty as the primary elements of customer loyalty (Chaudhuri and Holbrook, 2001). Today, research generally agrees that loyalty 'represents a mix of attitudes and behaviors that benefit one firm relative to its competitors' (Day, 1969; Dick and Basu, 1994; Melnyk, Osselaer and Bijmolt, 2009). Day was the first, in 1969, to define attitudinal loyalty as 'a biased behavioural response over time in favour of a brand as a result of a psychological evaluative process' (Melnyk, Osselaer and Bijmolt, 2009, p. 32). Attitudinal loyalty has been shown to derive from various components, such as: satisfaction with the brand; perception of the alternatives (even if dissatisfied, the customer doesn't switch); importance of brand choice (if brand choice is unimportant, she is 'uninvolved'); degree of ambivalence (the greater the ambivalence, the more likely that brand choice will be delayed until the last moment – market variables become important). Satisfaction with the brand, though not the only driver of customer loyalty, plays an important role.

Customer satisfaction is the extent to which a product's perceived performance matches expectations. If the product's performance falls short of expectations, the buyer is dissatisfied, but if performance matches or exceeds expectations, the buyer is satisfied. Starting from the late 1980s, many approaches have been introduced to measure and foster customer satisfaction. Before long, customer satisfaction programmes started putting emphasis on customer retention (Bolton, 1998). For many companies, it was not enough to have high satisfaction scores. Rather, customer satisfaction scores needed to be demonstrably linked to key outcomes such as customer retention. Typically using techniques such as correlation or regression analysis, firms calculated the relationship between satisfaction and repurchase intention. For instance, using such a model, it was estimated that for a service industry, a one-unit change in overall satisfaction produces a 6% change in likelihood of continued use, the so-called repurchase intention.

In 1990, Reichheld and Sasser published a seminal paper entitled 'Zero defections: quality comes to services' which disseminated the idea that loyal customers generate more revenues and profits thanks to a combination of the following:

- repeat purchases
- lower service costs
- low remarketing costs
- cross-category purchases
- purchases on and off promotion
- premium charges
- lower dissatisfaction costs
- employee satisfaction
- higher percentage of acquisition costs covered

- more referrals thanks to word-of-mouth advertising
- reduced company need for acquisition.

In the paper, and his subsequent book *The Loyalty Effect* (1996), Reichheld employs 'loyal' as a synonym of a 'retained' customer, focusing on the value that a company derives from customers who remain (i.e. continue transacting) with the company. The early 1990s were the years in which the total quality management – or 'zero defects' – philosophy swept across the corporate world and attracted management attention to the idea that prevention (of defects) is more economical than treatment or fixing afterwards. Hence the analogy drawn in the title of the article by Reichheld and Sasser, the former of which later revised his original thesis that companies should strive to retain all customers to retaining the 'right' customers. The attention on retention, however, stuck, and retention rate started being employed as a popular measure of loyalty and a company's health.

The retention rate is the ratio of the number of retained customers to the number of customers at risk. The retention rate expresses the average likelihood that a customer purchases from the firm in a period (t), given that this customer has also purchased in the period before ($t - 1$). In contractual situations, it makes sense to talk about the number of customers currently under contract and the percentage retained when the contract period runs out.

Firms that keep acquiring new customers but are unable to retain them are unlikely to see positive bottom-line results. The revenue stream from a retained customer is lost when the customer leaves. The firm not only loses sales but also the benefits of retaining customers listed above, such as lower service and remarketing costs. The loyal customer has to be replaced, at a high acquisition premium, by a new customer who buys less frequently and in smaller quantities, requires more service, and is less likely to bring new customers. Consequently, to make the same level of sales, a firm with a low retention rate must incur higher costs. The deleterious impact of customer defection can be much larger than the benefit reaped from retaining a customer. The retention rate is a common measure today of a company's 'health', and a proxy for future profits.

In 2000, Anderson and Mittal introduced the satisfaction–loyalty–profit chain to illustrate the intuitive connections at play: customer satisfaction driven by product, service and employee performance results in retention/loyalty and company revenue/profit. According to their analyses, firms that manage to create superior customer satisfaction should enjoy commensurate profits: research at the aggregate level showed a positive correlation between aggregate satisfaction scores for the firm and overall profitability measures. However intuitive that may seem, the links are far from straightforward. One cannot assume that a 1% increase at one end of the chain drives an $x\%$ increase in one of the other nodes, especially towards the other end of the chain.

Anderson and Mittal (2000) explained two important characteristics of the links in the satisfaction–loyalty–profit chain. First, the links are often asymmetric. That is, the impact of an increase is different from the impact of an equivalent decrease, not only in terms of direction but also in terms of size. Second, the links can also be non-linear. At certain points in the chain, non-linearity appears in the form of diminishing returns. That is, each additional one-unit increase in an input has a smaller impact than the preceding one-unit increase. For the links between performance and satisfaction, consecutive performance increases in certain types of product attributes (e.g. speed) will have less of an impact on satisfaction. At other points in the chain, there are increasing returns. Focusing on the satisfaction–retention link, the shape of the relationship, and especially the 'elbows' or points at which customers cross the threshold and become either 'customers for life' or 'customers never more', varies enormously across industries. The aggressiveness of competition, the degree of switching barriers, the ability of customers to accurately assess quality, and their level of risk aversion in the face of such uncertainty are some of the key factors influencing the shape of the link between satisfaction and repurchase intent.

The relationship between retention and revenue/profits is also non-linear. In fact, not all customers are as attractive in terms of revenue generation (Zeithaml, 2000). Furthermore, the successive acquisition of customers is also likely to be more expensive. As a firm keeps acquiring more and more customers, the quality of customers acquired may decline, resulting in higher maintenance costs and lower revenue. Thus the diminishing returns to acquiring new customers. The idea is that a firm should operate at a steady state and focus on acquiring and keeping the 'right' customers, rather than just blindly expanding its customer base. Central to this aim is the calculation of customer lifetime value discussed earlier. This is regarded as 'today's foremost CRM metric' (Winer and Neslin, 2014). Customer lifetime value is the total amount of value derived by a company from a customer over the full lifetime of her engagement with the company or product.

In the early 2000s, another measure of satisfaction and repurchase intention was introduced, one that has proven very successful in terms of the number of companies adopting it: the net promoter score. It is calculated based on responses to a single question: how likely is it that you would recommend our company/product/service to a friend or colleague? The scoring for this answer is most often based on a scale of 0 to 10. Those who respond with a score of 9 or 10 are called 'Promoters', and are considered likely to exhibit value-creating behaviours such as buying more, remaining customers for longer, and making more positive referrals to other potential customers. Those who respond with a score of 0 to 6 are labelled 'Detractors' and are believed to be less likely to exhibit such value-creating behaviours. Responses of 7 and 8 are 'Passives', and their behaviour falls in the middle. The net promoter score is calculated by subtracting the percentage of customers who are Detractors from the percentage of customers who are Promoters. Its straightforwardness has made it popular in several industries and with e-commerce sites, although it has been shown to be no more superior to other approaches to forecasting retention or future profits (Keiningham et al., 2008).

In our more than 20 years of experience with loyalty projects for business, as well as research, we have noticed that what a company defines as 'loyalty', and therefore sets as the target for their loyalty strategy, varies across companies and industries. Above all, the narrative, the image of the 'loyal customer', is one thing; the metric(s) that are adopted (if they are adopted) as guidance to monitor loyalty and manage loyalty building efforts is another.

In 2012 we conducted an extensive survey with Italian companies from a range of industries that included retail and manufacturing with the aim of understanding (1) how companies defined a customer as loyal to their brand and (2) what measures of loyalty they employed. The survey was run for mere exemplificatory purposes since no generalization to other countries was attempted (although several of the surveyed companies were part of multinational operations that are likely to share the same vision and metrics). We found that the most common conceptualizations of a loyal customer were:

- one who repeats purchases ('frequency' perspective)
- one who chooses our brand most or all the time for need *x* ('share' perspective)
- one who has an emotional bond with our brand ('attitude' perspective)
- one who does not cede to competitors' promotions and offers ('switching barrier' perspective).

Respondents in retail tended to cite frequency as the proof of loyalty, while manufacturers preferred a share-of-requirement/share-in-handlers perspective. Behaviours, rather than attitudes, tended to be 'working definitions' of loyalty for companies. The most-cited metrics were behavioural measures: frequency and spending for retailers, frequency and share of requirement for manufacturers. Respondents also declared the 'secondary' metrics they employed: retailers cited share of wallet and manufacturers brand awareness. Retailers also employed customer satisfaction measures, and we also found two emerging metrics among them: engagement in loyalty-building activities (e.g. enrolment or active participation in loyalty programmes), and engagement with the company's digital assets.

Measures that relate to loyalty programmes have become part of the customer loyalty dashboard in companies that use such schemes. This began in the 1990s in countries where loyalty programmes first diffused, such as the US and the UK. In Italy, however, such programmes had been in use for no more than a decade. In the early days, essential aggregated measures were conducted, such as percentages of transactions and of sales going through the loyalty card. Later, other aspects started to be monitored, among them earned/burned points balances, activity rates in programmes (percentage of active cards/customers) and response rates to 'members only' offers. In our study, loyalty programmes were less frequent among manufacturers than they were among retailers. In regard to consumer goods, engagement and retention were more commonly measured by manufacturers relative to their brands' digital assets, which are a vital means of direct contact with the customer base – touchpoints, as they have come to be known as today. We found that visits, interactions, likes, shares and a variety of other actions were monitored.

At the time of writing, we are looking at the results of a new comprehensive survey run by our Observatory with 363 companies on loyalty management practices, which we discuss in Chapter 8. It is worth noting here that, despite a history going back many decades, loyalty measures still have ground to gain when one considers that only 50% of companies calculate retention rates and less than one in three companies employs customer lifetime value, RFM or share of wallet. The diffusion of these metrics varies from industry to industry but, overall, we were struck by the fact that only 50% of the surveyed businesses regularly measured the effectiveness of their loyalty strategies. There is a need for this book after all.

References

Anderson, E. W. and Mittal, V. (2000) 'Strengthening the satisfaction-profit chain'. *Journal of Service Research*, 3(2), pp. 107–120.

Anderson, P. F. (1982) 'Marketing, strategic planning and the theory of the firm'. *Journal of Marketing*, 46(Spring), pp. 15–26.

Ascarza, E., Neslin, S. A., Netzer, O., Anderson, Z., Fader, P. S., Gupta, S. and Provost, F. (2018) 'In pursuit of enhanced customer retention management: review, key issues, and future directions'. *Customer Needs and Solutions*, 5(1–2), pp. 65–81.

Baier, M. (1967) 'Zip code: new tool for marketers'. *Harvard Business Review*, 45(1), pp. 136–140.

Bluesea Research (2018) 'Alibaba replicates Amazon's success'. *Seeking Alpha*, 16 November. Available at: https://seekingalpha.com/article/4222826-alibaba-replicates-amazons-success (Accessed: 30 January 2019).

Bolton, R. N. (1998) 'A dynamic model of the duration of the customer's relationship with a continuous service provider: the role of satisfaction'. *Marketing Science*, 17(1), pp. 45–65.

Brennan, T. (2017) 'Alibaba, Marriott team up to redefine travel'. *Alizila*, 7 August. Available at: https://www.alizila.com/albaba-marriott-team-up-to-redefine-travel/ (Accessed: 30 January 2019).

Chadha, R. (2018) 'Nearly half of US households are now Amazon Prime subscribers'. *eMarketer*, 31 January. Available at: https://retail.emarketer.com/article/nearly-half-of-us-households-now-amazon-prime-subscribers/5a72304cebd40008bc791227 (Accessed: 29 January 2019).

Chaudhuri, A. and Holbrook, M. B. (2001) 'The chain of effects from brand trust and brand affect to brand performance: the role of brand loyalty'. *Journal of Marketing*, 65(2), pp. 81–93.

Chou, C. (2017) 'Alibaba's new 88 membership club redefines loyalty'. *Alizila*, 18 August. Available at: https://www.alizila.com/alibabas-new-88-membership-club-redefines-loyalty/ (Accessed: 29 January 2019).

Columbus, L. (2018) '10 Charts that will change your perspective of Amazon Prime's growth'. *Forbes*, 4 March. Available at: https://www.forbes.com/sites/louiscolumbus/2018/03/04/10-charts-that-will-change-your-perspective-of-amazon-primes-growth (Accessed: 26 January 2019).

Copeland, M. T. (1923) 'Relation of consumers' buying habits to marketing methods'. *Harvard Business Review*, 1, pp. 282–289.

Dardi, M. and Gallegati, M. (1992) 'Alfred Marshall on speculation', *History of Political Economy*, 24(3), pp. 571–594.

Day, G. S. (1969) 'A two-dimensional concept of brand loyalty'. *Journal of Advertising Research*, 9(3), pp. 29–35.

Dick, A. S. and Basu, K. (1994) 'Customer loyalty: toward an integrated conceptual framework'. *Journal of the Academy of Marketing Science*, 22(2), pp. 99–113.

Green, D. (2018) 'Prime members spend way more on Amazon than other customers – and the difference is growing'. *Business Insider*, 21 October. Available at: https://www.businessinsider.com/amazon-prime-customers-spend-more-than-others-2018-10? (Accessed: 29 January 2019).

Grönroos, C. (1990) *Service Management and Marketing: Managing the Moments of Truth in Service Competition*. Lexington, MA: Lexington Books.

Grönroos, C. (2006) 'On defining marketing: finding a new roadmap for marketing'. *Marketing Theory*, 6(4), pp. 395–417.

Gummesson, E. (1987) 'The new marketing – developing long-term interactive relationships'. *Long Range Planning*, 20(4), pp. 10–20.

Harris, R. J., Sleight P. and Webber, R. J. (2005) *Geodemographics, GIS and Neighbourhood Targeting*. London: Wiley.

Harrison, B. (1991) 'Industrial districts: old wine in new bottles?' *Regional Studies*, 26(5), pp. 469–483.

Hotel Business (2018) 'Alibaba Group, Marriott trial facial recognition check-in technology'. *Hotel Business*, 12 July. Available at: https://www.hotelbusiness.com/alibaba-group-marriott-trial-facial-recognition-check-in-technology/ (Accessed: 29 January 2019).

Howland, D. (2018) 'Amazon opens "4-star" store in New York City'. *Retail Dive*, 27 September. Available at: https://www.retaildive.com/news/amazon-opens-4-star-store-in-new-york-city/533388/ (Accessed: 26 January 2019).

Huston, C. (2017) 'Grocery stocks tank as "Amazon effect" strikes fear in investors'. *Market Watch*, 16 June. Available at: https://www.marketwatch.com/story/grocery-stocks-tank-as-amazon-effect-strikes-fear-in-investors-2017-06-16 (Accessed: 26 January 2019).

Jacoby, J. and Chestnut, R. W. (1978) *Brand Loyalty: Measurement and Management*. New York: John Wiley & Sons.

Johnson, M. D. and Seines, F. (2004) 'Customer portfolio management: toward a dynamic theory of exchange relationships'. *Journal of Marketing*, 68(2), pp. 1–17.

Keefe, L. M. (2004) 'What is the meaning of marketing?'. *Marketing News*, 15 September, 17–18.

Keiningham, T. L. and Vavra, T. G. (2001) *The Customer Delight Principle: Exceeding Customers' Expectations for Bottom-Line Success*. Chicago: McGraw-Hill.

Keiningham, T. L., Aksoy, L., Cooil, B., Andreassen, T. W. and Williams, L. (2008) 'A holistic examination of Net Promoter'. *Journal of Database Marketing & Customer Strategy Management*, 15(2), pp. 79–90.

Kilgore, T. (2017) 'Costco shares' worst stretch since Great Recession was after Amazon–Whole Foods deal'. *Market Watch*, 24 June. Available at: https://www.marketwatch.com/story/plunge-after-amazonwhole-foods-deal-is-costco-shares-worst-stretch-since-great-recession-2017-06-23. (Accessed: 26 January 2019).

Kolodny, L. (2017) 'Amazon's web site will be flooded with Whole Foods brands, meaning more competition for food sellers'. *CNBC*, 28 August. Available at: https://www.cnbc.com/2017/08/28/whole-foods-brands-compete-with-groceries-on-amazon.html (Accessed: 26 January 2019).

Kumar, V. (2015) 'Evolution of marketing as a discipline: what has happened and what to look out for'. *Journal of Marketing*, 79(1), pp. 1–9.

Kwok, S. (2018) 'Alibaba launches top-tier membership loyalty programme for RMB 88'. *Marketing Magazine*, 9 August. Available at: https://www.marketing-interactive.com/alibaba-launches-top-tier-membership-loyalty-programme-for-rmb-888-or-rmb-88/ (Accessed: 30 January 2019).

Leaver, K. (2018) 'The Alibaba playbook: a guide to how the world's best ecommerce company thinks'. 27 April. Available via: https://www.slideshare.net/kenleaver/the-alibaba-playbook (Accessed: 30 January 2019).

Mandelli, A. (2018) *Intelligenza artificiale e marketing: Agenti invisibili, esperienza, valore e business*. Milan: EGEA.

Mandelli A. and Accoto, C. (2014) *Social Mobile Marketing*. Milan: EGEA.

Marshall, A. (1961) *Principles of Economics*. London: MacMillan.

Melnyk, V., Van Osselaer, S. M. and Bijmolt, T. H. (2009) 'Are women more loyal customers than men? Gender differences in loyalty to firms and individual service providers'. *Journal of Marketing*, 73(4), pp. 82–96.

Parasuraman, A., Zeithaml, V. A. and Berry, L. L. (1988) 'Servqual: a multiple-item scale for measuring consumer perceptions of service quality'. *Journal of Retailing*, 64(1), pp. 14–40.

Payne, A. and Frow, P. (2005) 'A strategic framework for customer relationship management'. *Journal of Marketing*, 69(4), pp. 167–176.

Petrison, L. A., Blattberg, R. C. and Wang, P. (1993) 'Database marketing: past, present, and future'. *Journal of Direct Marketing*, 7(3), pp. 27–43.

Reichheld, F. (1996) *The Loyalty Effect*. Boston, MA: Harvard Business School Press.

Reichheld, F. and Sasser, Jr, W. E. (1990) 'Zero defections: quality comes to services'. *Harvard Business Review*, September–October. Available at: https://hbr.org/1990/09/zero-defections-quality-comes-to-services (Accessed: March 1, 2019).

Retail News Asia (2018a) 'Alibaba announces smart mobility initiatives with partners'. 17 October. Available at: https://www.retailnews.asia/alibaba-announces-smart-mobility-initiatives-with-partners/ (Accessed: 30 January 2019).

Retail News Asia (2018b) 'Alibaba plans technology boost'. 17 March. Available at: https://www.retailnews.asia/alibaba-plans-technology-boost/ (Accessed: 30 January 2019).

Ringold, D. J. and Weitz, B. (2007) 'The American Marketing Association definition of marketing: moving from lagging to leading indicator'. *Journal of Public Policy & Marketing*, 26(2), pp. 251–260.

Shen, L. (2016) 'This is why Starbucks might not be the best stock to buy right now'. *Fortune*, 12 April. Available at: http://fortune.com/2016/04/12/sdtarbucks-stock-downgraded/ (Accessed: 12 November 2018).

Sheth, J. (2005) 'The benefits and challenges of shifting strategies'. *Customer Management* (MSI conference summary). Cambridge, MA: Marketing Science Institute, pp. 4–5.

Sonenshine, J. (2018) 'Amazon could make Whole Foods cheaper than most grocery stores'. *Business Insider*, 2 May. Available at: https://markets.businessinsider.com/news/stocks/amazon-stock-price-whole-foods-could-be-cheaper-than-most-grocery-stores-2018-5-1023168688 (Accessed: 30 January 2019).

Springer, J. (2017) 'Amazon's Whole Foods vision: "Affordable for everyone". *Supermarket News*, 24 August. Available at: https://www.supermarketnews.com/news/amazon-s-whole-foods-vision-affordable-everyone (Accessed: 26 January 2019).

Takala, T. and Uusitalo, O. (1996) 'An alternative view of relationship marketing: a framework for ethical analysis'. *European Journal of Marketing*, 30(2), pp. 45–60.

Tapp, A. (1998) *Principles of Direct and Database Marketing*. Harlow: FT Pitman (Pearson).

Thakker, K. (2018) 'Amazon Prime savings expands to all Whole Foods stores'. *Grocery Dive*, 26 June. Available at: https://www.grocerydive.com/news/grocery–amazon-prime-savings-expands-to-all-whole-foods-stores/533903/ (Accessed: 29 January 2019).

Webster, Jr., F. E. (1992) 'The changing role of marketing in the corporation'. *Journal of Marketing*, 56(October), pp. 11–17.

Whitten, S. (2016) 'Dunkin' Brands shares jump as loyalty program hits milestone'. *CNBC*, 22 August. Available at: https://www.cnbc.com/2016/08/22/dunkin-brands-shares-rise-tracking-for-best-day-since-july-14.html (Accessed: 31 January 2019).

Williamson, O. E. (1975) *Market and Hierarchies: Analysis and Antitrust Implications*. New York: Free Press.

Winer, R. and Neslin, A. (2014) *The History of Marketing Science*. Singapore: World Scientific.

Zaratiegui, J. M. (2004) 'Marshallian industrial districts revisited. Part I'. *Problems and Perspectives in Management*, 49(2), pp. 80–97.

Zeithaml, V. A. (2000). 'Service quality, profitability, and the economic worth of customers: what we know and what we need to learn'. *Journal of the Academy of Marketing Science*, 28(1), pp. 67–85.

2

THE EVOLUTION OF LOYALTY MANAGEMENT

Cristina Ziliani

The origins of loyalty management

In this chapter we tell the story of the tools and techniques that have enabled marketers to encourage customers to return and repurchase, with the aim of shaping their habits in favour of the brand or store. It is a story that begins two centuries ago with premiums and tokens and, passing through plastic cards, lands today on our smartphone screens.

In Chapter 1 we showed that the relationship with the customer has been central to marketing throughout its history. Even during the decades of the marketing management paradigm, when companies focused on acquisition rather than retention, the brand emerged as a way to capture and hold on to customer preferences. Ever since, advertising – in that it told the narrative of the brand – has attracted the most attention as the way to communicate with the customer with long-term goals in mind, including loyalty. So much so that marketing textbooks started in the early twentieth century to make a clear distinction between advertising and sales promotions, making sure to stress that the latter have short-term goals, notably sales.

This is a misconception. The business historian Alberto Guenzi (2015b) suggests we blame economists for framing sales promotion as a tactical, price-reducing tool that merely increases sales. These economists were mostly concerned with studying price promotions – which are easy to model – and their impact on competition, and largely ignored promotional activities that employed incentives other than price reductions. This contributed to keeping such promotional activities outside the purview of academic speculation.

If we read the fascinating guidebooks of Henry Bunting (1913) and Frank Waggoner (1939), however, we learn about the prominent role of 'premium promotions' in the economy of the early twentieth century. Premium promotions did not reduce the price of a product but instead employed premiums that the custo-mer received immediately with her purchase – direct premiums – or, after several purchases, through the redemption of coupons.[1] They were

> to be used where immediate and volume results are important, but the latter imply the diligent collection of proofs of purchase (like wrappers, box tops, stamps, coupons or tokens) by the customer to be given the right of receiving the item offered, and are to be employed *where sustained series of purchases from loyal customers are the objective.*
>
> (*Waggoner, 1939, p. 35: my emphasis*)

The link between non-price-incentive-based promotions and the goal of repeat patronage by loyal customers was quite clear.

Waggoner provided a clear nomenclature of the world of premium promotions that can still be usefully employed today. A direct premium is

> one that is given outright with a specified purchase made at no advance beyond the regular advice. It can be over-the-counter if handed out by the retailer, but can take the form of a container premium, or enclosure premium if it is enclosed in the package of the product [today this is also called 'gift in/ on pack'].
>
> (*Waggoner, 1939, p. 25*)

Premium promotions can both affect sales and shape habits when the reward is deferred, that is, postponed in time. The attractiveness of collecting was well known: for example, Waggoner (1939, p. 26) distinguished 'continuity premium offers' that occur when 'a number of premiums are offered, to be secured one at a time, over an extended period, such as items comprising sets'. A premium coupon was generally a printed slip of paper issued to the purchaser of a product with a redemption value determined by the issuer. It could be part of a label, wrapper or container. By extension, 'any evidence of purchase designated by a premium user, to which a redemption value is assigned is called [a] premium token. It can be a coupon, wrapper, label, box top, bottle cap, trademark and more' (ibid.). A trading stamp was a gummed premium token usually sold by an issuing company to retailers or others, and given by the latter to customers paying cash – generally at a rate of one stamp for every ten cents represented in the respective purchase – and pasted by the customer in stamp books supplied for that purpose. These books, when filled, were redeemable for cash or merchandise provided by the issuing company. A premium catalogue was a printed booklet or folder illustrating and describing the premiums, and how they could be secured.

---

1   It is worth clarifying that premiums are different from prizes, as the latter are awarded by chance to some customers and not to others (and are consequently treated like lot-teries), whereas premiums are available to all customers.

The marketing and competitive effects of premium promotions were already well known to business at the beginning of the twentieth century. By reading Bunting (1913) we can clearly understand that premium promotions increased sales, as was tested with controlled experiments, and supported the differentiation of new entrants in a crowded retail market. They were significant in helping small retailers fight established department stores and helped create profit for stores in unfavourable locations. They could also be used to help fight competition from catalogue companies, thanks to the fact that premiums are visible and tangible, and can be prominently displayed in a store.

Not only did premium promotions support manufacturer-to-consumer and retailer-to-consumer marketing efforts, but they were also successfully used within the marketing channel – to secure cooperation on the part of wholesalers and retailers and to motivate agents and salespeople. The use of premiums in business-to-business (B2B), alone or in schemes that extended over time, was a common practice: W. & H. Walker Co. of Pittsburgh – manufacturers, importers and distributors of toilet and food specialities – were known to say 'Our premiums are our salesmen' (Bunting, 1913, p. 135).

Bunting defined premium promotions as 'the highest possible form of attracting and holding the attention of individual buyers … . The premium is an advertisement in the true and literal meaning of the word' (1913, p. 38). Certainly, it is not 'space' advertising, that is to say, words and images printed in newspapers and magazines; it reconnects to much older forms of grabbing people's attention: with objects, which happened well before print media was invented. It is precisely its tangible nature that makes it attractive: 'The premium is the concentration and condensation of an invisible vapor called discount into a concrete parcel of actual property which the consumer can feel with his fingers' (Bunting, 1913, p. 39). For practitioners in those years, premiums appealed to the heart, to the emotions and to sentiment, and not to reason and intellect as space advertising does (Woloson, 2012). Premium use was encouraged by any manufacturer or distributor whose goods were used up with sufficient rapidity to result in quick and recurrent demand from the same consumer; when the goods were in slow demand, premiums worked if the slow-moving goods could be lumped together with fast-selling goods in the same sale or if the premiums could be given not to the consumer but to the distributor himself. Each of the above effects of premium promotions was known to practitioners but ignored in academia, probably because the mentioned authors were practitioners themselves. A few academics went as far as to extend to premium promotions the criticism that was reserved to lotteries, probably failing to understand the differences.

Premium promotions would be 'rediscovered' by academic research more than half a century later when studies of the effects of loyalty programmes began. They increased along with the development of mass production of consumer goods, and that of advertising. In 1928 the status of premium use was brought before the American Advertising Federation which, 'after an exhaustive hearing, officially recognised and declared premium use a form of advertising, on a parity, legally, ethically and economically, with all other media' (Waggoner, 1939, p. 6). By then, in fact, American corporations such as General Foods and Colgate-Palmolive were investing a significant proportion of their display advertising to communicating some premium offer or another to consumers, and those major campaigns were reporting record sales (for manufacturers and advertising agencies alike). Guenzi (2015b), through five stories of companies whose success was due to the pro-longed, strategic use of direct premium plans often spanning several decades, sheds light into their significance in marketing history.

A survey by Slichter (1916) covering the years 1900–15 showed that proof-of-purchase collection was by far the most widespread type of premium offer. It showed, for instance, that in 1913, an estimated ten million American consumers were collecting tokens (Slichter, 1916). Wright (1958) tells the story of the Jewel Tea Company, a seller of tea and coffee which widely employed premiums and introduced a surprising innovation that made it grow and assume leadership in its industry: the advanced premium. The company salesmen presented customers with a complete set of tableware, that they could immediately have and use, and entrusted the customer with 'paying' for the premium by continuing to purchase tea and coffee from Jewel. A detailed record of the individual customer's 'profit and loss' (i.e. where the customer was in terms of the balance) was kept by the company in order to contact her when the end of the scheme was approaching (i.e. when she had paid the premium off through her series of purchases) and attract her into a new one before she switched to a competitor. This story is particularly meaningful for three reasons: the peculiar faith that the company showed in its customers; the individual customer accounting prac-tice, similar to that of the catalogue business; and the power of a well-chosen reward.

Wright (1958) explained how some companies that employed premiums were so good at testing and choosing rewards that were going to be appreciated by consumers, that they played a role in introducing American society to new products, such as aluminium ware, and later, small electrical appliances. Meredith (1962) outlined three phases in the development of premium pro-motions in the US. The first phase (1851–1900) involved illustrated cards and lithographs, the second (1900–30) saw the growth of token redemption, and the third phase (1930–50) was that of direct premiums. The collection of tokens – that is, promotions employing premiums deferred in time – is most relevant to our history of loyalty management tools. We therefore focus on these in the remainder of this section.

The early days of token-based premium promotions can be then traced to the late eighteenth century, although there are accounts of a New Hampshire mer-chant who, back in 1793, gave customers small copper tokens that could be used, once a certain number was collected, to get goods for free at his store (Lonto, 2000/2013). In 1851 the B. A. Babbitt Company began putting certificates in packages of Sweet Home laundry soap. When a specified number of certificates were collected, they could be exchanged for colour lithographs. In 1872 the Grand Union Tea Company introduced the use of issuing cardboard tickets to customers in its stores, which were later redeemed for merchandise in a company catalogue

(Lonto, 2000/2013). It was, however, a department store in Milwaukee that first issued trading stamps to the public in 1891. One stamp was handed out for every dime spent, and customers pasted them in booklets provided, which were redeemed for merchandise in the same store. The requirement that the stamps be affixed in books not only gave the customer a convenient place to put them, but it also helped prevent fraudulent misuse. Independently, trading stamps had first appeared in the UK in 1851 (Beard, 2016).

The trading stamp

> is essentially the retailer's system for accomplishing the same result as the coupon for the manufacturer … [however,] while the coupon is centred on producing loyal customers for specified products and those only, the stamp or other retailer token embraces store-wide sales. The retailer's aim is to create loyal customers for the store and all the merchandise it handles.
>
> *(Waggoner, 1939, p. 131)*

What would be a distinctive feature of token schemes was already in place in the last years of the nineteenth century. It was not individual retail companies that launched the token scheme – although some did, and in some cities large department stores issuing their own stamps even permitted smaller retailers or traders in non-competing lines to use the same stamps, in a sort of 'loyalty village' (as we discuss in the following section) – but third parties, sort of 'loyalty intermediaries' that performed all necessary activities to promote the scheme, affiliate retailers and supply them with sheets of stamps and booklets for their customers.

These third-party companies developed premium catalogues and even managed dedicated premium stores, the so-called 'redemption centres', where the items featured in the catalogue could be seen, touched and purchased – with stamps only. The history of these token schemes in the US develops alongside that of the most famous of those intermediaries, the Sperry & Hutchinson Company, founded in 1896, whose 'S&H' logo identified the most popular brand of stamps, the Green Stamps. A few years later, Green Stamps were handed out to customers by department stores, grocers and supermarkets, while many entrepreneurs started their own stamp companies. In the early years, frauds abounded, not only in the form of poor-quality premiums: it was not infrequent that start-up stamp companies suddenly closed, the owner vanishing, leaving long lines of outraged consumers outside redemption centres. In 1905 a 'riot' of stamp-holding housewives required police intervention: when they arrived, the redemption centre had already been stripped of all content.

In 1910 the Kroger Grocery & Baking Company – a leader in loyalty today – started building its retail empire 'with a chain of a few small retail stores organised on the premium system' (Bunting, 1913, p. 81). It would give a premium coupon with every purchase, from a nickel's worth of soap upwards. Mr Kroger himself supervised the programme, preaching the following principle:

> See that the customer gets the premium, push the premium on the customer diplomatically, whether he cares for it or not … . Get the customer into the habit of wanting his premium, and of saving his coupons for that specific purpose. In a word, get your customer into the premium habit.
>
> *(Bunting, 1913, p. 82)*

The Kroger company was not a price-cutter, nor a big advertiser, and was entering a territory ridden with competitors: nevertheless, in less than a decade it went from distributing $3,000 worth of premiums a year to $300,000.

Despite the fact premium offers became popular in Europe in the 1920s, much later than in the US (Guenzi, 2015a), both continents experienced similar waves of 'trading stamp fever' during the twentieth century – that is, periods of five to ten years during which stamp schemes proliferated. It became a social phenomenon, attracting the intervention of regulators, until interest faded due to significant economic changes or dramatic events such as the two world wars. The years 1910, 1930 and 1950 marked the peaks of stamp collection in the US. Betty Crocker introduced its box top programme in 1929: box tops, as mentioned above, were coupons that were printed directly onto product packages that could be later redeemed for premiums. As in the US, promotions based on token redemption in Europe were much more common than direct premiums. In Italy three waves peaked in 1937, 1967 and 2007, as the Barilla success story shows (see Chapter 9). In the UK the 'golden' period of stamps was from 1958 to 1980 (Jones and Tadajewski, 2016).

On both sides of the Atlantic, several parties opposed stamp schemes from the start: consumer associations, trade associations, politicians, retailers. The most common critiques involved the allegation that these schemes increased retailers' costs, which in turn were transferred to retail prices, and that these promotional activities pushed consumers to spend more, getting less in return. The first US economist believed to have tackled premium promotions – Isaac Max Rubinow – severely criticized them, suggesting they hinder competition and lure customers into spending more, hence building early arguments for a kind of dismissive, critical attitude that has often surrounded the topic since. Pressure from retailers led Chambers of Commerce in Sweden, Germany, Poland and Switzerland to press for legislation to outlaw, or at least limit, the spread of premium offers. Several US states put forward bills to outlaw stamp schemes or tax them, and Canada forbade them altogether. Manufacturers, and to a lesser extent, wholesalers formed groups and associations to defend the use of premiums in Austria and Germany.

Despite these concerns, premium promotions and stamp or token schemes enjoyed a great revival after World War II as consumer markets boomed and welcomed any novelty. In 1951 King Soopers, a major US supermarket chain, relaunched Green Stamps, soon followed by competitors, all resorting to stamp companies. Consumers witnessed a real 'stamp war' as supermarkets offered double, triple and quadruple stamps on designated days, then every day, to attract customers, until stamp companies forbade the practice. In the late 1990s the Loyalty

Observatory at the University of Parma monitored a similar 'points war' in the UK supermarket industry, this time related to card-based loyalty schemes, as Tesco's competitors hurried to erode Tesco Clubcard's first entrant advantage. Industries other than department stores, supermarkets and fast-moving consumer goods (FMCG) manufacturers adopted stamp schemes: petrol stations, chemists, laundrettes, cinemas and independent grocers and retailers started offering them, opening up new markets for 'loyalty intermediaries', while bigger players such as the national chains looked at stamp schemes more as a necessary evil to stay in business.

During the 1950s, stamp fever again peaked in the US. Attempts by some retailers to eliminate stamps and pass the savings on to customers through lower prices (the practice of 'everyday low price', EDLP) proved unsuccessful, even attracting antitrust condemnation for below-cost sales. A new wave of legislative attempts to regulate premium practice gained momentum (Ziliani, 2008): Kansas outlawed stamps, Washington placed a heavy tax on them, New Jersey claimed $7.6 million from S&H – the value of unredeemed stamps – on the grounds that derelict property becomes the state's property. North Dakotans, on the other hand, invoked a referendum to repeal the anti-stamp law that had just gone into force. The result? Stamps won!

The continuous growth of stamp schemes is testified by the success of stamp companies through the 1960s: S&H was the major single client of General Electric for small home appliances and, with over a million redeemed coupons to manage every week, the company had to take care of increasingly cumbersome operations, including building incinerators next to its warehouses to avoid the theft and reuse of filled booklets, which would compromise the economic balance of the company. During the same years, supermarket chains created 'coalitions' to cooperatively launch and manage their own brand of stamps, for example in California. In 1965, 83% of American families were collecting points, but the downward trend had begun: modern, low-priced retail chains such as Kmart and Target were flourishing across the US, and the oil shock and subsequent spike in consumer goods prices and plunge in consumer confidence swept stamps away for more than a decade. Later they would be subsumed into another extremely successful promotional tool – the card-based loyalty programme.

The age of the loyalty programme (1980–2000)

As Figure 2.1 shows, after trading stamp schemes held the stage for decades, the next step in the history of loyalty management tools was the birth of modern loyalty programmes in the 1980s. Traditionally, 1981 is seen as the start of the loyalty programme era since it was that year (on 1 May) that American Airlines launched its AAdvantage frequent flyer club.

So, what *is* a loyalty programme? According to Butscher (1993, p. 20),

a loyalty program or customer club is a union of people or organisations, initiated and operated by an organisation in order to contact these members

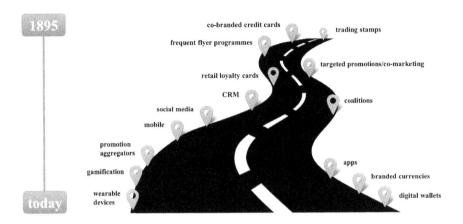

FIGURE 2.1 The history of loyalty management tools

directly on a regular basis and offer them a benefit package with a high perceived value, with the goal of activating them and increasing their loyalty by
creating an emotional relationship.

To be considered as such, loyalty programmes ought to have means for individual
member identification, and for collection and retrieval of individual member data.
Typically, since the 1980s, this has been done by means of a plastic card – the
loyalty card – and a customer database. The 1980s was the decade of database
marketing. Advances in information and communication technologies, notably in
processing power and data storage (well illustrated by Moore's Law: see Chapter 4
in this volume), made it possible to process growing amounts of data for organizations of all sizes. IBM had launched DB2, one of the first databases that, thanks
to its SQL operating language, became one of the most successful tools to aggregate and analyse customer data. Customer databases came to support a variety of
marketing activities, from analysing customer characteristics, to testing commercial
communication, to calculating the return on investment on marketing activities, to
spotting niche segments or determining catchment areas for stores. Marketers star
ted to use databases for one or more of the following reasons: enhancing marketing
productivity, creating a sustainable competitive advantage, and creating and
enhancing customer relationships (see Blattberg et al., 2008, chap. 2).

Plastic cards and customer data

Several industries and companies began to adopt database marketing coupled with
some form of loyalty programme, as defined above. Commercial aviation was the
first industry to adopt data-based, card-based loyalty schemes. In the US, following
deregulation of pricing in 1978, airlines flooded the market with discount coupons
to attract frequent flyers. To fight fraud related to the birth of an illicit coupon

market, airlines built customer databases and started the systematic management of discounts and incentives through mailings and loyalty cards.

The AAdvantage club launched the first modern loyalty programme, based on a plastic card to identify its members and a customer database. It also introduced a loyalty programme 'currency' – air miles – which corresponded to how many miles a member had flown. Members could accumulate points (equivalent to miles of free air travel) by buying airline tickets and other products and these points would be redeemable against the cost of air travel with that particular airline. AAdvantage was soon followed by similar schemes from United Airlines, Trans World Airlines and Delta Airlines – and other airlines around the world quickly replicated the practice (see Table 2.1). In 1987, Southwest Airlines launched a programme which rewarded members with points for trips flown, irrespective of the number of miles, starting a debate that has not ceased today on whether loyalty programme rewards should be based on spending or frequency (as shown by the Starbucks case study in Chapter 9). Soon after the launch of these airline loyalty programmes, hotel and car rental companies began partnering with airlines to offer

TABLE 2.1 Timeline of the rise of modern loyalty programmes

Year	Key event
1981	American Airlines launches AAdvantage
1983	Holiday Inn becomes the first hotel to launch a loyalty programme; shortly followed by Marriott
1986	Discover launches cashback; Canadian retailer Zellers launches the Club Z rewards programme
1987	National Car Rental launches the Emerald Club; Ukrop's introduces the Valued Customer Card programme
1988	Air Miles begins operating in the UK, managed by the Loyalty Management Group
1990	AMC Theatres launches MovieWatcher, thought to be the entertainment industry's first loyalty programme
1991	Nordstrom launches Fashion Rewards
1993	Programmes follow worldwide, launched by Superquinn (Ireland), Delhaize Le Lion (Belgium), Morgan Tuckerbag (Australia)
1994	Launch of flybuys in Australia; Air Miles introduced in the Netherlands; loyalty programmes launched in Italy by supermarket retailer Esselunga and department store Rinascente
1995	Tesco introduces its loyalty card Tesco Clubcard in the UK
1996	Sainsbury's follows with its Reward card (forerunner to the Nectar Card)
1997	Boots, the UK's leading chemist, launches its Advantage Card
2000	Payback, Germany's first coalition loyalty programme, is launched
2002	The Nectar scheme, run by Loyalty Management Group, is launched in the UK, merging several existing loyalty programmes
2006	The Malina coalition loyalty programme is launched in Russia

miles or points as a way to grow their share of the lucrative world of business and high-value leisure travel. Thus were created the first cross-industry loyalty alliances.

During the 1990s, loyalty programmes were adopted in several industries. The Loyalty Observatory was born in those years with the original goal of studying the adoption of loyalty management and use of customer data in European retailing, and overseas. For this reason, the tracking of loyalty practices of over 130 retail groups began in 1997 and provides the foundation for our understanding of the loyalty management phenomenon between 1980 and 2000, when we expanded the monitoring to loyalty programmes in other industries. Our data set of loyalty programme information allowed for a variety of analyses: how the customer was identified; what rewards were available; how customers qualified for rewards; whether rewards were direct or deferred in time; what level of segmentation programmes reached; what direct personal communication was employed; what media were in use, what customer relationship management (CRM) systems, and much more.[2]

Below we share some insights gained from this work of the Loyalty Observatory. Rather than going into detail about how individual loyalty programmes worked, it is more interesting, and critical to this book, to outline how they developed specific characteristics in different countries and different industries. This is no mere historical curiosity: as more industries and companies adopt new loyalty management tools, there are lessons to be learned on how market and country-specific factors may impact success. Think, for example, of the influence market structure may play in favour of non-price promotions – avoiding dangerous price competition in the UK, considering the role of consumers' readiness to accept new payment methods in France or legislation that forbids targeted direct communication in Germany. Unique national factors all play a part in understanding how and where non-price promotion has flourished, or not, and why they differ.

In Europe it was the supermarket industry that led the adoption and advancement of loyalty programmes. Retail in Europe was, in the 1980–2000 period, a collection of very diverse markets: some were concentrated and competitive, and the territory dense with modern retail formats operated by large, managerial, publicly traded companies (Ziliani, 1999). Others counted tens of thousands of mom-and-pop stores organized in local or regional distribution groups, where a 'buy cheap to sell cheap', rather than a marketing mentality prevailed. Such structural differences played a role in the adoption of loyalty programmes. In countries where the supermarket industry was most concentrated, such as the UK, Finland, Norway and Sweden, where three to four groups held 60% or more of the market, two to three large-scale loyalty programmes emerged and quickly dominated the landscape. Awareness of these programmes was high among consumers, and their strategic valence was clear to the management that ran them.

---

2   See Ziliani (1999), Lugli and Ziliani (2004) and Ziliani (2008) for details of the companies monitored and the primary and secondary sources used.

The cycle of loyalty in the UK

In the UK, the concentrated, oligopolistic market and the prevalence of the chain store strategic group, as opposed to small-scale organized distribution, certainly played a role in determining a very fast 'launch–imitation–diffusion–shake out' cycle for loyalty programmes. A saturated market – the average Briton could find all top three supermarkets within ten minutes of their home, largely offering very similar ranges – made it very difficult to grow by opening new stores, as good locations were already taken, or by buying competitors' stores – which antitrust law disallowed on the grounds of obstructing competition. Growth by acquiring competitors' customers by means of price offers yielded diminishing results, as consumers would move back and forth among their two or three stores of reference to take advantage of temporary price cuts, in a zero-sum (and zero-profit) game that in the end left each retailer with the same, but increasingly price-sensitive, customer base.

In such a scenario, non-price promotion looked to Tesco like a promising approach. Several advantages accrued from offering to regular customers advantages that were different from immediate price reductions and which grew progressively over time with the customer's spending. First, the shelf price remained untouched, so the manoeuvre could not be easily imitated in the short term like a classical price cut and did not ignite immediate competitor response. Second, the delayed benefits stimulated repeat patronage and consolidation of customers' share of wallet with Tesco[3] in a virtuous circle. Third, Tesco would be the first to offer such a programme in the UK and would thus enjoy a certain visibility and the first-mover advantage (Lugli and Ziliani, 2004). It is interesting to note that collecting customer transaction data to improve marketing and operational decision-making was not among the company goals at the beginning: it would take a few years, and the intuition of Tesco's consultants – dunnhumby – to turn management attention to the non-visible advantage of a loyalty programme: customer insight. But more on this in the next section.

Having a nationwide network of stores and centralized management of information systems and marketing decisions made it quicker, if not easier, for Tesco to launch and run the programme nationwide. By contrast, we had observed at the Loyalty Observatory that organized distribution groups and, in general, network organizations where decisions are negotiated among peers, are much slower in the adoption of marketing innovations, even when these can be freely observed and imitated because of a first successful and conspicuous entrant in the market or neighbouring markets.

In 1995, Tesco Clubcard was launched. One might wonder why, given the UK market situation, it was Tesco, and not one of the other prominent players, to take this step. This is no idle question since, in our opinion, it helps shed light on the relevance of internal, company-specific, not only external factors, in determining a

---

3   Tesco rewarded customers with vouchers worth 1% of their total spent over the preceding quarter, that could be spent in the store.

business's adoption of loyalty management. At the time, Tesco was a follower, second-in-command in the UK supermarket industry to Sainsbury's. However, it saw the opportunity to gain leadership by consolidating a few points of individual share of wallet, multiplied by ten million loyalty cardholders, into the few points of national market share that separated it from Sainsbury's. The latter had been the leader for decades and, possibly suffering from 'marketing myopia' (Levitt, 1960), did not deem a retention investment necessary – after all, loyalty programmes cost 1.5–2% of annual turnover, which, for a large group, meant tens of millions of pounds. Asda, on the other hand, had a cost leadership orientation that kept it away from extra marketing costs such as those of loyalty programmes: in other words, it preferred to put a discount on the final price, rather than through a card.

In an industry that is traditionally cautious if not risk-averse, Tesco had proven its bold mentality. Back in 1964, it was the first to launch trading stamps in the UK, in a move that contrasted with suppliers' pressures for respect of resale prices (Corporate Watch UK, 2004). So successful was the initiative, that it played a key role in persuading the UK Parliament to liberalize retail prices through the Resale Prices Act the same year. Thirteen years later, in 1977, Tesco was not afraid to eliminate the still hugely successful stamps when it felt consumer preferences were changing due to the economic crisis. In the same year, it introduced Operation Checkout, a massive price cut plan that shook the market profoundly and initiated a price war with Sainsbury's.

In oligopolistic markets it seems that once a first player introduces a loyalty programme or some sort of loyalty management approach, this becomes a requirement for staying in business for all major competitors. At least, they need to 'take a stand' – that is, incorporate in their positioning a clear proposition regarding what they offer as far as customer retention strategy is concerned. Consumers become familiar with the nationally advertised scheme and start evaluating retailers also along their loyalty propositions. Sainsbury's is a case in point. After dismissing Tesco's Clubcard as nothing more than 'the electronic version of trading stamps' and initially refusing to do the same, it rushed to introduce its own Reward Card a year later, after realizing that Clubcard holders were spending 28% more at Tesco and 16% less at Sainsbury's (Shabi, 2003).

The imitation phase had begun. Safeway introduced its version, the ABC (Added Bonus Card) loyalty scheme, in 1995 but ditched it in 2000, after it failed to be distinctive and have any impact on customer behaviour. Boots rolled out the Advantage Card in 1997 and scores of other operators in other retail industries developed similar schemes, including Barclaycard, BP, Shell and WHSmith. Card adoption rates were high during this phase, reaching 20–30% growth per year. National advertising and communication supported the effort. When a scheme introduced a successful perk, the others followed, trying to differentiate it at the same time. For example, significant investments were made in loyalty programme magazines available to cardholders, which would remain a typical feature of such programmes for several decades. In 1997, Tesco's *The Clubcard* magazine (4.5 million copies), *A Taste of Safeway* (2.75 million) and *The Marks & Spencer Magazine* (2.5 million) were among the highest circulated magazines in the country (Ziliani, 1999). From these early, untargeted exercises many retailers will develop segmented approaches to communicating in print with customer base segments, such as through the famous 'clubs' approach that dunnhumby devised for Tesco (Humby, Hunt and Phillips, 2003), from 'mother and child' to 'healthy living' and more (see Table 2.2).

When the number of loyalty programmes increases but existing loyalty programme member bases grow at a slower pace, we enter into the diffusion phase. In 1999 the penetration of loyalty cards among the UK population was growing at a 3% rate, against the 25% growth rate of 1997. In this phase, businesses such as petrol suppliers, restaurants and telecommunication companies that had familiarized themselves with loyalty programmes by partnering with supermarket schemes – for points earning or points burning (redeeming points) or both – began to launch their own loyalty programmes. Multi-business companies started using the loyalty programme to drive traffic to the business unit in need. For example, in response to petrol companies setting up their own loyalty schemes, supermarket chains began offering double points to members patronaging the retailer's petrol stations. In attempts to attract more customers, points earning thresholds were lowered, point conversion rates were doubled, and ever more aggressive moves took place, such as when Asda began accepting vouchers issued by competing schemes or when Tesco converted the points balances of Safeway customers to the Clubcard after the closure of the ABC programme.

The fourth and final phase of the cycle – shake out – soon starts. Out of a total of 150 loyalty programmes recorded in the UK by Marketing Week in 2004, more than half would disappear within ten years. According to Euromonitor, in 2000 the UK had the highest card-to-person ratio in Europe (2.2), followed by the Scandinavian countries. France's was 1.6, Italy's 1.3 and Germany's only 0.6 (Lugli and Ziliani, 2004).

TABLE 2.2 Price and non-price benefits of loyalty programmes

Price	Non-price		
	Premium/prize/game	*Services*	*Self-segmentation*
Immediate discounts	Direct premiums:	Payment (debit)	'Life stage' clubs:
Deferred discounts	– single	Payment (credit)	– Mother and
(points or spending	– piece a week	Financial services	child
or time threshold)	Deferred	Insurance	– Families with
Vouchers (to spend	premiums:	ISP (email box)	children
in store/to spend	– catalogue	Home delivery	– Students
with partners)	– self-liquidating	Shopping evenings	– Seniors
	Sweepstake	Free parking	'Lifestyle' clubs:
	Instant win	Self-scanning	– Gourmet
		Remote ordering	– World of wine
		Partners for points	– Healthy living
		earning and burning	– Quit smoking
		Private sales	– Me time
		Tastings/demonstrations	– Free time
		Customer magazine	

Loyalty schemes go global

In Sweden, Norway and Finland the highly concentrated market situation was coupled with a peculiar feature: the strong tradition of cooperatives. The customer-member is by definition at the centre of the company's attention: she is the actual owner of the cooperative, she pays a membership fee when she joins, and she is rewarded at the end of the year with a rebate that is calculated thanks to the tracking of her purchase history facilitated by the membership card. It is easy to see that the main conditions for a loyalty programme were already in place in these markets. Swedish cooperative Ica had launched its own card in 1990 in three versions: credit, debit and points only. The payment cards were developed completely independently of the banking system, based on the typical expertise and strength of cooperatives in savings collection and management. S-Group in Finland offered the same proposition of credit, debit and membership/rewards only cards. The dominant position of the cooperatives' loyalty programmes in both Sweden and Finland forced competitors to follow suit – as had happened in the UK – and even join efforts to bridge the gap: in 1997 the Finnish group Kesko – a competitor of S-Group – signed a partnership deal with Ica to secure its support for the development of the recently launched loyalty programme.

Payment cards paved the way for loyalty programmes in France too. Here, hypermarkets dominated retail and had been offering credit and debit cards for years: Carrefour launched Pass in 1981, Auchan introduced Accord in 1983, and Castorama, Darty, Conforama and Picard Banners have shared Aurore since 1985. In 1993 there were 25 million active retail payment cards in circulation (Ziliani, 1999). Hypermarkets, though, were slow to add loyalty features to their payment cards: it was supermarkets, struggling to compete, that saw the opportunity. Spurred on by their second-best position while not burdened by a financial services orientation, they embraced loyalty programmes to provide consumers added reasons for repeat patronage. They looked at experiences in neighbouring Belgium and to Tesco and introduced points-based schemes that rewarded customers with vouchers entitling them to reduced prices on selected items in store or with premiums from a catalogue. With this move most supermarkets aimed to reduce advertising spend, especially the costly flyer, which is still common in many European countries, where it accounts for the largest part of supermarket retail ad expenditure (Gázquez-Abad et al., 2014).

France was also home to the longest running scheme in Europe – that of Galeries Lafayette, which is said to have started in 1965. Department stores introduced loyalty management activities well before the supermarket industry: Dutch group KBB and British store Debenhams in the mid-1970s, Zellers in Canada and Coin in Italy in 1986. When the grocery industry was still dominated by independent, traditional, family-run stores, the department store format was in a much more advanced stage of development. Many department stores originate from a trading company of the nineteenth century, involved in importing luxury goods from overseas to supply the leisure class of European capital cities. The type and value of the goods sold may explain why these companies developed payment cards first, and only a decade or so later, following the loyalty programme trend, added a loyalty card or loyalty functionalities to the original payment card. Possibly due to lower penetration rates of payment cards compared to ordinary loyalty cards (30% against 80% of the average customer base), department stores were slow in leveraging insights and developing targeted communication, even if they did make use of direct mailing, if for no other reason but to send customers payment balance information.

Italy saw the first wave of payment cards introduced by selected retail groups in the late 1980s. However, in a country where cash was the dominant means of payment and use of debit and credit cards lagged behind most markets, consumers were not ready to adopt retailers' cards and all projects failed. Those early failures probably contributed to making retailers cautious if not sceptical of card-related projects for some time. The Italian retail market was, and still is, very fragmented into dozens of regional organized distribution networks, and the two major groups, Coop and Conad, are consortia of independent cooperatives with complex decision-making processes. Individual companies lacked the culture and critical mass to develop and communicate marketing innovations effectively. The two foreign players in the market – Carrefour and Auchan – at the time only operated hypermarkets (and their related payment cards) in Italy, and this was hardly an inspiration to others to follow their example on loyalty management. Moreover, retailers in Italy depended strongly on suppliers' contributions for advertising and promotion, a situation that hindered the development of an autonomous marketing orientation and played in favour of preserving long-established practices. Even by the time loyalty programmes became common practice – the end of the 1990s – suppliers were only modestly interested in paying contributions for targeted promotions by means of loyalty card data since the small scale of retail companies made the numbers very small and to have an impact would require signing multiple agreements with many retailers – provided there were enough who not only had a loyalty programme but the necessary human resources and actionable databases too (Ziliani, 2008). By contrast, suppliers in the UK were keen to invest in Tesco's targeted promotions since they knew doing so would mean reaching 30% of British consumers through Tesco's mailing activities.

There were exceptions, of course. The Italian supermarket chain GS was a pioneer and, once absorbed by Carrefour, it contributed to fostering a loyalty management mentality within it. Some cooperatives had excellent information systems and so soon experimented with CRM as well as e-commerce. Esselunga became the 'best in class' example of loyalty management and is still regarded today as a benchmark. Its intuition was, among others, that loyalty management is a long-term strategy and thus should be treated as a brand: it needs an image, positioning and consistency so that it can 'envelop' activities and promotions that evolve over time.

In Belgium, planning and commercial laws had hindered the modernization of the retail trade and the landscape was polarized between three large, modern retail chains and a plethora of traditional grocers organized into buying groups and voluntary chains. The two market leaders – Delhaize and GB – both offered loyalty programmes, with distinct flavours. Delhaize, in alignment with its EDLP strategy, geared its programme towards lower prices for members, while GB opted for a point collection scheme for direct and differed premiums from a catalogue.

Switzerland had an extraordinarily concentrated retail trade, where Migros dominated not only the supermarket business but also others such a petrol stations, DIY hardware stores and bookshops. Despite the reluctance of market leaders to innovate, around the time that Sainsbury's declared its indifference to loyalty programmes, Migros's unsatisfactory financial results and poor customer satisfaction is recognized as being the reason for their launch of its M-Cumulus card in 1997.

Spain is the home of an early experiment with targeted loyalty promotions in the grocery industry. The discounter Dia – owned by Carrefour – ran a very successful card-based programme that rewarded cardholders with reduced prices and special offers printed on till receipts to stimulate repeat visits. While the Spanish hypermarket sector was dominated by French groups (that 'exported' the payment-card approach described above), it was smaller supermarket chains that developed loyalty programmes: Caprabo, for example.

Legislation in Austria and Denmark banned the collection and use of customer transaction data: this kept loyalty programmes at bay for years in those countries. A similar legal ban was in force in Germany until 2000. That, coupled with Germans' reluctance to disclose personal information and a checkout scanner penetration rate that was lower than the European average, contributed to a delay in the adoption of loyalty programmes.

What was happening outside Europe, during the same period, between 1980 and 2000? While Japan, China and India would only see loyalty programmes develop from 2000 onwards, one would reasonably assume that US loyalty programmes would be the most advanced, given the pioneering experiences of the airline industry and the legacy of the direct marketing industry. As far as the supermarket industry is concerned, however, this was not the case. Again, market factors provide some background for understanding this.

According to Supermarket News, 60% of US grocery retailers had a loyalty programme in place in 1996. However, this represented 'very low cost, low technology investment in some kind of short-term incentive programme' (Reynolds, 1995 p. 34). Typically, US supermarket loyalty programmes provided benefits in the form of reduced shelf prices for cardholders (so-called 'two-tier pricing'). One of the reasons that lured US retailers to loyalty programmes was to get rid of the cumbersome burden of managing the billions of print coupons that manufacturers pushed to consumers, and that stores had to manage. In other countries the coupon phenomenon was totally marginal compared to the US, where one of the most popular slogans to advertise the launch of a loyalty card[4] was 'The Clipless Coupon'. Retailers declared to

4   Americans generally prefer to call these plastic cards.

industry press that the reason for the launch was to 'improve customer service and convenience by eliminating coupons, to reduce the high costs of the Hi-Lo price model, and to improve image by adopting a modern tool' (Lugli and Ziliani, 2004). Immediate discounts were communicated with two-tier pricing, that is, shelf labels showing two prices: the regular price and a discounted price for cardholders only. Customers had to show their card at the till to be entitled to the reduced prices.

The Great Atlantic & Pacific Tea Company loyalty programme applied a progressive immediate price reduction approach and was considered 'advanced' at the time, although no analysis was undertaken of customer data. Such immediate price reductions made US supermarkets 'essentially no more than glorified sales promotions exercises with a dose of technology thrown in' (Reynolds, 1995, p. 35). The US technological advancement, the tradition of co-marketing with FMCG manufacturers, notably through coupons, the absence of a national leader in loyalty management – for historical reasons, the US market had been dominated by regional, not national chains – played in favour of a formidable spread of instant reward systems, be it supermarket loyalty programmes or checkout couponing networks such as Catalina's. It would take a full ten years before Kroger embraced loyalty management, significantly under the guidance of dunnhumby, the authors of the Tesco Clubcard success.

Features of the first phase of loyalty management

The 1980–2000 period of loyalty management can be broadly summarized as follows:

1. Loyalty programmes were the main tool for loyalty management. They adopted plastic cards to identify customers at every transaction.
2. They operated a basic segmentation of the customer base into two groups: cardholders and non-holders. Subgroups, such a 'life stage' or 'lifestyle' clubs, where they existed, were mass advertised to the whole customer base who were invited to join by opting in (self-segmentation).
3. Rewards took the form of points, premiums, services and statuses. Table 2.2 classifies the benefits to members identified by the Loyalty Observatory in its cross-industry analysis of loyalty programmes.
4. There was very little or no use of data to generate customer insight. One US supermarket retailer admitted to having 'thrown away' the first five years of transaction data before realizing it could be put to use. Tesco itself focused initially on rewarding customers for their loyalty, not on the insight it could derive from loyalty programme data.
5. The first entrant advantage was real.
6. The simplistic idea that it is sufficient to distribute a card for customers to spend more was common in the early days. Little was known about the impact of the loyalty programme on customer behaviour. Overconfidence in loyalty programme impact on behaviour led to poor planning of programme

costs.[5] Underestimation of some loyalty programme costs, such as the need to revamp the programme periodically to maintain engagement or the costs associated with database maintenance, hindered results. Moreover, companies that knew little about the economics of retention – such as the need to wait in order to see customer lifetime value grow in a loyalty programme after the initial erosion of profits – and expected immediate results from loyalty programmes were soon disappointed, and when projects lacked strong internal support, they were simply closed.

7.   Exits were numerous. Many loyalty programmes were opened and then closed within a year or a few, such as in the case of Safeway, which folded the ABC scheme notwithstanding its 6.5 million active users.

CRM and the promotion revolution (2000 to today)

With the dawn of the twenty-first century, loyalty management ceases to be identified with a single promotional tool (first trading stamps, then loyalty programmes) and broadens its boundaries to encompass an ever-increasing variety of instruments and processes, as shown in Figures 2.1 and 2.3. This is the consequence, on the one hand, of opportunities generated by what has become known as the information revolution, in the form of new data collection and analytical instruments, statistical techniques, new digital media and new devices. On the other hand, it is the consequence of companies' search for differentiation in a market increasingly crowded with 'traditional' loyalty programmes. The powerful catalyst of this evolution in loyalty management was the global economic crisis of 2008–13 which forced companies to invest in innovative promotions to sustain slumping sales. The economics of retention and its benefits were well known by then, so marketers set out to innovate not only price promotion but also loyalty promotion. An increasingly sophisticated digital world allowed new hybrid forms of promotion to be born and for the rise of entirely new players in the promotional arena.

This part of the story of loyalty management starts with the increased presence and competition of loyalty programmes that characterized the early 2000s. According to McKinsey, in the year 2000 both in the UK and the US, 50% of major retailers across grocery, mass merchandisers, department stores, chemists, petrol stations and clothing stores operated loyalty programmes (Cigliano et al., 2000). In Italy the top 20 supermarket groups all had a loyalty programme in place. To distinguish their own loyalty proposition from those of competitors, companies looked to innovate their loyalty programme structure.

Over the years, different models had become established. The simplest loyalty programme model is the 'stand-alone', a closed system where members earn and

5   Holiday Inn's Priority Club, for example, was too generous. After spending 75 nights in one of its hotels, members were entitled to two airline tickets to Europe, a free week in a hotel in Paris and a week of free car rental! Unsurprisingly, the company was forced to restructure the scheme in 1986.

spend points with the issuing party only. Another form, the 'affinity' model, is typically used by credit card companies: points are earned wherever the card is used but can be spent only with the card issuer. Soon stand-alone programmes became the exception to the rule, as businesses, in an effort to provide customers with greater convenience and higher value rewards, created 'villages' of partner companies that supported point collection (earning partners) and/or redemption (burning partners). In the village model, it is the primary brand/retailer that progressively expands the network of involved parties by adding partners to the original loyalty programme. For example, in 2000, Tesco Clubcard points could be earned (or burned) in 7,000 stores in the UK, of which only 700 were Tesco's own stores. Another model that gained momentum in the 2000s was the 'coalition' – although early examples of it originate in the 1980s. As with villages, coalition members can get benefits and rewards through a number of different organizations across several industries; the difference lies in the fact that the programme is not run by one of the partner companies, but rather, it is jointly owned and managed by all partners, typically through a joint venture.

A consequence and sign of the multiple ownership at play in coalition programmes is the choice of a fantasy name for the programme and its card, marking it as a different entity from its partner organizations: Air Miles (Canada), Nectar (UK), Payback (Germany), S'Miles (France), Dotz (Brazil), Malina (Russia), Plenti (US) and I-Mint (India) are among the most well-known cases of coalition loyalty programmes. Some academics and practitioners employ the term coalition in a broader sense, to include all loyalty programmes that have partners (therefore including villages). There are, however, from a business viewpoint, distinctive advantages and challenges posed by the coalition model that make the case for treating the two as separate. For example, in a coalition several loyalty management costs are shared among partners – technology and systems, database analysis, campaign set-up and management, customer care and administration – which makes the model attractive, especially for latecomers to loyalty management that want a loyalty strategy to be up and running quickly. The fact that the major coalitions that operate today around the world, such as those named above, originated from the idea of a few innovators that replicated them in different countries favoured the rise of an international loyalty management services industry and makes the story of coalitions one worth telling.

Rise of coalition programmes

Air Miles was the first coalition programme. The concept was created by Keith Mills, the man who was also behind the Nectar Card, and began operating in the UK in 1988. Consumers who bought products from participating companies were given banknote-like scripts that they could redeem for flights on British Airways. Mills took the idea to the US and Canada in 1991. In the US the idea failed because consumers had to 'clip' barcodes from products of participating manufacturers and mail them to earn miles to redeem as flights from participating airlines – at the very time when retail loyalty programmes were substituting 'clipping' with the modern plastic card and when Americans were already strongly engaged with the programmes of individual brands (especially airlines) that had enough partners to fulfil the function of multi-brand coalitions. In Canada, by contrast, the coalition recruited large retailers such as Sears, which issued air miles to its loyalty programme cardholders, and the scheme flourished – so much so that this retail-driven version was exported to the Netherlands in 1994. In 2003, about 65% of Canadian households and over 53% of Dutch households were collecting Air Miles points.

Once the new ventures were established, Mills and his partners opted to sell their stakes. Air Miles UK was sold to British Airways and the Canadian operation was sold to Alliance Data Systems, a provider of database and CRM solutions. In 2000, Mills began to look again at the UK, where he sought to apply the lessons learned internationally to design a better coalition programme and founded Loyalty Management UK. He decided to seek as core partners retailers who were not happy with their own loyalty programmes and were keen to enhance their impact by joining forces with other companies. With major companies such as Sainsbury's (which had lost the loyalty programme battle with Tesco), BP, Debenhams and Barclaycard among its members, a massive advertising campaign introduced the Nectar scheme to UK consumers in 2002, costing a reported £50 million. Within six months, Nectar had signed up 11 million, or 50%, of UK households (Shabi, 2003).

Coalitions, with their national scale and heavy advertising, contributed to accelerating the diffusion of loyalty programme membership among consumers, especially in countries where loyalty programmes lagged behind, such as Germany, the South American nations and India. The coalition card was everywhere pitched to consumers on the ease of attaining rewards by earning points in one combined account across all sorts of businesses and the simplicity of carrying a single card.

The coalition management venture typically operates by selling to partner companies the right to issue points and buy them back at prices and spreads agreed with each partner (based on each partner's contribution to earning or burning points in large amounts), and by managing promotions and communication to customers on partners' behalf. In addition, they charge partners a fixed fee for administering the programme in all its aspects, from planning and developing the strategy, to managing data, points, rewards and IT systems, to providing communication and customer service across various media with individual customers. Exploring the coalition model's pros and cons is outside the scope of this section; suffice it to say that it is vulnerable to conflicts among partners regarding the price of points, conflict due to the overlap of merchandise sold (for example, both Sainsbury's and BP sell gasoline), the different positioning of some partners that might hinder the image of higher profile ones, the ownership of detailed customer purchase histories, the exit of valuable partners that might reduce appeal for consumers, and partners' fear of fostering a brand different from their own. Despite these risks, for over a decade, coalitions have been hugely successful and subject to acquisition and consolidation among the founding ventures, so much so that today we can count on one hand the number of groups running these large schemes worldwide.

An industry is born

The rise of 'loyalty intermediaries' such as the above-mentioned ventures that ran coalition schemes mark the fact that a market for loyalty management services was born. Coalitions were, in essence, cross-industry behavioural databases and applied scientific rigour and state-of-the-art analytical techniques to analyse members' data. They developed segmentation approaches and predictive models to make promotional offers more attractive, hence increasing redemption rates for offers and promotions. Coalitions spun off their own consulting divisions to offer their expertise to other companies seeking greater effectiveness and professionalization in their loyalty activities. Their highly trained promotion and loyalty specialists were frequently hired by client companies in need of professionals to establish, run or improve their own loyalty management strategies.

In the mid-2000s, the need for structured, scientific and efficient loyalty management efforts was no longer a niche requirement; it was felt across industries by a growing number of organizations. Additional testimony of this is the fact that, during the decade, international strategic consulting groups such as KPMG, PWC and A.T. Kearney opened specialized loyalty divisions and offices. To gain the sustainable advantages of loyalty management strategies, businesses gradually began to embrace the idea that CRM tools were necessary, as the returns of simply having a loyalty programme in place had worn off. In turn, the diffusion of loyalty programmes stimulated academics and practitioners to develop CRM applications to support the design and management of loyalty programmes (Neslin, 2014). Their work sought to address problems such as upselling and cross-selling to members, reducing churn, enhancing loyalty and making the best use of multiple channels, and they provided industry with recommendations based on their research.

Loyalty management was developing an invisible side (CRM) to the visible tools it had been identified with up until then: plastic cards, points, direct mailings, websites, e-newsletters and so on. This is the CRM stage in the history of loyalty management. In the 2000s, coalitions had captured large percentages of the population in the countries in which they operated (around 50% in Germany and UK, for instance) and an increasing number of proprietary customer databases, such as Tesco's, had reached a considerable size. The top 20 retail loyalty programmes in Europe, for example, had in excess of a million active cardholders each. Ten of them had over five million. That was more than the hardware and software available in those days could handle (Lugli and Ziliani, 2004).

With retail loyalty programme databases recording more and more numbers of customers, FMCG manufacturers, who lacked direct contact with the final customer, developed an interest in partnering with retailers to target consumers with direct offers and targeted promotions. Retailers, on the other hand, were keen to show how effective this type of co-marketing could be because they aimed to increase the amount of marketing contributions from suppliers (to cover the costs of their own loyalty management strategies). In the mid-2000s, international manufacturers started introducing specific clauses in supply contracts regarding contributions for targeted marketing activities to loyalty programme members by means of 'cooperative CRM' (Lugli and Ziliani, 2004).

It must be acknowledged that, over the years, supplier–retailer relationships have become more and more transparent as far as data sharing is concerned. Cooperating to share sales data, for example, or inventory data, was beneficial for both parties in that it led to cost savings. Hence a trend of investments in supply-chain IT was in full swing in North America and Europe. The arrival of loyalty programme data-bases and the new types of available insight – data regarding who bought what products or brands – therefore found fertile ground. For retailers such as Tesco or Carrefour, both of which had already set up platforms for sharing sales data with suppliers, sharing customer analysis looked like a natural next step. Tesco moved forward with dunnhumby, which it had acquired in 2001; other groups set up similar agreements with ad hoc companies as data intermediaries. The favourable trends in hardware and software costs continued throughout the decade and made it affordable even for small and medium-sized companies to start investing in CRM tools and services for the analysis of their own loyalty programme customer data-bases. This too contributed to expanding the market for loyalty, customer databases and CRM, thus attracting more entrants to it.

The new digital age

As we review what happened to loyalty management from 2000 to today, we should not forget the bigger picture: the explosion of the Web and of big data. At the beginning of the century, marketers were focused on the dot-com bubble, the exponential growth of the Web and the turbulence of a rising e-commerce era. Companies invested in building websites, intranets and extranets to connect the store network (in the case of retailers), to share supply chain data and to experiment with e-commerce. At the same time, the proliferation of the Web and new mobile devices generated a plethora of available new media that diffused quickly through the first decade of the twenty-first century. SMS text messaging, websites, email, rich media such as video and animation, instant messaging, blogs, forums and early social networks all showed potential for day-to-day communication with the customer base. The availability of these new channels gave new impetus to customer service and loyalty strategies, including loyalty programmes, that have communication with the individual at their core.

New digital media allowed entire industries to embrace loyalty management. Think of low-frequency retail sectors: when a customer visits a store only two or three times a year, she is unlikely to make room for a plastic card in her wallet; but she can register online to the store digital loyalty programme website, and receive emails and mobile promotions. Put simply, CRM and the new digital touchpoints that have emerged in the last two decades have made a retention strategy possible for everyone.

A feature of this new media is the fact that it is bidirectional in nature. The customer can employ the same channel of communication she was contacted through to respond directly to the marketing stimulus. And she can initiate that contact at will. Interactivity – the holy grail of relationship strategies – becomes easier to achieve and new digital tools make the interaction measurable. Engagement becomes the buzzword. Although several definitions of engagement have been provided in the literature, one that has enjoyed a degree of success with practitioners is that proposed by Forrester Research (Cooperstein et al., 2011), which sees it as composed of three aspects: a deep emotional connection with the brand, a long-term relationship, and high levels of active participation. The 'active' part, just as was the case with the 'behavioural' component of attitudinal loyalty, captured marketers' attention because an observable behaviour is easier to register and acts as a litmus test of the non-observable, emotional side of the concept. With digital media, all sorts of active behaviours are recordable: click, share, post, comment, like, contribute, dwell … these, and others, have become engagement measures. For some time, engagement obscured loyalty, as the desirable outcome of marketing activities.

It is no wonder that, with the increased focus on engaging customers, interest in gamification as the 'science of engagement' also emerged. According to Paharia (2013, p. 65) gamification 'takes the motivational techniques that video game designers have used for years to motivate players, and use [sic] them in nongame contexts'. Such techniques included giving users goals to accomplish, awarding badges, engaging them with competition, encouraging collaboration in teams, giving them status, and enabling them to earn points. Some of these features had already been known in the field of promotions and loyalty programmes for several years; others were now being adopted. Social science research on the drivers of motivation was advocated to support the inclusion of these motivational techniques in the design of promotions, digital media and loyalty management tools. Gamification was hailed by some as the new life needed to inject into the loyalty programmes that had proliferated but which were no longer able to set the brand aside and change consumers' habits. One consequence of the adoption of gamification techniques to engage and sustain customers and loyalty scheme members has been to blur the boundaries between the domains of price and loyalty promotion. However, this is one consequence among many the information revolution has had on promotions.[6]

6   Reprinted/adapted by permission from Springer: 'Innovation in brand promotion: reacting to the economic crisis with digital channels and customer insight' by C. Ziliani and M. Ieva (2014). In Gázquez-Abad, J. C., Martínez-López, F. J., Esteban-Millat, I. and Mondéjar-Jiménez, J. A. (eds) *National Brands and Private Labels in Retailing: First International Symposium NB & PL, Barcelona, June 2014*, Cham: Springer, pp. 151–59.

The most tangible change in how individuals now experience promotions is the fact that the physical interface has become digital: specifically, it has become the smartphone screen. Promotional vehicles traditionally had their own individual character – the plastic card, the glossy customer magazine, the paper coupon, the letter from the customer club arriving in the mail. They had their own specific gestures and rituals: clipping coupons, opening letters, flipping through a magazine, pasting stamps into a booklet, swiping a card at the till. Today each of these exists in a digital, successful version, such as e-cards and digital coupons. Consumers experience all of them through the same interface. It is by tapping and swiping on a smartphone screen that we access points, discount codes, loyalty programmes, the digital weekly flyer from our supermarket, the customer magazine and so on. Is this changing their nature, their distinctive character? And what about their impact, their memorability? Research is still lagging behind on these questions and certainly, there are no studies yet written of the long-term effects of substituting physical with digital promotional tools.

The second pervasive impact of the information revolution on promotions has to do with the increasing personalization made possible by the availability of individual customer data from a variety of touchpoints. Loyalty promotions have utilized personalization for several years thanks to CRM, but they are now growing ever more sophisticated as advanced algorithms are employed to predict behaviours, moods and events, and target customers. Meanwhile, the same personalization power is being applied to price promotion, which used to be the domain of one-size-fits-all price cuts but which is now taking quantum leaps in a very different direction. Take, for example, the traditional print promotional flyer. Today, its digital version is available online at retailers' websites. In some cases, this is simply a PDF file; in others, it is enhanced with everything that digital can offer. By clicking on product images on the flyer, consumers are taken to product descriptions, recipes, shopper ratings, and to brand websites for a one-click purchase. Different versions of the flyer are made available online. Consumers can register their brand and category preferences with the retailer so they can regularly receive (via email or in the retailer app or an all-purpose digital wallet) a flyer targeted to their individual needs. A flyer is no longer solely a price promotion vehicle; it also serves relationship purposes. As with the adoption of gamification techniques, this increased level of data-based personalization has contributed to blurring the lines between price and loyalty promotion.

As we move up the pyramid in Figure 2.2, we find the third impact of the information revolution: digital enables new types of promotion that could not have existed before since they are impossible or impractical to deploy in the physical world (Grewal et al., 2011). Think of group deals or flash sales, where consumers who are geographically dispersed and unaware of each other come together on an online platform to express interest (in a short time bracket) in purchasing a product at a discounted price: the discount is granted once a critical mass of prospective buyers is reached.

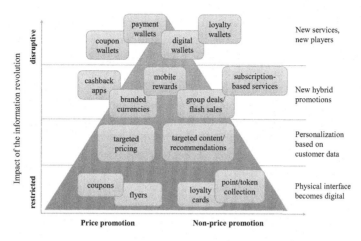

FIGURE 2.2 Impact of the information revolution on promotions

Digital also revives a long-established type of promotion: the subscription club. Subscriptions are lock-in loyalty activities where customers pay in advance for a repeated service over time. Subscription-based e-commerce gives companies regular income, a greater ability to upsell and deeper relationships with customers, which can generate customer loyalty. Customers benefit from lower costs, time savings and more efficient purchases. Minor brands such as Dollar Shave Club have launched nationwide following a subscription club business model that challenges established FMCG brands. Competition in the healthy snacks category was revived by subscription-only start-up Graze, followed by General Mills's experimental app Nibblr and then Kellogg Company's subscription snack service (Stanford, 2015). Colgate announced in July 2018 that it's investing in Hubble, an online start-up that sells subscriptions for contact lenses (Copeland and Terlep, 2018). Subscriptions deliver solutions regularly to consumers and since bundling related products can deliver increased value, it seems that Colgate will focus on building personalized collection schemes based around all the tools consumers need for oral care. The explosion of this phenomenon has led business analysts like McKinsey and Forbes to employ the expression 'subscription economy' (Columbus, 2018), noting that, for example, 50% of online shoppers in the US belong to at least one subscription service (Chen et al., 2018). Amazon Prime's success has led many others – including Alibaba – in recent years to add a subscription-based 'layer' to their loyalty programmes (Hu, 2018).

Digital reward platforms – the online version of points-based repeat-purchase promotion – used to require consumers to enter product codes via a personal computer (e.g. Coke Rewards). They now reward customers for specific behaviours, brand purchase or visits to stores, thanks to apps that localize shoppers, read till receipts, collect user-generated content such as product photos and can credit customers with cash, discounts or points. Kellogg's Family Rewards counts millions of customer records in its database and promotes loyalty to the company's brand portfolio. Mobile devices have made digital reward programmes much more convenient. The Ibotta app in the US and T-frutta in Italy, for example, allow consumers to take a photo of the till receipt showing the purchase of the promoted products: the amount saved by the brand-buying shopper is automatically credited to their account for later use (cashback) or conversion into coupons. Start-ups in this area abound and compete for consumer engagement and brand investment. Cashback programmes offer members a partial cash rebate on their purchases. This money is collected in a virtual pot before being transferred directly into the customer's bank account or converted into another form of 'currency', as we discuss below.

New promotional intermediaries were born to capitalize on opportunities like these. Some of their models show a clever, hybrid use of both price and loyalty promotion to attract shoppers and make them stay. For example, the Aisle50 app provides savings to consumers who buy a branded product online and are willing to pick it up at their local grocery store using their loyalty card to facilitate the transaction. The programme gives shoppers convenient access to special buys and strengthens their relationship with the retailers that offer the programme. It also gives FMCG marketers a way to sell directly to consumers without risking conflict with important retailers. At first, Aisle50 offered daily deals, thus operating more on the price promotion side, but it soon moved to a subscription model. It extended the saving offers into 'continuous prepaid subscription deals': meaning it offered customers who showed an interest in specific brands the opportunity to buy at a reduced price in the future by subscribing to the deal, for a fee. The new 'subscription deals' allow shoppers to get products repeatedly from the participating retailer at the same price as Target or Walmart, and sometimes even cheaper, and provide revenues and loyalty to brands, participating retailers and the promotional intermediary, in a win-win-win scenario. In 2015 the start-up behind the app was acquired by another promotion intermediary: Groupon.

Another very interesting case of price and retention approaches being blurred by new intermediaries is that of flyer aggregators, platforms that shoppers around the world increasingly use to browse retail flyers conveniently. These information intermediaries group online flyers by retail sector and geographical area down to zip/postal code and allow customers to compare prices and offers across flyers in real time. They support retailer and manufacturer promotional efforts in many ways. Depending on the level of investment, greater visibility, delivery of previews, reminders of flyer and other communications can be pushed to the customer segments of choice. It has been demonstrated by the research company Nielsen (2011) that aggregators give retailers access to non-loyal customers, a different audience from the retailer's own digital assets visitors. The flyer intermediary thus closes an insight gap, in that it traces the behaviours of customers who are not in the loyalty programme database.[7]

7   We have dedicated previous work to digital flyers and flyer aggregators (see Ziliani and Ieva, 2015).

The next innovation?

Innovation has come to loyalty management from several industries, over time. We believe that the payment industry will have the most significant impact in the coming years, not least because of the growing importance of subscription services in every aspect of our lives. The payment industry has already been radically transformed by the information revolution. E-commerce has spurred the development of online payment methods. According to Worldpay (2018), over 300 alternative online payment methods exist, that is, methods other than credit and debit cards (of which PayPal is possibly one of the best known[8]) and account for 50% of total e-commerce payments worldwide. Brands and retailers have been looking at the retention potential of means of payments for some time. In the early 1980s, many retailers had launched payment cards well before loyalty cards. Today, digital wallets (also called e-wallets or virtual wallets), where money can be stored – by preloading them or taking funds from another payment method like a credit card – to use later on brand purchases, are quickly spreading. They are predicted by Worldpay (2018) to grow from 18% to 46% of global payments by 2021. The Starbucks case is a success story of a loyalty programme that morphed into a payment method and will possibly become a payment platform for third parties (Chapter 9). Following Starbucks, Subway and Dunkin' Donuts have launched similar digital wallet-based schemes in recent years.

Not every brand will be able or see fit to invest in the development of its own branded currency like Starbucks has. But integrating payment methods into one's loyalty strategy is seen as imperative today, and many will do it by partnering with services such as Samsung Pay or Apple Pay, with credit card company digital wallets, or by offering peer-to-peer payments. In August 2018, Abercrombie & Fitch, the clothing retailer, integrated the PayPal-owned peer-to-peer money transfer platform Venmo within its mobile app (Williams, 2018). In adding Venmo, Abercrombie & Fitch hope to win over millennials and Gen Z customers, who have been quick to embrace the use of digital payments. Google, Apple, Samsung and Alipay digital wallets not only store everything we used to carry in our physical purses – cash, ID, coupons, loyalty cards, credit and debit cards – but, given that they have access to a wealth of data on individual customers, they can act as information and promotional intermediaries for any business that wants to invest. The Alibaba case is a testimony of how integrated payment services and loyalty management solutions are becoming.

---

8   At the end of the twentieth century, PayPal emerged as the first online money transfer company. In recent years, the rise of fintech has flooded this sector with new players such as InstaRem and TransferWise. And with the emergence of blockchain technology, cryptocurrencies such as bitcoin, and ongoing breakthroughs in artificial intelligence (which has led to talk of possible voice-based cross-border money transfers), the future of the industry looks set for more rapid change.

When the financial crisis hit the US and Europe, loyalty programmes were commonplace. From the Loyalty Observatory evidence base[9] we know that in 2008, 93% of US retailers – across all industries – had a loyalty programme in place and that 80% of credit cards and 25% of debit cards were linked to a loyalty programme. In the supermarket business, 49% of companies had a programme, reaching on average 90% of the customer base. Overall, the retail industry was top of the tree in terms of numbers of active cards: retail company loyalty databases counted 153 million consumers. In the UK, 41% of the 250 British companies had a loyalty programme, while in France in 2009, 100 million cards registered to 300 programmes were in circulation.

In times of economic downturn, consumers typically reduce their grocery bill by buying more private label products, shifting a portion of their spending to discount stores and buying on promotion. During the past crisis years, however, shoppers resorted to even more drastic measures. Reducing volumes and giving up certain purchases altogether were the two main saving strategies. The steep drop in sales across all consumer goods sectors called manufacturers and retailers to take action and in order to obtain quick results, they increased promotional investments.

However, this came after decades of increasing promotional pressure. More than one in four products in the average European supermarket was sold on promotion (i.e. at a discounted price) before the crisis (Ziliani and Ieva, 2014). Price cuts became ubiquitous but did not make consumers buy more. We analysed how indexes of promotional effectiveness in the US and Europe declined for several years in a row in a previous study (Ziliani and Ieva, 2014). A vicious circle of increasing investment and decreasing effectiveness led manufacturers and retailers to take action.

Innovation in promotion was chosen by many as a strategy to sustain sales in the post-crisis economy. In fact, simply decreasing promotional spending was not possible for most players since it would make them vulnerable to competition. The increased price sensitivity of consumers in recession also meant that they did not forget their loyalty cards and showed them at every possible occasion (Aimia, 2013). The more intense use of the card allows for better tracking of behaviour and thorough data collection at the individual level. This sustained brands' interest in loyalty strategies. In an effort to sustain sales and reconnect with shoppers, manufacturers and retailers looked at all available options for innovation in promotions. What they found was a rich and diverse range of new options that had been deeply transformed or ushered in by the information revolution.

Brands' interest in experimenting with new promotion types, channels and intermediaries fuelled the development of these new technologies, and as the impact of the global financial crisis came to an end, the loyalty management landscape emerged thoroughly transformed. As Figure 2.1 showed, the new frontier of loyalty is one equipped with a diverse set of new tools made possible by the age of

9   The data in this paragraph is drawn from various research reports compiled by the Loyalty Observatory (Osservatorio Fedeltà) over the course of the last 20 years. Some of these reports have yet to be made available digitally and others are protected by confidentiality agreements. Those that are available are in Italian and can be accessed at the Observatory website: http://www.osservatoriofedelta.it.

digital. With these tools have come a host of new players (retailers, manufacturers, e-commerce-only enterprises, promotion intermediaries) that have flooded the loyalty sector and offered new and more innovative options to consumers. Twenty years ago, only retailers were offering loyalty programmes. Today the picture is very different (Figure 2.3).

What loyalty means today

In the previous section, we called the period from 1980 to 2000 the age of the loyalty programme. Continuing this theme, we might call the phase from 2000 to today the age of CRM. Let us recall some of its main features.

1. Loyalty management is no longer synonymous with loyalty programme but encompasses an increasing variety of ever more sophisticated tools.
2. Due to the diffusion of CRM, loyalty management begins to mean managing the customer relationship along its lifecycle by means of individual customer data (collected via the loyalty programme or otherwise).
3. New types of loyalty programmes diffuse, notably coalitions.
4. New digital media are adopted en masse in loyalty management and price promotion.
5. Promotional intermediaries are born which demonstrate how customer data can be effectively leveraged and which offer loyalty management services and consulting.
6. Loyalty management practices are embraced by new industries that did not have direct access to final consumers or were impaired by a low frequency of visits or long repurchase cycles.

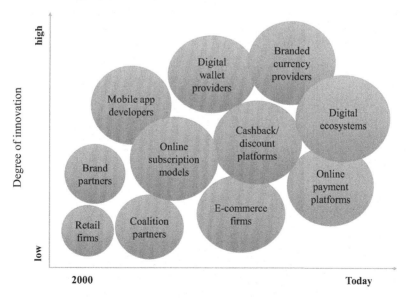

FIGURE 2.3 The new players in loyalty management

7. Mobile devices profoundly change marketing and because of their intimacy and potential for continuous and ubiquitous interaction are immediately embraced in loyalty management.
8. The industry of loyalty management tools and services is born, comprising CRM vendors, loyalty management platforms and a host of other players.

From 1980 to the end of the twentieth century, managing loyalty basically meant running a loyalty programme (Figure 2.4). Since 2000, companies have turned to the 'invisible' advantages of loyalty schemes (and related customer databases) – that is, the insight they unlock and its use for targeted marketing activities for retention, upselling, cross-selling and reactivation of selected members of the customer base. Today, in 2019, we believe we are entering a new phase in which loyalty management is identified with the design and management of a quality customer experience across the various touchpoints that connect the customer and the brand.

If we look at the evolution of loyalty management it is possible to notice a continuous attempt by marketers to extend the benefits, privileges and moments in which a customer is recognized as a member. What was the purpose of villages and coalitions, after all? We could say that loyalty management efforts have continuously focused on creating and expanding a space of free circulation for the customer – in which she is identified as an individual customer with unique characteristics derived from data collection at various touchpoints – and provide superior value doing so. The development of CRM tools and the impact of the information revolution only furthered such a trend by spurring on advances in systems for customer identification across touchpoints and in personalization algorithms. Mobile and wearable devices played a major role. In China, services like WeChat truly show how a customer can be placed at the centre of an ecosystem, not to mention Alibaba's vision of a digital loyalty ecosystem that we discussed at the beginning of this book.

FIGURE 2.4 The three phases of loyalty management

In order to make a customer loyal, companies now consider it necessary that she encounters the brand at the relevant touchpoints along which her shopping journey evolves, be it traditional touchpoints such as the store or newer ones such as apps, digital wallets or promotional aggregators. If she feels that such an encounter positively contributes to the journey in some way, this translates as a quality customer experience. This might be generated if she feels that her encounter with the brand at the touchpoint is relevant or engaging or personal, is consistent with the stage of the shopping journey or even with the emotional state she is in, or if it adds value in some other way to her journey. Research suggests, as we discuss in Chapter 6, that a positive customer experience leads to loyalty.

In order to orchestrate touchpoint encounters across channels to improve the customer experience, a new framework is emerging: customer experience management (CEM). As stated by the influential work of Homburg, Jozić and Kuehnl (2017), the final goal of CEM is to achieve long-term customer loyalty by designing and continually renewing touchpoint journeys. CEM and loyalty management, therefore, share the same goal: making customers loyal. CEM is, however, only a theoretical framework at the moment, whereas loyalty management has proven to be an effective set of tools and approaches that work. These tools and approaches can be the enabler of the CEM framework. A loyalty programme, for example, serves the purpose of identifying customers, and CRM serves to provide insights that help create personal and relevant interactions.

In their search to translate the CEM framework into action and put in place a seamless management of touchpoints so that the customer is identified consistently across them and treated accordingly, marketers should look at loyalty management. Since most companies today have some sort of loyalty programme or CRM activity already in place, this could be the starting point to move into the next phase that is CEM. We elaborate on this in Chapter 8.

References

Aimia (2013) *The Rise of the Savvy Shopper: The Impact of the Recession on Customer Loyalty.* Paid access only, summary available at: https://engageemployee.com/the-rise-of-the-savvy-shopper/ (Accessed: 14 December 2018).

Beard, F. K. (2016) 'A history of advertising and sales promotion'. In Jones, D. B. and Tadajewski, M. (eds), *The Routledge Companion to Marketing History*, Abingdon: Routledge, pp. 203–224.

Blattberg, R. C., Kim, B. D. and Neslin, S. A. (2008) *Database Marketing: Analyzing and Managing Customers.* New York: Springer.

Bunting, H. S. (1913) *The Premium System of Forcing Sales: Its Principles, Laws and Uses.* Chicago: Novelty News Press.

Butscher, S. A. (1993) *Customer Loyalty Programmes and Clubs.* Aldershot: Gower.

Chen, T., Fenyo K., Yang, S. and Zhang, J. (2018) 'Thinking inside the subscription box: new research on e-commerce consumers'. *McKinsey*, February. Available at: https://www.mckinsey.com/industries/high-tech/our-insights/thinking-inside-the-subscription-box-new-research-on-ecommerce-consumers (Accessed: 14 December 2018).

Cigliano, J., Georgiadis, M., Pleasance, D. and Whalley, S. (2000) 'The price of loyalty'. *McKinsey Quarterly*, 4, pp. 68–77.

Columbus, L. (2018) 'The state of the subscription economy, 2018'. *Forbes*, 4 March. Available at: https://www.forbes.com/sites/louiscolumbus/2018/03/04/the-state-of-the-subscription-economy-2018/#15bec14d53ef (Accessed: 14 December 2018).

Cooperstein D. M., Bernoff, J., Hayes, A. and Ryckewaert, E. (2011) *Competitive Strategy in the Age of the Customer, Forrester Research*, 6 June. Available (subscribers only) at: https://www.forrester.com/report/Competitive+Strategy+In+The+Age+Of+The+Customer/-/E-RES59159# (Accessed: 2 February 2019).

Copeland, R. and Terlep, S. (2018) 'A toothpaste club? Colgate to invest in online startup'. *Wall Street Journal*, 2 July. Available at: https://www.wsj.com/articles/a-toothpaste-club-colgate-to-invest-in-online-startup-1530537593 (Accessed: 14 December 2018).

Corporate Watch UK (2004) 'Tesco company profile'. 18 October. Available at: https://corporatewatch.org/tesco-company-profile/ (Accessed: 12 December 2018).

Gázquez-Abad, J. C., Martínez-López, F. J. and Barrales-Molina, V. (2014) 'Profiling the flyer-prone consumer'. *Journal of Retailing and Consumer Services*, 21(6), pp. 966–975.

Grewal, D., Ailawadi, K. L., Gauri, D., Hall, K., Kopalle, P. and Robertson, J. R. (2011) 'Innovations in retail pricing and promotions'. *Journal of Retailing*, 87S(1), pp. S43–S52.

Guenzi, A. (2015a) 'Building brand awareness with a bowl of cherries'. *Journal of Historical Research in Marketing*, 7(1), pp. 113–132.

Guenzi, A. (2015b) 'Le origini americane delle operazioni a premio'. In Ziliani, C. (ed.), *Promotion Revolution*, Milan: EGEA, pp. 251–279.

Homburg, C., Jozić, D. and Kuehnl, C. (2017) 'Customer experience management: toward implementing an evolving marketing concept'. *Journal of the Academy of Marketing Science*, 45(3), pp. 377–401.

Hu, K. (2018) 'A look at Alibaba's Amazon Prime-like loyalty program'. *Yahoo Finance*, 10 August. Available at: https://finance.yahoo.com/news/look-alibabas-amazon-prime-like-loyalty-program-195547419.html?guccounter=1 (Accessed: 14 December 2018).

Humby, C., Hunt, T. and Phillips, T. (2003) *Scoring Points: How Tesco is Winning Customer Loyalty*. Sterling, VA: Kogan Page.

Jones, D. B. and Tadajewski, M. (eds) (2016) *The Routledge Companion to Marketing History*. Abingdon: Routledge.

Levitt, T. (1960) 'Marketing myopia'. *Harvard Business Review*, 38(July–August), pp. 24–47.

Lonto, J. (2000/2013) 'The trading stamp story (or: when trading stamps stuck)'. Available at: http://www.studioz7.com/stamps.html (Accessed: 12 December 2018).

Lugli, G. and Ziliani, C. (2004) *Micromarketing: Creare valore con le informazioni di cliente*. Turin: UTET.

Meredith, G. (1962) *Effective Merchandising with Premiums*. New York: McGraw-Hill.

Neslin, S. (2014) 'Customer relationship management'. In Winer, R. S. and Neslin, S. A. (eds), *The History of Marketing Science*. Singapore World Scientific, pp. 289–317.

Nielsen (2011) 'From print to digital, slowly the evolution of the circular'. Available at (registration required): www. nielsen.com/us/en/insights/reports-downloads/2011/the-evolution-of-circulars-q42011.html (Accessed: 14 August 2017).

Paharia, R. (2013) *Loyalty 3.0: How to Revolutionize Customer and Employee Engagement with Big Data and Gamification*. New York: McGraw-Hill.

Reynolds, J. (1995) 'Database marketing and customer loyalty: examining the evidence'. *European Retail Digest*, 7(Summer), pp. 31–38.

Shabi, R. (2003) 'The card up their sleeve'. *Guardian*, 19 July. Available at: https://www.theguardian.com/lifeandstyle/2003/jul/19/shopping.features (Accessed: 12 December 2018).

Slichter, S. (1916) *Coupons, Trading Stamps and Premium Systems*. New York: Alexander Hamilton Institute.

Stanford, D. D. (2015) 'Kellogg said to plan snack subscriptions as General Mills exits'. *Bloomberg*, 9 June. Available at: https://www.bloomberg.com/news/articles/2015-06-09/kel logg-said-to-plan-snack-subscriptions-as-general-mills-exits (Accessed: 14 December 2018).

Waggoner, F. (1939) *Premium Advertising as a Selling Force*. New York: Harper & Bros.

Williams, R. (2018) 'Abercrombie & Fitch cashes in on Venmo for mobile payments'. *Mobile Marketer*, 8 August. Available at: https://www.mobilemarketer.com/news/abercrombie-fitch-cashes-in-on-venmo-for-mobile-payments/529613/ (Accessed: 14 December 2018).

Woloson, W. A. (2012) 'Wishful thinking: retail premiums in mid-nineteenth-century America'. *Enterprise and Society*, 13(4), pp. 790–831.

Worldpay (2018) *Global Payments Report*. Available at (registration required): https://worldpa y.globalpaymentsreport.com/#/insights (Accessed: 15 September 2018).

Wright, J. (1958) 'A brief marketing history of the Jewel Tea Company'. *Journal of Marketing*, 22(4), pp. 367–376.

Ziliani, C. (1999) *Micromarketing: Le carte fedeltà della distribuzione in Europa*. Milan: EGEA.

Ziliani, C. (2008) *Loyalty Marketing: Creare valore attraverso le relazioni*. Milan: EGEA.

Ziliani, C. and Ieva, M. (2014) 'Innovation in brand promotion: reacting to the economic crisis with digital channels and customer insight'. In Gázquez-Abad, J. C., Martínez-López, F. J., Esteban-Millat, I. and Mondéjar-Jiménez, J. A. (eds), *National Brands and Private Labels in Retailing: First International Symposium NB & PL,* Barcelona, June 2014. Cham: Springer, pp. 151–159.

Ziliani, C. and Ieva, M. (2015) 'Retail shopper marketing: the future of promotional flyers'. *International Journal of Retail & Distribution Management*, 43(6), pp. 488–502.

3

MAKING CHANNEL PARTNERS LOYAL

Cristina Ziliani

Managing relationships with channel partners[1]

A vast body of research on retailing and channel relationships has pinpointed the fact that the evolution within distribution channels – the modernization, concentration and proliferation of formats and new channels – and parallel changes in consumer habits have pushed manufacturers to take action to orient channel players to support their brands. At the same time, distributors have developed an increasingly autonomous marketing mindset that makes them less ready to accept manufacturers' proposals. The rise of trade marketing activities and the establishment of trade marketing roles within manufacturers' organizations, as well as the business-to-business (B2B) roots of the relationship marketing paradigm, is testimony to a long-felt need to manage channel relationships. According to Narus and Anderson (1996), firms are constantly busy finding new and creative ways to motivate intermediaries by way of direct or indirect sales force activities and other initiatives for distributors.

Academic attention has mostly focused on *contractual* incentives and instruments: discounts, street money, free goods, bill back, inventory financing and slotting allowances, calendar marketing agreements, display allowances, co-op advertising, co-marketing and more. Gilliland's (2003) analysis of standard contracts offered by manufacturers to independent resellers identified 173 different incentives in the IT industry alone. Contractual incentives are, for the most part, monetary in nature.

By contrast, the non-price, non-monetary forms of channel promotion have received little attention in the literature, with some exceptions. Kasulis et al. (1999) categorize trade promotion incentives according to the distributor's interest and

---

1 Reprinted/adapted by permission from Springer: *European Retail Research*, 26(2), Ziliani, C. (2012) 'From "trade loaders" to "online channel partner programs": how trade promotion changed its face from 1990 to 2010', pp. 77–95.

their effects. Those effects could be: (a) compliance, in the short term, with the requested behaviour; (b) identification, that is, cooperation limited to the initiative at hand; (c) internalization, also defined as 'attitude and behaviour consistency', that is, long-term cooperation rooted in the alignment to common goals. Kasulis et al. note that price incentives determine short-term compliance with supplier demands but do not bring about an attitudinal change from channel partners. Price incentives are welcomed by resellers because they can be easily put to the service of their own objectives, in that they result in higher margins to utilize. However, Frazier and Sheth (1985) and Kasulis et al. (1999) point out that channel partner initiatives need to produce attitudinal, not only behavioural results. Non-price promotional activities that develop brand or image and involve distributors and their personnel can, in fact, result in internalization or long-term cooperation. Such a desirable situation in behaviour and attitude consistency bears a striking resemblance to attitudinal loyalty as we defined it in Chapter 1.

In industries – and countries – where the distributors' landscape is fragmented and where, because of the nature of the goods sold or the purchase process, assisted sales rather than self-service is the rule, manufacturers tend to adopt non-price promotional activities. However, with power increasingly shifting towards retailers, including e-commerce behemoths, will these increasingly powerful players push suppliers to provide price incentives only, hence eroding the ground for non-price trade promotion? Any player along the marketing channel could benefit from adopting loyalty management tools and techniques to support their relationship with the others. Is this opportunity being missed?

Non-price promotions in channel relationships

With these questions in mind, we decided to investigate the use of loyalty management tools – loyalty schemes, point collection, customer clubs and so forth – in channel partner relationship management. By means of three research projects conducted in 2008, 2011 and 2015, we explored B2B non-price promotions along their many dimensions: goals, type of recipient in the channel, techniques, incentives and duration. The first study had two core research objectives:

1.   to put forward a classification of B2B non-price promotional activities based on goals, rather than techniques, in order to explore if and how non-price incentives were used to control channel partners and motivate their behaviours, with a specific focus on retention and loyalty goals
2.   to compare, with specific reference to loyalty programmes, its results with previous findings for B2B and draw conclusions on the opportunities for loyalty management in the B2B context.

In 2011 and 2015 the analysis was repeated in order to capture possible signs of change in B2B promotions that might have descended from the impact of the promotion revolution described in Chapter 2 and from the onset of the economic crisis. In fact, analyses conducted over the years by the promotions industry body Incentive Performance Center in the US show a surge of B2B promotion and motivation activities during periods of economic downturn (Incentive Performance Center, 2008). We chose to focus on loyalty management activities directed at resellers/distributors and salespeople alike. Both categories are targets for manufacturers' efforts to control and manage the channel, although in business and academic literature where the target is salespeople the words 'motivation' and 'incentives' are employed, while 'trade promotion' is generally reserved for promotions targeting retail or wholesale distributors.[2]

Several campaigns illustrated well how marketers create promotions that target both types of channel partners simultaneously. Brembo, a multinational manufacturer of automotive brake systems with a headquarters in Bergamo, invites garages to join its Professional Club programme: in return for a minimum purchase obligation, the garage owner, mechanics and end customers receive gadgets and premiums. Garages also earn points with purchases and by setting up special Brembo brand displays. Garage owners can check their points, claim premiums from a catalogue and convert points into discounts on future orders, all online on the programme website.

In this section we use the expressions 'channel promotion' and 'B2B promotion' interchangeably to encompass non-price promotion directed at players in the channel, both organizations and individuals. The various categories of recipients for B2B promotions that we identified in our analyses can be classified as follows. A first general distinction can be made between 'trade', i.e. firms that purchase and resell brands' products and services (be they independent retail stores, chain stores or wholesalers), and 'sales force', i.e. persons who act independently (e.g. agents) or as employees of brands and resellers (e.g. direct sales force and third-party salespeople for the sale of the brands' goods and services). For example, a brand of cosmetics might target their B2B promotional activities at Sephora (a chain store), to Sephora employees (third-party salesforce), to a wholesaler of cosmetics, to independent perfume shops, to their own salespeople or to agents and dealers who, in turn, sell to the various types of trade just mentioned.

The promotional activities included in our study went beyond loyalty programmes since considering only these would have been restrictive and it was common knowledge that other promotional techniques such as 'trade loaders' and 'sales contests' were in use to support retention, relationship and loyalty goals. We therefore included the following types of non-price promotion:

- direct premiums (also known in B2B as trade loaders)
- sales contests

2   *promuovere* means 'showing the way to go', and the Latin for incentive – *incentivum* – derives from 'setting the tone for someone to sing'.

- various forms of token scheme (based on a point or proof-of-purchase collection mechanism and offering just one premium or a wide range of rewards/ points redemption options)
- clubs entitling members to privileges and/or special services
- sweepstakes and draws
- games.

The above activities are categorized as 'premium and prize promotion' by Mullin and Cummins (2008) and share the feature of rewarding non-price benefits. Given that it includes prizes (awarded by sweepstakes, games and sales contests), the resulting group of non-price promotions is larger than what we defined in Chapter 2 as sole premium promotions.

The methodology for our studies is presented in detail in Ziliani (2015). Here we introduce the major points, before discussing the results. In 2008, after conducting in-depth semi-structured interviews with four experts and managers of promotion agencies with experience in sales promotions and incentives to explore available approaches for data collection, a database of promotional campaigns was set up using secondary sources. After the first round of research, it contained data on 149 campaigns carried out in Italy between 1992 and 2008 by 111 different companies in 14 industries. In 2011 a new set of 70 campaigns relative to the years 2009 and 2010 and 63 companies (36 in common with the previous set but with new, different promotions) was added. Lastly, in 2015, 200 new campaigns were added, relative to the period 2012–14, 20 industries and 112 companies (of which, 20 were in either of the previous sets). Overall, the complete data set of B2B premium and prize promotions contained 420 cases, spanning 20 industries and 25 years, from 1990 to 2015.

In addressing the first research objective we adopted a 'grounded theory' approach, instead of employing existing frameworks referring to distribution channel incentives such as those developed by Heide (1994) and Gilliland (2003), or those referring to sales force management (e.g. Eisenhardt, 1985; John and Weitz, 1989; Challagalla and Shervani, 1997; Krafft, 1999). This allowed us to examine promotional activities close to reality, in great detail, reflecting their breadth, variety and creativity, rather than forcing them to fit a given classification framework. We examined qualitative data from the 420 campaign records in order to derive a classification scheme inductively and adopted an open coding procedure or constant comparative method (Glaser and Strauss, 1967). A record card for each campaign was drawn up containing 16 pieces of information. The description of each campaign was analysed, conceptualized and labelled with a code. Each one was compared with the previous, and if similar, received the same label. Otherwise, it was classified as different. It is important to note that the codes were not predetermined; they were determined item by item. Once all activities had been labelled, they were grouped around similar phenomena.

As a result, the 420 campaigns were classified into 13 categories according to their goal. Of these 13, three can themselves be considered as broader overarching frameworks that encompass all the categories identified:

(A) *Sell in*: partners are enticed to purchase a product, a range of products, make larger volume orders and so on, compared to past purchase history. Any promotional technique can serve this goal: trade loaders, contests, sweepstakes, scratch and win, point collection, loyalty schemes.
(B) *Sell out*: partners are rewarded for sales volume and specifically for selling slow-moving items, whole ranges, selling above a certain threshold over the previous year, and so forth.
(C) *Retention/relationship*: mainly loyalty schemes, clubs and point collection mechanisms that encourage repeating purchases/sales. We develop this point below.

The other ten categories are as follows:

(D) *Acknowledge best performance*: typically achieved by means of sales contests. Used for the sales force and franchises.
(E) *Facilitate partner's sales*: by providing a sales pitch. Examples are contests and sweepstakes for end customers advertised in store with point-of-purchase (POP) material, rewarding the partner as well as the winning customer.
(F) *Improve partner's service to product*: typically the case with premiums rewarded to personnel responding to mystery shopper enquiries.
(G) *Support product listing*: in order to gain access to retail store ranges, manufacturers reward store owners with premiums for the purchase of special displays containing the product.
(H) *Support new product launch*: to stimulate channel partners' adoption of a new product.
(I) *Improve product/brand awareness*: in order to make channel partners aware of the product/brand distinctive features and characteristics.
(J) *Partner qualification*: rewarding partners for participating in training courses or taking advantage of support and marketing services devised by the manufacturer.
(K) *Enrol new partners*: to expand the number of stores carrying the product in existing channels or to gain a foothold in new channels.
(L) *Enrich database*: rewards for providing names of potential new customers/partners or uploading sales data.
(M) *Develop new channels*: to enter a channel that the company was not using before for the distribution of its products/services.

We'll discuss later in this section the finding that actions directed towards data capture and enrichment are booming. However, after identifying these goals, we sought to understand how to group them into the three broad frameworks of sell in, sell out and retention/relationship. As the goals of supporting product listing (G), enrolling new partners (K) and developing new channels (M) all result in more purchases from partners, it makes sense to include these goals in the general category of sell in. In the same way, improving partners' service to product (F) and product/brand awareness (I), supporting a new product launch (H) and facilitating partners' selling activity (E) are clearly sell out goals since they translate into greater end sales. Lastly, acknowledging best performances (D), partner qualification (J) and database enrichment (L) are different sides of the same coin: the company's orientation to foster a lasting relationship with partners. The three-category classification contributes to a better understanding of the role of non-price channel promotion in channel partner management. The tables below present examples of promotional activity identified by the research organized by this classification.

Between 1990 and 2008, retention and relationship goals were never pursued for their own sake but to complement sell in or sell out goals. Between 2009 and 2011, however, campaigns oriented around relationships became more frequent, some of them having no other stated goal than supporting the relationship with channel partners. Between 2008 and 2015 creating a database of channel partner information became central in all industries: with 60% of campaigns aiming to do this, it became the most frequent goal. Since we included this goal (L) in the retention/relationship goals of channel promotions, its boom contributes to a shift in balance between the three overarching goals observed in 2008 (sell in: 33%, sell out: 31% and relationship/retention: 32%) to a situation where, in 2015, 20% of promotions aimed to sell in, 33% to sell out and 47% to build and maintain the channel relationship.

TABLE 3.1 Examples of 'sell in' channel promotional activities

Category	Activity
Sell in (A)	Coca Cola issues a scratch card offering bar and restaurant owners purchasing two cases of Burn energy drink an exotic holiday
	Conserve Italia runs a loyalty card with point collection for any case of fruit juice purchased. Points can be redeemed for hi-tech gifts
	Vaillant offers ready-to-collect trade loader premiums of different value for purchases of three, seven or ten boilers in a single order
Support product listing (G)	Pharmacies ordering a self-standing display of a chocolate snack can win a weekend for two at a chocolate fair offered by snack producer Costruttori di Dolcezze
	Kellogg's rewards retailers who buy a pre-pack of the new product Biscuit Moments with new headphones
Enrol new partners (K)	Galbani dairies offers a catalogue of direct premiums to deli shops that purchase a certain quantity of products over the first quarter of their becoming customers
Develop new channels (M)	Infostrada rewards small-scale national lottery agents for selling telephone contracts

TABLE 3.2 Examples of 'sell out' channel promotional activities

Category	Activity
Sell out (B)	Campari declares that wholesalers increasing sale volumes of the drink by 10% or more can win a Porsche car
	Helena Rubinstein cosmetics brand rewards points redeemable for premiums to perfume shop sales assistants who improve sales of slow-moving products
Facilitate partner's sales (E)	Soco hair products rewards hair salons and perfume shops that order and display Cielo Alto hair product POP window dressing material, as well as hairdresser staff who answer mystery shopper questions and engage consumers, with scratch cards for Soco products
Improve partner's service to product (F)	Kuwait Petroleum (Q8) runs a contest for teams of petrol station workers who accumulate points redeemable for premiums from a catalogue for best service to mystery shoppers
	Beiersdorf rewards tattoo studio owners with technology products if they correctly display all POP material for skin moisturizing product Aquaphor and suggest its use to mystery shoppers
Support new product launch (H)	Nestlé support the launch of new premium cat food called Gourmet Diamant with a gift of a real diamond to each of the first 100 pet shop owners who reach sales targets set by Nestlé
Improve product/ brand awareness (I)	Philips run a contest for electricians, with no purchase obligation, aimed at improving their knowledge of a new energy-saving lamp

At the same time, we observed a sort of polarization between, on the one hand, simple 'old-school' promotions with sell in goals, on the other, innovative and articulate activities merging sell out and retention objectives. Unsurprisingly, with sell out becoming increasingly challenging due to the market changes we discussed in Chapter 1, investing in the relationship with the partner becomes necessary, particularly since moving the product or brand down the channel requires partners' involvement and commitment.

The employed methodology did not allow for generalizations to be made across industries, and it would be interesting to investigate if a correlation exists between goal and sector. For instance, it is interesting that in the electrical equipment and plumbing and heating sectors, where manufacturers' first concern is making their way into wholesaler ranges, all campaigns we analysed were geared towards sell in goals.

When considering the preferred targets for channel promotions, several interesting elements emerge. First, brands tend to design separate promotions for consumers and for channel partners: campaigns with both B2B and business-to-consumer (B2C) targets decreased in number over time. The most frequent target of channel promotions was 'trade'. Specifically, it is 'normal trade', i.e. independent retail stores, that is most often targeted. In the words of a sales manager we interviewed, 'the chance of influencing chain stores decisions has almost vanished for brands, the same can be said for third party salespeople: as a consequence, we all flock to channels where some margin for manoeuvre is left'.

TABLE 3.3 Examples of 'retention/relationship' channel promotional activities

Category	Activity
Retention/ Relationship (C)	La Roche-Posay invites pharmacy owners and employees to participate in a team-based online game. Prizes include an in-store event for consumers, holidays, visits to La Roche laboratories and product kits
	Lexmark Printers offers its Channel Value Programme with three membership levels. Benefits are based on different sales thresholds. The programme is completely online
	Bocchiotti rewards a rechargeable Visa card to installers of electrical panels based on sales
	Conserve Italia develops two separate clubs (Granchef Royal and Granchef Privée) for retailers and restaurants respectively, offering training and management tools
Acknowledge best performance (D)	IBM launches a competition for the best video illustrating the benefits of IBM middleware products. Winners are rewarded with a TV set and an upload of their video on YouTube. Creators of the most viewed videos win a free holiday
	Carrefour runs a contest for franchisee stores to increase sales of own-label Carrefour brand products
Partner qualification (J)	Epson (the printer company) enrols retailers in its Best Seller loyalty programme providing access to discounts, training courses, technical support and consumer referral. Requires commitment to purchase
	Samsung offers a point collection scheme to redeem rewards from a catalogue to sales representatives and sales assistants who qualify by completing at least one of its online training courses every quarter
Enrich database (L)	Several food and drink manufacturers reward bars and restaurants for reporting detailed sales information, in order to create a file of loyal purchasers of their brands

The majority of campaigns we analysed were aimed at only one type of channel partner, but some target more than one. For instance, promotions aimed at wholesalers, where sell in goals such as getting wholesalers to list a product do not translate into end sales unless the sales personnel are directly involved, are often structured to incentivize both the company and its sales force. Kasulis et al. (1999) suggest that supplier promotions aimed at retailers' or wholesalers' employees are a sign that the wholesalers are willing to allow suppliers to influence their employees. And Burnett and Moriarty (1998) show that this can result in lasting goodwill when the initiatives successfully cement ties between employees and supplier. Employees involved in promotional activity become more effective and successful in selling the product, and their acquired competencies and rewards reinforce the relationship with the supplier brand so that the promotion results in supplier-favourable behavioural and attitudinal changes.

As for the duration of the promotional activities, the mean value of six months remained unchanged across the 20 years. However, the total amount of short-term campaigns (up to six months) dropped from 75% to 50% during the same period.

This is in line with the rise in the number of promotions that have retention/ relationship goals, which need to be developed over a longer period of time. However, we should not overlook the fact that, in times of economic downturn, promotions ought to allow partners extra time to build the purchase or sales volumes required to qualify for rewards.

Loyalty programmes and premiums in channel management

Different promotional techniques are used interchangeably to achieve various goals, and some of the campaigns we looked at combine more than one technique. Contests and draws were most often 'added' to other techniques, such as to bring some excitement to long-running schemes. We acknowledge as a limitation that the methodology we employed for data collection inevitably favoured loyalty promotions and prize draws and the results showed that indeed these were the most common types of promotions employed in B2B: Token schemes, loyalty programmes and clubs (41%), sweepstakes and draws (37%), direct premiums (26%), sales contexts (11%) (Note: total frequency exceeds 100% as some campaigns included more than one technique).

Despite this limitation, one cannot question the fact that loyalty promotions are employed in every industry and have been gaining in popularity over time. This might reflect the popularity enjoyed by loyalty schemes in consumer markets and the diffusion of relationship-building goals in channel activities.

The following types of loyalty-building promotion were identified in our research:

- loyalty programmes and clubs, promoting a sense of belonging to a group that lasts over time (such as the Lexmark Channel Value Club), which may be accompanied by a loyalty card and/or by point collection mechanisms
- point or token collection schemes enabling members to redeem premiums from a catalogue
- point or token collection schemes that reward a single premium, often a trip or holiday package
- premiums rewarded for cumulative purchases or sales, calculated by the supplier, with no need for point or token collection, i.e. trade loaders.

Collection schemes differ from trade loaders in that while the latter issue the premium immediately, the former require time for the partner to build the amount of purchases or sales requested by the supplier. However, all of the listed types of loyalty promotions are intended to encourage repeat behaviour (purchases or sales), but evidently, a one-month 'free gift for cumulated purchase' campaign is a different proposition (and investment) from a multi-year club providing training or exclusive services and offers.

The first appearance in our database of loyalty programmes and clubs was in 1992 when Fiat, the Italian car manufacturer, pioneered incentives for the distribution of lubricants. The next case was in 1999 when national airline Alitalia launched Volare Club, an annual points scheme. In 2001, printer manufacturers Epson and Lexmark introduced channel programmes that operated for more than a decade, while all other loyalty programmes launched in 2007–8 or later. A diachronic perspective shows that over the years the basic mechanism of proof of purchase to support sell in has evolved to incorporate new features. These include points schemes, premium catalogues, and loyalty cards, member accounts and clubs, and these new features all have longer durations.

We also note a shift from changing the promotion or programme claim or name every year towards an 'umbrella brand' for the company's channel promotion initiatives, a trend that has strengthened since 2000. B2B loyalty management appears to be undergoing something of a 'branding revolution' following the path described by Mauri for B2C (Castaldo and Mauri, 1993). Two cases make interesting examples: Vaillant and Heineken. Vaillant, a heating and plumbing manufacturer, has been active in channel promotion since 1995 when a yearly tradition of offering trade loaders to wholesalers' customers purchasing boilers began. It was only in 2007 that Vaillant changed its approach with the launch of the biannual Vaillant Club point collection scheme. Points are now earned when boilers are installed, not simply bought: a simple tweak of the programme that unveils a new orientation away from sell in towards sell out goals.

Heineken's wholesaling division Partesa first introduced channel non-price promotions in 2002 when a six-month point collection scheme for ho.re.ca. customers tied to customer specific sales targets was linked to agent incentivization. Partesa agents were rewarded for the number of ho.re.ca. customers who reached their targets, with credit accumulated on a payment card accepted for purchases in 65,000 affiliate stores. Six years later, building on the 2002 experience, Heineken launched its Horeca Street Club. Bars and restaurants pay a small annual fee for the Partesa Card and gain access to discounts on utilities, financing plans, furniture and fittings, pay TV and other services of interest. Store managers receive the *HS* magazine containing product information, targeted promotions, and information about training courses for wine, beer and spirits tasting, service skills and so forth. In 2010 a point collection campaign was added temporarily to the club proposition: an interesting example of the degrees of freedom available when an 'umbrella brand' – the Horeca Street concept – is developed to encompass the company's loyalty management activities. Under the club 'roof' new activities can be added and substituted over time providing novelty and excitement without interrupting the dialogue with customers. Both the Vaillant and the Heineken campaigns show a commitment to fostering lasting relationships with channel partners by means of loyalty programmes and clubs.

Clubs, in particular, are proposed as 'containers' of activities that change over time, to keep partners engaged: they are enriched with contests, draws and short-term point collection schemes with premiums changing frequently over time. Technology company Bosch runs a club for car part resellers whose members have exclusive access to instant wins, sweepstakes and apps, along with a two-year point collection scheme.

The same pattern is shown by the Myhome PRO club for installers of electrical equipment primarily intended for educational purposes, whose offer of courses and training materials is coupled with various types of non-price promotion.

As with the polarization we discussed earlier between sell in goals on the one hand and sell out and retention/relationship goals on the other, something similar can be identified when we look specifically at loyalty promotions. On one side we find three-month and six-month point collection schemes that deliver single premiums which are, in fact, simple variations on the trade loader theme, with sell in rather than relationship-building objectives. On the other, we find one, two, or three-year loyalty programmes or clubs with no closing date, which suggests a greater commitment to relationship goals – in fact, these longer promotions display three goals we've discussed: retention, acknowledgement of partners' best performance and partners' qualification.

We might make another observation about the variety of reward options. More than 10 years ago, our analyses of B2C loyalty schemes singled out the trend towards the creation of a 'free circulation space' for members; that is, the expansion of opportunities for being recognized as a member and rewarded or treated accordingly. All schemes – not only coalitions – were adding rewards and recognition options to that purpose. B2B programmes were different in 2008 and even in 2015, in that half of them offered one single type of reward (among physical goods, vouchers, experiences and charity donation), and 30% only two types. The reason might be connected to the higher homogeneity of B2B promotional target groups compared with those of B2C loyalty schemes. In other words, identifying the preferences of a narrow target group such as perfume shop sales assistants or bartenders or wholesalers' agents might look easier to the promotion designers when compared with devising the right rewards for a more heterogeneous group of final consumers. When we look at campaigns diachronically, we also find that B2B loyalty promotions tend to move from offering very simple choices when they first launch, typically one type of reward only, to a slightly wider variety over time.

Given that channel partners are organizations or individuals working with others within organizations, we wondered whether promotions rewarded individual rather than group behaviours, and cooperation rather than competition. Before 2015, promotions rewarding group behaviours were almost non-existent. In 2015, when skill-based contests become common, especially in the food and drink industry – a sort of 'MasterChef effect', we believe, due to the international popularity of the competitive cooking TV show – it was still individual results that were rewarded. We argue that more needs to be done to explore the opportunity of designing promotions that reward group behaviour, in that group cooperation can produce longer-lasting effects such as team-building, all in favour of relationship goals. Moreover, digital today makes it extremely easy to act, communicate and share information and activities as a group.

This brings us back to the digital impetus. New technology has energized loyalty promotions not only in B2C but B2B too. In our 1992–2008 data set, only 20% of campaigns used the Internet to reach the target group; another 20% was run entirely online. In the 2009–11 sample, the Internet and email gained momentum as optimal channels for partner contact and interaction: 30% of recorded activities were online only, and these were exclusively loyalty schemes. In 2015 online was the majority media for communicating with target participants (56%).

Online media has many advantages for channel loyalty activities. An online loyalty scheme enables cheaper, faster communication and delivery, and allows for the better control of elements such as data entry, personalized communication, offers and prizes, and continuous monitoring of participation, results and costs. Digital premiums such as vouchers can be rewarded online. Participants can interact with the programme at their own convenience and check their progress towards rewards. Research published by channel marketing organizations shows that there is a higher level of participation in online schemes thanks to the frequency of communication and interaction.[3] It is possible to test recipients' responsiveness to different objectives and different point thresholds and adjust 'on the go' according to early results. For example, slow-moving rewards can be substituted with more appealing ones, thresholds raised when redemption is higher than expected, and goals and time frames tailored for each participating partner.

Campaigns differed too in the actions requested of partners to qualify for rewards. We grouped all requested behaviours according to whether they oriented towards sell in, sell out or relationship goals. Here are some examples of the sell-out-oriented behaviour we identified:

- employ the POP material provided by the brand to set up a window display, a store corner or space on the shop counter to give prominent visibility to the product
- respond to mystery shoppers' questions and requests by providing satisfactory answers on product features or merits, or by suggesting the correct product
- recruit or introduce a new customer
- stimulate final consumers to provide data, collect tokens or join a B2C promotional initiative
- encourage payment via the brand's preferred option (e.g. co-branded credit card, digital wallet)
- meet sales goals.

Among sell-in-oriented behaviours, we encountered the following:

- meet purchase volume/value thresholds or % increase on purchase volumes against previous periods
- purchase a specified mix of products from the supplier's portfolio
- order online
- join the club when visited by the brand's salespeople.

3   https://www.incentivemarketing.org/resources.

Our study demonstrated that loyalty promotions that target channel members have evolved over time, proving to be responsive to new opportunities such as online media, gamification and expanding the variety of reward options to things such as vouchers, educational content and experiences. There were, however, limitations to our research. The first was inherent in the methodology in that our classification of channel promotions was a function of the data set and does not necessarily conform to other frameworks put forward in the literature. Secondly, we were only able to cover the Italian market, although it was at the time the third largest in Europe and our sample included over 100 multinational companies. Thirdly, promotional activities were analysed separately from other incentives, notably contractual incentives, and from other marketing mix decisions. Trade promotion, in fact, is just one area among many that feel the impact of evolving channel relationships – but this is a broader subject that goes well beyond the scope of this book.

References

Burnett, J. and Moriarty, S. E. (1998) *Introduction to Marketing Communication: An Integrated Approach.* Upper Saddle River, NJ: Prentice Hall.

Castaldo, S. and Mauri, C. (1993) *Promozioni-fedelta` della distribuzione moderna. Un'indagine empirica.* Milan: EGEA.

Challagalla, G. N. and Shervani, T. A. (1997) 'A measurement model of the dimensions and types of output and behavior control: an empirical test in a salesforce context'. *Journal of Business Research*, 39(3), pp. 159–172.

Eisenhardt, K. M. (1985) 'Control: organizational and economic approaches'. *Management Science*, 31(2), pp. 134–149.

Frazier, G. L. and Sheth, J. N. (1985) 'An attitude-behavior framework for distribution channel management'. *Journal of Marketing*, 49(July), pp. 38–48.

Gilliland, D. I. (2003) 'Toward a business-to-business channel incentives classification scheme', *Industrial Marketing Management*, 32, pp. 55–67.

Glaser, B. G. and Strauss, A. L. (1967) *The Discovery of Grounded Theory: Strategies for Qualitative Research.* Chicago: Aldine-Atherton.

Heide, J. B. (1994) 'Interorganizational governance in marketing channels'. *Journal of Marketing*, 58(1), pp. 71–85.

Incentive Performance Center (2008) *Why Incentive Programs Endure Recessions.* Report no longer available, but summary at: http://enterpriseengagement.org/articles/content/8288915/why-incentive-programs-endure-recessions/ (Accessed: 14 December 2018).

John, G. and Weitz, B. (1989) 'Salesforce compensation: an empirical investigation of factors related to use of salary versus incentive compensation'. *Journal of Marketing Research*, 25(1), pp. 1–14.

Kasulis, J., Morgan, F.W., Griffith, D. E. and Kenderdine, J. M. (1999) 'Managing trade promotions in the context of market power'. *Journal of the Academy of Marketing Science*, 27(3), pp. 320–332.

Krafft, M. (1999) 'An empirical investigation of the antecedents of sales force control systems'. *Journal of Marketing*, 63(3), pp. 120–134.

Mullin, R. and Cummins, J. (2008) *Sales Promotion: How to Create, Implement and Integrate Campaigns that Really Work.* 4th ed. London: Kogan Page.

Narus J. A. and Anderson, J. C. (1996) 'Rethinking distribution: adaptive channels'. *Harvard Business Review*, 74, pp. 112–120.

Ziliani, C. (2012) 'From "trade loaders" to "online channel partner programs": how trade promotion changed its face from 1990 to 2010'. *European Retail Research*, 26(2), pp. 77–95.

Ziliani, C. (2015) *Promotion Revolution: Nuove strategie e nuovi protagonisti della promozione 2.0.* Milan: EGEA.

4

THE IMPACT OF BIG DATA AND ARTIFICIAL INTELLIGENCE

Cristina Ziliani

The information revolution

Before the expression 'big data' became popular, scholars and practitioners had been talking about an 'information revolution' for decades. In the late 1980s, Peter Drucker, widely regarded as the father of post-war management thinking, identified that the world economy was shifting from being organized around the flow of goods and money to the flow of information. Nicholas Negroponte, architect and founder of the MIT Media Lab, introduced in his book *Being Digital* (1995) the image of the 'atom' society – based on the production of tangible goods – giving way to the 'bit' society – based on the production of information and knowledge and of products and services derived from that information and knowledge.

Relationship marketing scholars predicted in the 1990s that emerging information and communication technologies (ICTs)[1] were going to play a major role in businesses' orientation towards customer loyalty. They were right. Computers, databases and other software applications – from call centre management to analytics – were indeed at the basis of the evolution of direct, database marketing and customer relationship management (CRM). Blattberg, Glazer and Little (1994) clearly saw that developments in ICTs were creating an explosion in the quantity and variety of information available to a growing number of individuals and organizations across the globe. This was going to be a 'marketing information revolution'.[2]

1 Although several definitions exist, we follow Khyade and Khyade (2018, p. 2) and understand ICT to broadly mean 'any product that will store, retrieve, manipulate, transmit or receive information electronically in a digital form, e.g. personal computers, digital television, email, robots'.
2 The volume of information worldwide is ever expanding. This is due largely to the fact that the majority of the information that is being produced today is digital; that is, produced in the binary numeric form that can be manipulated by computers. This transformation from analogue to digital information is enabled by technological

Since their introduction, ICTs have had a close and significant relationship with both marketing and loyalty management. Given the incessant pace of technological progress, amplified – among other things – by the increasing availability of the Internet to half of the world's inhabitants, the embedding of computing power in everyday objects (the so-called Internet of Things), and the rise of ever more sophisticated software to make sense of the available data, it is worth reflecting on what all this means for marketing, and for loyalty management in particular.

As we articulated in Chapter 2, we see loyalty management as going through three phases in its history. Each is marked by the availability of new technologies and by the progressive expansion they make possible of the ecosystem in which the individual customer is identified and treated accordingly as he or she moves freely across touchpoints. We are now living in the 'loyalty as experience' phase where customer loyalty is pursued and fostered by means of the design (and redesign) of a superior customer experience. Technology, data and the information unlocked by software such as artificial intelligence (AI) algorithms are transforming what human experience is. We 'experience' through a network of touchpoints, many of them new, digital and enriched with sensors whose inputs produce the hyperpersonalization of communication, content and offers in a way that is increasingly relevant to the moment we are at in our journey, regardless of where we or the brand are physically located. This is how far the information revolution has come. Not only it is making ever new tools available to marketers, but it is shaping and redefining the human experience of perception.

This chapter provides some reflections on how this revolution played out in the world of marketing on the evolution of loyalty management and customer experience management (CEM) – and asks what might follow in the future.

Big data marketing

In recent years, the phrase information revolution has been substituted by 'big data revolution', an expression that signifies the prominent role of data – and big data – in the transformation of business and society as the product, or by-product, of ICTs. Big data is 'an intentionally subjective definition that refers to datasets whose size is beyond the ability of typical database software tools to capture, store, manage and analyze' (Manyika et al., 2011, p. 1). In incorporating a moving definition of how big a data set needs to be in order to be considered big data, the expression captures how technology is continuously advancing.[3]

Mandelli (2017) describes big data marketing as the evolution of marketing into a new data-based, automated approach whose keywords are: data-driven, customer journey, omnichannel, programmatic, platform economy, automation and hyperpersonalization. She sees this evolution as enabled by the continuous

---

3   Yet no universal definition exists. In 2014, UC Berkeley School of Information asked 40 thought leaders how they would define big data. See the results at https://datasci ence.berkeley.edu/what-is-big-data.

flow of data from the environment and from interactions between customer and brand at various touchpoints, and by newly available intelligence to make sense of and use such data.

Specifically, the big data revolution impacts marketing on two fronts:

1. *Understanding markets and customers.* Thanks to the improvements in online and offline tracking of individuals and content, it is possible to introduce novel segmentation approaches (think of computer image recognition and image analytics applied to images and videos posted by users) and to understand customer journeys. In turn, journeys that show similarities can be clustered together to define 'personas', which may serve as the basis for:

2. *Managing the customer experience.* This takes the form of not only managing contents and channels/media for communication, but also managing interactions with customers, including personalizing offers, introducing smart and robotic services and designing new intelligent touchpoints, ambients and servicecapes, as will be discussed later in this chapter.

The transformation of marketing by big data does not take place at the operational level alone. It has strategic consequences too. Processes become adaptive and interactive, new business models are possible and automation can be applied even to creative aspects of marketing such a content production and service design.

Stitch Fix is a telling case in point. Founded in 2011 as a personal styling e-commerce website, it delivers a selection of clothes guaranteed to match each customer's preferences for a monthly subscription fee (Hollis, 2018). The company now boasts in excess of 5,000 employees (including 80 data scientists), $1 billion in revenues, more than 700 brands in its assortment and more than two million customers (Lake, 2018; Marr, 2018). A new customer starts by filling out a survey describing her fashion and style preferences and provides a rating and feedback on each and every item she receives. The company's data scientists can then parse through her survey responses and data of how she navigated the Stitch Fix website and other platforms she uses – e.g. social media sites rich in fashion ideas such as Pinterest – to quickly refine suggestions and deliver clothes she is likely to prefer. They employ image recognition and natural language recognition tools (take, for example, a comment like 'I don't like to show my arms') and feed all that data through recommender engines that select products based on customer preferences, later validated by human stylists who take the final decision regarding what five pieces of clothing will go in the customer's box that month (Planet Retail, 2018).

Not only is this a new business model for fashion retailing, but their use of analytics brings creativity in fashion retail to a new level (Bhattarai, 2018). In fact, AI tools analyse clothing items that have been top sellers during a specific season and pinpoint best-selling distinctive 'traits' – like, for example, the colour purple, string tops, lace, shoulder-showing sleeves, and so on. Each top-selling item in the season has one or more of such traits but not all of them, and only in some combinations: for example, purple string tops and black lace shoulder-showing blouses sold very well. Why not 'cross' successful items and see what 'offspring' they could generate, carrying some of the 'parent' features with them? Genetic algorithms combine automatically successful features in hundreds of novel ways thus creating fictional items of clothing that do not 'exist' (Gershgorn, 2017). Human stylists eliminate 'ugly' combinations – since algorithms do not have aesthetic taste ... yet! – and select a few styles. They then request that partner manufacturers produce a batch of each for trial shipment to customers. In 2018 Stitch Fix successfully marketed 17 AI-designed pieces of clothing under their own label Hybrid Designs, unique to their assortment, thus setting themselves apart from competition and giving marketers a glimpse of a future in which human–machine cooperation will support creative processes.

This case illustrates well how far loyalty management has been transformed by technology. The subscription model is a well-known lock-in approach to retention. The business goal of providing customers with superior value hasn't changed. The processes for the extraction and delivery of such value have, and they are increasingly data-based and AI-powered. The emphasis within the marketing information revolution, then, is on the endless possibilities opened up by the analysis and use of data by means of advanced software and algorithms, especially in domains comprised under AI. Below we reflect on the growing availability of data and its impact on business and marketing, before turning to AI specifically.

The moving frontier of data availability and its impact on business

The word 'data' has been with us since well before computers were invented. It comes from the Latin word *datum*, meaning 'fact', 'description of something that has happened'. To 'datafy' means to describe phenomena in quantitative form so that they can be analysed and easily compared. Datafication refers to observing anything, even things we never thought of as information, such as vibrations of an engine or a person's location, and transforming it into data format; that is, quantifying it (Mayer-Schönberger and Cukier, 2013).

Datafication began well before the digital revolution. Humans have always felt the need to translate phenomena into data in order to analyse it and make sense of reality. Throughout history we have continually added ways of measuring the world: weight, distance, time and so forth. Mayer-Schönberger and Cukier (2013) recall some key milestones:

- In 3000 BC, in Mesopotamia, writing was developed to record and keep track of information about production and business transactions.
- In 200 BC, in Greece, the first version of latitude and longitude was developed to determine where locations were and how long it took to travel from A to B.
- The Romans ran censuses to gather data sets of information in order to levy taxes.

- Arabic numerals, invented in India, travelled to Persia and were later adopted in the West in the twelfth century (and entered common use from the fifteenth century).
- In the late fifteenth century, double-entry bookkeeping was invented in Italy by Luca Pacioli, a Franciscan friar, and marked the beginning of the standardized recording of business information.

Clearly, datafication is something that is inherent to human nature. Technology is not its cause, but it has been a powerful enabler of the datafication of phenomena not yet quantified. The technologies that support datafication and make digitization and digitalization possible we refer to as ICTs.[4] When talking about ICTs we distinguish three categories: (1) Core technologies are those that enable the storage of data, such as memory discs, and those that process data, such as devices that perform operations and execute instructions: typically, microprocessors. Since data needs to be entered into memory and processors, sensors and readers of various kinds are included here. (2) Access technologies have to do with networks for telecommunication and allow access to data wherever it is located. One example would be routers. (3) Applications are software that enable the actual use of information for specific purposes. Think here of Web browsers or analytics tools.

The development of these technologies began in the early 1950s when the first computer – the mainframe – was invented. They have evolved ever since, thanks to the peculiar dynamics of their production processes. These have been popularized as the 'laws' that have governed the development of ICTs to date: Moore's Law, Gilder's Law and Metcalfe's Law. The evolution of marketing and loyalty management is intertwined with the availability of data enabled by advances in ICT: for this reason, we briefly recall the laws that govern it and their implications.

In 1965 Gordon Moore, co-founder of Fairchild Semiconductor and Intel, wrote that the number of transistors on a computer chip was doubling every year. The number of transistors expresses the processing power of a microchip. In 1975 he revised that to a two-year doubling period, although looking back at the data it was closer to 18 months (Wilson, 2012). Moore's Law means the number of components doubles on each chip and that the device size gets smaller allowing more to be put in the same space. The fact that the power of the computer chip was doubling in a comparatively short time meant that tasks that are hard to perform today will be feasible tomorrow and the cost of equivalent computing power is halving on a similar timescale (Wilson, 2012). Today we speak also of a 'generalized' Moore's Law to indicate various trends of exponential improvement in many aspects of ICTs (both computing and communication) such as storage capacity/cost, clock frequency, performance/cost, size/bit, cost/

---

4   Throughout the book we distinguish between digitization and digitalization, two terms often used synonymously. In this we follow Brennen and Kreiss (2014) who, in line with *The Oxford English Dictionary*, define digitization as the 'material process of converting individual analogue streams of information into digital bits' and digitalization as 'the way in which many domains of social life are restructured around digital communication and media infrastructures'.

bit, energy/operation, bandwidth/cost and others. These trends impact productivity, efficiency and economic growth (Mack, 2015) and enable the current development of AI, which needs massive computing power.

Gilder's Law, proposed by George Gilder, author and prophet of the new technology age (Pinto, 2002), is about communication networks. It states that the bandwidth – that is, the rate of data transfer – of communication systems triples every year. Bandwidth, which is measured in bits per second, grows faster than computing power. While computer power doubles every 18 months (as seen above), communications power triples every year. Latest developments seem to confirm that bandwidth availability will continue to expand at a rate that supports Gilder's Law (Shankar and Carpenter, 2012). This supports the possibility of making data and information, and information-based products and services, accessible to growing audiences, even in remote regions of the globe.

Last but not least, Metcalfe's Law, attributed to Robert Metcalfe, originator of the Ethernet and founder of 3Com (Pinto, 2002), asserts that the value of a network is proportional to the square of the number of nodes, that is, the connected users on the system. The number of connected users of the network grows by linear progression and the value of the system – the value of being connected – grows exponentially, while the cost per user remains the same. In marketing, this is known as the network effect, which in the simplest terms states that the value of a system is dependent on the number of people using it. Metcalfe's Law was advocated to support investment in the Internet, e-commerce and social network booms and draws attention to business models and marketing strategies that promise to connect users and create communities.

The above trends combined explain the accelerating pace of digitalization, digitization and the big data revolution. Moreover, the frontiers of this revolution are expanding every day, pushed by the embedding of the Internet in objects and by humans carrying the Internet with them wherever they go in their mobile and wearable devices. In this respect, individuals are contributing to datafication enthusiastically by subjecting themselves to regimes of self-measurement that go far beyond the familiar habits of stepping on a weighing scale every morning ... We now count steps, calorie intake, hours of sleep and more, so much so that some scholars speak of 'the quantified self' (Lupton, 2016).

Ever more personal aspects of our lives are being quantified: our relationships, our experiences, our moods. Social networks take intangible elements of our daily life and transform them into data. LinkedIn datafies work experiences. Twitter datafies sentiments. In 2011, scholars were able to discover the 'pattern of global mood' by analysing the content of a global sample of tweets during each day of the week and by attributing a valence (positive, negative or neutral) to the statements of millions of individuals (Golder and Macy, 2011). Country indexes of emotional states like optimism and anger can be created and fed into stock-trading systems (Mayer-Schönberger and Cukier, 2013). The 'social graph' of individuals on Facebook could be employed for credit scoring. As emotions become data, the opposite is also happening. Alibaba's financial arm Ant Financial calculates individuals' credit scores – named Sesami – based on e-commerce records and payments through the proprietary Alipay wallet, and on the customer's engagement activities such as posting, sharing and commenting online with friends and family. People in China post their Sesami score on dating sites to testify to their reliability and require others to reveal theirs to make sure they are 'real' and accountable (Hvistendahl, 2017).

These examples point towards another feature of the big data revolution. The value of data is shifting from its primary use (the purpose for which it was collected) to its potential future uses (Mayer-Schönberger and Cukier, 2013). Think of Amazon. It allows other merchants to sell through its websites, thus providing them a service and, at the same time, gains access to information regarding what consumers purchase, which is of significant value to Amazon's own assortment management. In pursuit of such opportunities, companies today strive to collect data about customers and partners – often employing loyalty programmes and loyalty-building approaches – because they understand the power of analysing, selling and using it for both primary and secondary uses. However, this opens up challenges in how to make customers and partners aware – and how to ask their permission – of the uses the data will be put to if such uses do not yet exist. As AI algorithms become better at recognizing and classifying human voices and image content, for example, audio and video information stored on platforms by users can be put to totally new uses.

Perhaps the largest contribution to datafication today is from the Internet of Things (IoT). Internet traffic already connects more things than it does people, and the economic impact of the IoT is estimated to be 11 trillion dollars by 2025 (DeNardis and Raymond, 2017). The IoT, according to scholars, is often equated with home appliances and consumer devices like wearable technologies and cars. However, the Internet has expanded into a vast array of everyday objects. Cyber-physical systems underlie almost all industrial sectors. They involve the acquisition of sensor data from, and the delivery of instructions to, devices that interface with or are part of the real world. Transportation and shipping companies use them for tracking vehicles and packages. Medical systems increasingly rely upon Internet-connected monitoring, diagnostic, and treatment devices. In manufacturing, digital networks are used to manage the handling of materials, optimization of inventories and connection of robotic systems. Local governments are increasingly an important IoT constituency in that street lights, utilities, traffic control systems, and other so-called smart city applications are now part of the Internet ecosystem. In all economic sectors today, cyberspace touches the material world. IoT-collected data are about the actual behaviours of objects and of people's real usage and interaction with objects and services. In consumer markets, as smart home devices (smart thermostats, lighting controls, motion sensors, etc.) become commonplace, brands that can leverage such devices as touchpoints will be able to collect massive amounts of actual usage data that can be put to use with varying degrees of innovation, from control and maintenance to new service design. Moreover, the availability of vast amounts of sensor-collected data is enabling the development of AI algorithms and systems.

How is the big data revolution impacting business and marketing? Traditionally, technological revolutions have been studied for their economic impact in terms of productivity and for the reorganization of industries and supply chains that came as a consequence (Mandelli, 2017). Since Johannes Gutenberg invented the printing press in the mid-fifteenth century, the world has witnessed several waves of technological innovation. Between 1780 and 1840 the application of steam power to production triggered the Industrial Revolution. The steam engine mechanized the great majority of manufacturing processes, beginning with textiles, the most important industrial commodity at the time in Britain, whose price fell by 90% in 50 years, while production increased at least 150-fold (Drucker, 2013). In 1829 came the railroad, an innovation that has been defined by many as the truly revolutionary element of the Industrial Revolution since it rapidly changed mental geography. Human beings had become truly mobile. As a new concept of distance was introduced, the horizons of ordinary people expanded for the first time. The next wave of technological revolution can be dated between 1890 and 1950, when both electricity and the automobile were introduced. The information revolution is thus the most recent of several waves.

However, it has some peculiar traits. It is happening at a faster pace and it is pervasive: new technologies find application in every industry. Moreover, its cornerstone technology, the computer, has evolved from number cruncher to medium. It has enabled the existence and diffusion of several digital media from email to the Web to social networks – with all the consequences on human communication and society that brings. At the same time, the computer has subsumed several other intelligent technologies. Today maps, calculators, clocks, and an array of other tools that support and expand human intellectual abilities are all accessed via a computer screen. With that computer screen becoming mobile, moreover, all these tools are accessible anytime and anywhere. We may adopt the traditional economic categories to interpret the impact of the big data revolution, but there is simply much more to it.

Economists have tended to argue that technological innovations are adopted for their positive effects on productivity, because they produce more output with the same input or reduce the cost of one input. ICTs are no exception. However, the input whose cost they reduce is peculiar: information. Changes in the cost of information, especially information connected to the use of markets instead of internal production – a component of so-called *transaction costs* – alter the structure of companies' value chains, markets and indeed entire industries. They enable disintermediation and reintermediation, that is, the reallocation of activities across several players, including new ones, who are connected in networks or ecosystems. This way, new sources of supply that were previously impossible or uneconomical are allowed to enter the product and labour markets. One only need to think of how Airbnb unlocked the supply of new accommodation options or how Uber brought more underutilized cars to our roads or how Amazon's Web services have provided scalable infrastructure that reduces the need for peak capacity resources. In Chapter 2 we discussed how, thanks to the information revolution, new intermediaries have emerged in the specific domains of marketing services and promotion, contributing to the evolution of loyalty ecosystems and of a market for loyalty management services.

If we consider demand, the big data revolution has unlocked the potential for customers not only to seek out information but to unbundle (or bundle) aspects of products and services that were formerly combined (or separated) by necessity or for profit. It will suffice to cite the practice of watching as many episodes of a TV series as we want. A subscription-based service such as Netflix analyses huge amounts of data on the viewing behaviour of its customer base to create successful TV programmes and deliver them in ways that enable new social practices like binge-watching.

At a general level, the literature that explores the impact of the information revolution on business and marketing is immense. Any attempt to summarize it would fall outside the scope of this chapter. However, we may say that most of it has concentrated on the contribution to value creation in terms of efficiency and effectiveness, as was proposed back in 1985 by Porter and Millar. Reflecting on the business impact of the ICT revolution, they stressed that the relevance of the latter is in the unlocking of information, which can create value in the following ways:

- It can improve the strategic decision-making process.
- It is a tool for the effective implementation of a given strategy.
- It is a source of product and process innovation at company, channel and industry levels.
- It enables the building of intangible assets based on information and knowledge.

The possibility to give customers what they want in new, more efficient ways translates into new value propositions that deliver what customers did not realize they wanted. Did we know we wanted the Internet in our pockets? Or that we wanted to share music? Many of the new propositions link digital and physical worlds across multiple touchpoints and exploit the availability of data and ubiquitous connectivity. The delivery of these new value propositions requires the rethinking and reimagining of business systems and industry value chains. Those who can access, analyse and exploit relevant information to create new value propositions for products, services or match-making have an advantage. The information revolution, for example, allows insurance companies to operate new touchpoints for enhanced customer convenience, such as paying premiums online. However, information on customers' car-related behaviour would allow for the creation of completely new insurance products and services: customers could pay based on the real use of their car, how safe they are as drivers, their car parking and maintenance habits, and so on. The enabling data for such innovation may reside with different players, ranging from car manufacturers to smartphone manufacturers, insurance companies, municipalities and more.

Who can (and will) take advantage of it? Existing players? New information brokers? Industries differ in terms of the potential for value creation from big data and the real possibility of extracting value. Where markets are turbulent, performance is highly variable, transactions are frequent and/or the numbers of potential partners or customers are high, the potential and incentive to mine data to improve understanding and value creation are higher (Brown, Chui and Manyika, 2011). However, capturing such value depends on several factors, starting with competitive pressure from incumbents and new entrants, and encompassing the actual accessibility of data (who owns Alexa's records of interactions with its owner? Who can access them?), the type of decision-making prevalent in the industry, and the adequacy of technological, human and financial resources and skills. Among the latter, the availability of smart software is emerging as a powerful catalyst for the exploitation of big data (Kumar et al., 2016).

AI in marketing

The advances we have discussed in ICTs have made unprecedented quantities of empirical data available and, at the same time, provided the means to access, store and process them. This has given new impetus to the scientific field of AI, as the renewed academic and investor interest in this area in recent years testifies. According to Shoham et al. (2017), academic papers on AI were nine times more numerous in 2017 than in 1996. The annual venture capital investment into US start-ups developing AI systems has increased six-fold since 2000. The number of active US start-ups developing such systems has increased fourteen-fold over the same period.

A hundred-year study report on AI published by Stanford University (Stone et al., 2016) recalls how in 1956 John McCarthy was the first to use the term 'artificial intelligence' in the proposal he co-authored for a workshop at the Dartmouth Summer Research Project. The goal was 'to investigate ways in which machines could be made to simulate aspects of intelligence' (Stone et al., 2016, p. 49). This can still be considered the essential idea that propels research in this area. The Dartmouth workshop created a unified identity for the field and a dedicated research community. The report offers a working definition: 'AI is a science and a set of computational technologies that are inspired by – but typically operate quite differently from – the ways people use their nervous systems and bodies to sense, learn, reason, and take action' (Stone et al., 2016, p. 4). Nilsson (2010) explains that AI is devoted to making machines intelligent, intelligence being that quality that enables an entity to function appropriately and with foresight in its environment.

Visual perception, speech recognition, decision-making and language translation are among the tasks – normally requiring human intelligence – that AI research is striving to enable software to perform. For example, Facebook is using AI to automatically translate into different languages 45 billion user posts per day

(Rouhiainen, 2018). How many human translators would be necessary to do this? The whole market for virtual assistant services accessible via smart devices, such as Siri (Apple) and Alexa (Amazon), would not exist if it weren't for the development of AI speech recognition and natural language processing, not to mention entirely new business models such as that of Stitch Fix described in the previous section. Despite the early promise of the 1950s, for decades practical results lacked behind, mainly due to the unavailability of computational power and data. Technological progress made it more feasible to build systems that derive solutions from real-world data made available by the Internet and supported by the availability of computing power for storage and processing. As Alibaba's founder Jack Ma put it, 'large scale computing and data are the father and mother of AI' (Ericson and Wang, 2017).

Such advancements have allowed AI to emerge in the past two decades as a profound influence on our daily lives. According to the Stanford University report, domains where AI is already having, or is projected to have, the greatest impact include transportation, healthcare, education, low-resource communities, public safety and security, employment and the workplace, home/service robots and entertainment. In their analysis of over 400 cases of AI applications, Chui et al. (2018) found that AI is presently used to support activities where classification, clustering and prevision are useful or necessary to solve problems and take decisions. They see AI today as applied with an incremental orientation, to add value and efficiency to existing processes and products or services. The majority of applications today are for process control, optimization of planning and logistics, customer service and personalization. Currently only 15% of cases represent solutions that are radically different from what is possible with traditional analytics and software tools (Chui et al., 2018). This is consistent with the beginnings of many technological innovations that later turned into real revolutions. Before reflecting on AI's impact on marketing it will be useful to introduce a few more concepts related to AI.

An additional driver of progress with AI was the shift in researchers' efforts from building systems that aim at encompassing all aspects of human intelligence – that is, ones that could perform different tasks typical of humans such as image recognition, speech recognition and decision-making, all in the same system – to concentrating on developing systems that focus on a single task, for example a machine that's great at recognizing images but nothing else. In the debate about AI, therefore, two categories of research exist: general (or strong) AI and narrow (or weak) AI. General AI research has not been abandoned, but it is today surpassed by the fast-advancing results obtained in narrow AI research. The applications we discuss in the remainder of this section regard different areas of narrow AI.

Within AI, machine learning and deep learning are research areas and types of applications which, based on algorithms and powerful data analysis, enable computers to learn and adapt independently. The phrase 'machine learning' was coined in 1959 by Arthur Samuel who defined it as 'the ability to learn without being explicitly programmed' (McClelland, 2017). He invented a computer-checking application that was one of the first programs that could learn from its own mistakes and improve its performance over time. Machine learning is a type of AI research that enables software applications to become more accurate in forecasting outcomes without being specially programmed. Instead of coding specific instructions to perform a particular task, machine learning is a way of 'training' an algorithm so that it can learn how to perform the task autonomously. There are several approaches to training algorithms,[5] which involve several ways of feeding them vast amounts of data with which they adjust themselves and improve. This aspect of AI algorithms is, in our opinion, a revolutionary advance for marketing, and we will elaborate on it further.

Within machine learning, a category of algorithms that can be employed define what is called 'deep learning'. Neural networks are systems based on simulating connected 'neural units', loosely modelling the way that neurons interact in the brain. Neural networks are organized in many layers of interconnected neural units. Each layer specializes in perfecting a specific task and it's this multilayered structure that makes the learning 'deep'. An important implication of deep learning is that the way results are obtained is non-understandable and non-replicable by humans – a sort of 'black box' – hence it is difficult to trace back to eventual biases. This is relevant to marketing when one thinks of the selection of customers for preferential or adverse treatment or the selection of products for recommendation.

The aspect of human intelligence that has to date been best mimicked by AI is the ability to make predictions (Mandelli, 2018). Agrawal, Gans and Goldfarb (2018) reason that the rapid interest in and adoption of AI systems is because these systems cause a drop in 'prediction costs' and consequently open up opportunities for informed action. In the countless areas of management and marketing (and indeed elsewhere) where the risk of action can be lowered by better prediction, adopting AI offers solutions. Specialists, in turn, are increasingly translating any sort of decision problem into a prediction problem in order to better address it within the framework of an AI approach and with AI tools. The development of the self-driving car is a case in point. It looked like an unsolvable problem until it was redesigned as the problem of making the predictions a human driver would make in different situations in order to perform the task of driving. The same approach led to success in the above-mentioned field of language translation. As long as translating was considered a task based on putting into a system all the functioning rules of a language, it was too complex to tackle. When looked at as making the agent able to predict what words a human would employ in a context similar to the one at hand, the problem became addressable with machine learning techniques. The same approach greatly improved the accuracy of Google's instant query autocomplete interface, as probably every reader of this book can attest to.

By introducing automation into one of the most critical goals of marketing management – optimizing decisions by making better predictions – machine

---

5   Researchers speak of supervised, unsupervised and reinforcement learning. See, for example, Yao, Jia and Zhou (2018).

learning (be it, or not, based on deep learning techniques) changes the role of human intervention and creates intelligent agents (Kumar et al., 2016). Humans will increasingly have to interact with such agents. In the future there will almost certainly be an increase in machine–human interactions that will result in totally new experiences and advances in intelligent agent technology (IAT). We are already experiencing this as consumers in the area of customer service robotic assistance, where today we encounter chatbots, communicate with voice assistants and interact with robots in hotels and airports.

According to Wooldridge (2002, p. 5), IATs are 'intelligent software or computer systems that are autonomous and possess important properties such as learning, social ability, reactivity, and pro-activeness to perform a set of complex tasks'. Furthermore, Kumar et al. (2016, p. 27) expand the definition in the context of marketing:

> Intelligent agent technologies (IATs) are computational systems that inhabit a complex dynamic environment and continuously perform marketing functions such as (a) dynamic scanning of the environment and market factors including competitors and customers, and firm actions impacting the marketing mix; (b) collaborating and interacting to interpret perceptions, analyzing, learning and drawing inferences to solve problems; and (c) implementing customer-focused strategies that create value for the customers and the firm within the boundaries of trustworthiness and policy.

As Kumar et al. suggest, AI is powering the development of a variety of IATs that perform marketing activities such as information search (e.g. Web spiders), customer acquisition (e.g. programmatic advertising and retargeting), retention (e.g. recommender systems) and interaction through communication (e.g. personalization and content generation engines), to name but a few.

Figure 4.1 provides a framework to capture how AI applications are impacting marketing. There can be little doubt that AI is one of the catalysts of the momentous advancement made by the big data revolution that has been with us for 30 years. We contend that AI will contribute to further transform both the management of the customer experience and the understanding of markets and customers. Figure 4.1 shows how AI has been applied to marketing and how this may lead to improvements in the customer experience.

Let's take some of these applications in turn. The nature of AI tools such as prediction machines dramatically improves searching, as we have discussed in this section. Successful search – the retrieval of sought and unsought but relevant information – is essential for businesses in markets where the available products and services are almost infinite but where consumers' patience is definitely finite. The average online clothing retailer, for example, can have a range easily exceeding 50,000 items: most of them will never be seen by prospects and customers – hence never turned – unless better search options are made available to them (uploading a snapshot of a friend's dress, for example, to search for the same or similar options) and better recommendation algorithms are employed (which can recognize

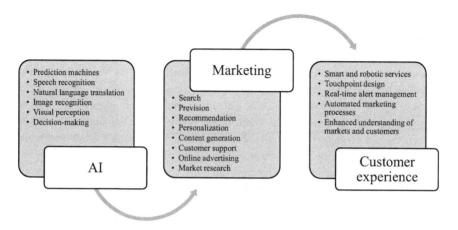

FIGURE 4.1 Impact of AI on marketing and customer experience

sophisticated attributes of the dress such as the type of garment, its colour, pattern, style and fabric, the brand, the context in which one would wear it – for a party, for the outdoors, etc. – and more).

Search and recommendation, in fact, are two sides of the same coin: the coin being the prediction problem. Improving this area would mean giving customers access to a wider yet relevant variety, allowing them to place themselves in a 'niche' instead of settling for the 'average'. From the point of view of the marketer, improved search results and recommendations help sell slow-moving items and thus increase revenues and profits and the ratings of sold goods, since recommended items typically score higher in customers' ratings than non-recommended ones. By streamlining how we search, companies can shorten the customer search-to-shop journey and capitalize on impulse buying. Consumers may experience feelings of discovery, excitement, gratification and empowerment – all of which become embedded in their perceived customer experience.

AI tools for image and speech recognition will have a significant impact in terms of improving search and recommendation, and consequently the customer experience. In a recent interview, the Pinterest CEO claimed that the future of search will be about images, not keywords (see Taylor, 2017). For millennials, both young and old, visual search is the technology they are most comfortable with (Wurmser, 2018). Visual search is good for questions that are difficult to verbalize, hence it seems not to cannibalize text search but rather complement it (Wurmser, 2018). Marketers are speaking of 'snap and search', as more and more businesses offer such functionality on their websites and apps: searching with images is as simple as snapping a photo of a pair of shoes or using a Web app to select a certain image that you found via a Google search. Ultimately, visual search brings online searching closer to the in-store browsing experience.

New AI-powered agents help customers to not only find specific items but also the right complements (Butterfield, 2018). Customers upload an image from any source and the software extracts the image's attributes, correlates it with a massive database of products and displays visually similar results as well as relevant recommendations of similar but also complementary products, such as accessories in the case of fashion. The information generated – uploaded photos, results, and customers' consequential actions (click, enlarge, save, discard, purchase, etc.) – enrich the user's profile. In November 2018, Zalando launched their Algorithmic Fashion Companion (AFC). Based on a 'training set of over 200,000 outfits created by stylists, the agent suggests those that best match recent customer purchases, hence offering a curated shopping experience' (Planet Retail, 2018).

The consultancy firm Gartner predicts that early adopters of visual search technology will experience a 30% increase in e-commerce revenues by 2021 (Panetta, 2017). Fashion is the consumer industry where marketers' attention is highest: e-commerce websites are adding visual search functionalities and encouraging customers to share their own photos (something that can be rewarded within a loyalty programme initiative, incidentally). For example, the French e-commerce group Vente-Privée has recently invested in Daco, a French start-up that develops AI image recognition tools for fashion retail (Balmat, 2018). Pinterest, Instagram, Google, Facebook and Alibaba have all invested in this area too: players that have access to vast repositories of images are in the position to extract value from offering them for algorithm training, for market research purposes and to support proprietary snap and search services. Moreover, marketers not only want to offer better search – and need tools and image banks to do it – but also to close the loop from search results to shopping. Amazon has launched a partnership with Snapchat to enable 'snap and buy'; such a move will benefit the app by boosting its usage, and expand Amazon's standing in mobile and in-app search markets (Heller, 2018). Image recognition enables the creation of new value propositions.

But it's not just images that are changing how we shop. AI is being applied to the customer experience in the area of speech recognition, too. Like image recognition, speech recognition builds on a natural human trait. Using our voice 'is more natural than using a touchpad or keyboard, takes less brain power, and creates even more opportunity for tech to move further into the background and reduce our reliance on screens' (Cakebread, 2019). The evident advantages of using one's voice to perform tasks, give instructions, search for products and services, place orders and, in general, be heard means that voice-operated services (from search to purchase to post-purchase assistance) will grow exponentially in the future. In late 2017, over 20% of Google searches conducted on mobile phones were executed through the voice service. WeChat claimed that five out of every six messages were sent using voice and WhatsApp alone processed over 200 million voice messages every day (Tiwari, 2017). Nie Zaiqing, a leading scientist at Alibaba AI Labs, predicts that the frequency of usage for voice interaction will surpass touchscreen interaction by 2023 (Chou, 2018). The accuracy of voice recognition algorithms has dramatically improved since IBM's first prototypes in 1995 when the word error rate (WER) – the common metric to gauge the accuracy of voice recognition systems – was 43% (Saon, 2016). It decreased to 15% in 2004, while

Google Assistant reached an impressive 4.9% in 2018, close to the average capability of humans, which is a WER of around 4% (van der Velde, 2018).

Since Apple launched Siri in 2011, followed by Amazon's Alexa in 2014 and Google Assistant in 2016, the tech giants have sustained the adoption of voice assistants by popularizing smart devices for the home. In this category smart speaker sales alone rose from 2.9 million units sold worldwide in the first quarter of 2017 (and 20 million in total in 2017) to 19 million in the third quarter of 2018, according to Canalys (Kinsella, 2018). An ever-growing number of smart devices, connected to the Internet and equipped with microphones, cameras, screens, sensors, voice and image recognition and computer vision capabilities will emerge on the market in the future. As more smart objects and devices permeate our daily lives, intelligent voice assistants will become indispensable (Chou, 2018). Moreover, these new smart objects and digital assistants will change the 'servicecape' as we know it. Just think of the last time you went to a hotel. It's quite possible that you interacted with a plethora of robotic assistants: your check-in was swift thanks to facial recognition, and a series of smart devices enabled you to manage the temperature and lighting of your room, order entertainment and book other services.[6] Data from such interactions can be used to enrich each customer's profile or derive insights on the needs and wants of the customer base (leading to the better understanding we presented as an outcome in Figure 4.1) and to inform the (re) design of services and of the customer experience.

Digital assistants, thanks to natural language processing, 'understand' voice commands (to ever increasing degrees of accuracy) and are able to produce voice output in natural language that resembles closely what a human would say in response to the command. Advances in this area have been rapid; today, natural language processing software can even manage dialects, in countries such as India where this is essential for business, or detect emotions. One area of application of natural language processing for CEM is the development of chatbots – automated customer support services powered by AI algorithms – that can process and respond in natural language by text and voice.

Chatbots are becoming increasingly common and represent a new touchpoint in the customer journey. Yao, Jia and Zhou (2018) have analysed hundreds of chatbots employed for the purposes of customer support in a variety of industries. Our own analysis of new services made available to members of major loyalty schemes (see Chapter 8) has found that some companies develop chatbots to provide exclusive services that are intended for retention as well as acquisition of new members to a loyalty initiative and/or to the company. Sephora, the beauty retailer, introduced a Facebook Messenger chatbot to let customers book in-store appointments with beauty consultants in the nearest store. Discount supermarket chain Lidl introduced a conversational chatbot to help customers take full advantage of the wine range in its stores. It finds wines by country, grape, colour and

6   Of course, not every hotel is powered by smart technology in this way. But many are, and in the future more and more are likely to be, as AI applications grow.

price, suggests wine for occasions and pairs wines with food (Kokoszka, 2018). Meanwhile, Jetblack is an invitation-only subscription service that finds what members want by interpreting their text or voice messages to the interface bot, delivers it, picks up returned goods and provides information and assistance 'to the busy moms of Manhattan' (Ricker, 2018). Launched by Walmart's 'Store 8' innovation lab, the service merges speech recognition, image recognition, chatbots and the subscription model to obtain a new retail format.

The game changer of AI in the customer experience raises questions about how customers will engage with touchpoints in the future. Today's customers live in an omnichannel world. The connected devices of the IoT and the opportunity to interact with them via natural language and image recognition via smart assistants and services are being woven into the fabric of everyday life. The landscape of touchpoints will change, and so will the customer's perception of her journey across new and old touchpoints. Brands' access to final consumers will change too. Connected objects and smart devices potentially allow more brands to enter the home. With this come several challenges. Intuitively, voice search will benefit those brands that appear first in search results, while their competitors fall into the shadows (how many pages of search results do you look through?). Thus businesses unable to compete with the resource-rich and technologically savvy brands risk becoming 'invisible' to customers. Experimental research conducted by Planet Retail shows that voice is better for searching for specific products rather than discovery (see Collins, 2018). Products that have already been present in the customer shopping basket are favoured in terms of their prominence in search results, and sponsored content doesn't necessarily come first. Marketers, therefore, will have to devise strategies to 'win' the intelligent agent, and have their product or brand selected by the smart assistant for suggestion to the customer who is ordering via voice. In other words, new touchpoints will find their unique place in customers' journeys and marketers need to understand and address this in developing appropriate customer experience design strategies.

The new intelligent touchpoints collect data that can be employed to gain insight and personalize the touchpoint interaction experience by making content and offers available to individual customers according to their tastes and preferences. By employing AI, personalization can be taken to new levels. For example, AI tools can help businesses adapt their offer to the context and indeed the specific moment in the customer journey and even to the emotional status of the customer. Not only has facial recognition software been able to map emotions for years; natural language processing software algorithms can now detect and decipher emotions, sarcasm and figures of speech (Dhanrajani, 2018). Think of the impact on customer service in a world where chatbots can tell the emotional state of the customer. With prediction capabilities built in, more real-time scoring of customers and prospects will be possible and personalization will be driven less by previously built profiles and more conversationally driven and oriented by contingency factors.

Programmatic online advertising is one area where this has important applications. More accurate predictions will result in improvements in the real-time A/B testing of different advertising solutions, in bidding for inventory and in real-time campaign optimization, thanks to the improved selection of an audience that is more likely to convert. These are just some of the marketing processes that will become automated by AI. Let's take another. As is pointed out by Mandelli (2018), real-time relationship risk management will become a genuine possibility since algorithms can do a better job of predicting churn from a variety of data (including those on emotions detected in spoken conversations) and can send alerts to marketers or automatically devise retention strategies. The human's role will shift to monitoring processes and choosing among a variety of automatically generated options – as we saw in the case of Stitch Fix's new product designs and as will be shown to be the case in the advertising and content creation examples below.

Offers, product descriptions and articles related to entire product lines will be automatically composed and personalized by machines. This is one example of how product information will be used to both personalize and automate formerly traditional marketing processes. During the 11.11 Global Shopping Festival in 2017 (Alibaba's mega 24-hour online sale and arguably the world's biggest shopping event to date), 6.7 billion personalized shopping pages were generated by more than 230,000 merchants on Taobao.com and Tmall.com.[7] Personalized landing pages had a 20% higher conversion rate compared with non-personalized ones (Alibaba Group, 2017). In 2018 Alibaba made an AI tool available to companies selling on their e-commerce platforms – Taobao, Tmall, Mei.com and 1688.com – that automatically produces advertising copy for the products, writing 20,000 lines per second (Handley, 2018). Advertisers can choose the tone among 'promotional, functional, fun, poetic or heartwarming' (Handley, 2018). AI has also been applied to generating captivating slogans for the launch of new car models, such as the Toyota Mirai, and even brands and names for new business ventures (see Yao, Jia and Zhou, 2018).

Creative human skills will increasingly be supported – if not substituted – by AI as far as content (not only advertising) creation. Today, a significant portion of sports and finance articles on news sites is written by machines, not by humans. Companies like Automated Insights and Narrative Science have developed AI tools that can turn data into readable texts, sometimes indistinguishable from those authored by human beings (Sachin, 2018). Wordsmith, for example, is a content generation agent used by the Associated Press to automate most of its financial earnings reports. It can produce over 4,400 quarterly earnings reports which translate into a 1200% increase compared to manual output (Parbey, 2018). Perhaps most fascinating is the neuro-storyteller developed by Ryan Kiros at University of Toronto, which combines recurrent neural network, skip-thoughts vectors and other AI techniques to generate stories based on the content of images. One of neuro-storyteller's models was trained on over 14 million passages from

---

7   Taobao.com and Tmall.com are subsidiaries of Alibaba in China and currently two of China's largest retail platforms.

romance novels and, when fed with images, generated a short fictional story based on the recognition of its content (samim, 2015).

The impact of AI undoubtedly goes well beyond marketing. Any discussion about content creation and personalization would not be complete without a reflection on the social consequences of people increasingly living inside their own 'filter bubble' (Pariser, 2011), that is, our own personal unique universe of information that we inhabit online. Ever since 2009 when Google first introduced individualized search results by using each user's past searches to display search results, personalization on the Web – and on digital touchpoints such as social media and apps that have emerged since – has skyrocketed. Pariser (2011) argues that although choosing one medium over another has always implied that we self-select ourselves for certain content (before the age of digital, we still *chose* to read one newspaper rather than another), the personalization bubble online is different. In fact, it is unique to each individual. It is invisible. Many people are not even aware of it. We do not know what gets edited out. With news sites mimicking search engines in (creating and) serving content that has a higher probability of being clicked on, read, forwarded and shared, and with less work performed by humans and more by algorithms, de-bundling and the disappearance of unpopular articles happens in minutes, if not seconds. Friends on social media whose content we do not interact with disappear from our newsfeed. We live inside a narrower image of the world. Because it is built around our behaviour and preferences, our bubble enhances our proclivity to consume content that does not challenge our beliefs. A non-challenging context blunts creativity and openness. This might be good for consumers, particularly if it simplifies choices, but it might not be as good for citizens who, in order to live constructively in peace, need to be aware of differences and learn to accept them (Pariser, 2011). The development and diffusion of ever more powerful AI will exacerbate this and other related risks, including the malevolent use of such technology. Because IATs act autonomously and produce unforeseeable results, there will also be unprecedented challenges in terms of tracing responsibility.

Blockchain, marketing and loyalty management

A chapter dedicated to the relationship between technology and the world of loyalty management would not be complete without some consideration of the blockchain. In 2018 Rakuten, Japan's largest retailer, announced a blockchain-based loyalty programme that would issue reward points in the form of an alternative currency called Rakuten Coin. According to a CoinDesk article (see Milano, 2018), Rakuten moved $9 billion worth of existing Super Points into the blockchain. Consumers will be able to freely trade their Rakuten Coins for bitcoin and other cryptocurrencies that are widely accepted by tens of thousands of merchants. The move has been explained as intended to appeal to international customers since the new, alternative payment method avoids exchange rate fees. In the same year Singapore Airlines developed KrisPay, the world's first blockchain-based airline loyalty digital wallet, in partnership with KPMG and Microsoft. Developments like these have turned many heads in the loyalty management industry and loyalty managers are starting to turn their attention to the blockchain and related technologies.

Blockchain, best known as the technology behind the bitcoin, is one form of distributed ledger technology (DLT), a term that broadly describes the dispersal and syncing of the same set of data across many parties at once rather than with one central party (Ray, 2018). There are many ways to achieve such syncing: the blockchain does it by structuring data into connected, secure blocks using cryptography. When a new transaction occurs (for example, a loyalty point is issued, redeemed or exchanged), a unique token is created and assigned to that transaction. Tokens are grouped into blocks (for example, every ten minutes) and distributed across the network, updating every ledger at once. New transaction blocks are validated and linked to older blocks, hence creating a verifiable record of all transactions that eliminates the need for centralized databases or intermediaries. Blockchain solves the so-called 'double-spend problem' because it makes it impossible to replicate the ownership of a digital asset but rather do an authorized transfer of it (Empirica, 2018). Every blockchain is a distributed ledger, but not every distributed ledger is a blockchain.

DLT is a breakthrough in managing information and there is little doubt that it will be adopted in every industry. We can draw a parallel with the introduction of the Internet protocol: DLT and the blockchain will be essential components of digital value chains, ecosystems and business in general. In fact, some authors have labelled the blockchain the 'Internet of Value' (Empirica, 2018). We are already seeing supply chains managed with blockchain applications and smart contracts. With reference to consumer goods, Walmart is using blockchain to track food products through its supply chain, while Unilever is applying it to increase transparency in their digital advertising ecosystem (O'Brien, 2018). Juniper Research (2018) forecasts that two-thirds of major companies are planning to integrate blockchain in their businesses. McKinsey, however, expresses scepticism and calls for caution (Higginson, Nadeau and Rajgopal, 2019).

In thinking about the relationship between the blockchain and loyalty management, it is important to separate the discourse regarding blockchain, the technology, from that of cryptocurrencies such as bitcoin, the applications of such technology. With that caveat in mind, let us ask: will loyalty programmes be based on blockchain technology or, more generally, DLT? In the future, some of the activity behind them probably will be. One current pilot is that of American Express, which is testing how DLT could improve efficiency and transparency in the information exchanges between the company and B2B partners of its Membership Reward programme (Cohen, 2018). The goal is to save on costs associated with reconciling and validating partners' activities with points, offers and rewards, a task that is typically performed centrally by the accounting department of the company that runs the loyalty programme. A DLT ledger 'would dictate and manage how all parties issue points, who can see and write transactions and what types of promotions mechanics are and are not permitted' – all in real time (Cohen, 2018).

It is worth noting, however, that in order to use the blockchain, a new private channel needs to be set up between two entities. In the above pilot, American Express is experimenting with online retailer Boxed. This should be replicated with any additional partner. But will companies see the investment worth? Cohen argues that if American Express is successful in giving merchants control over the offers it is making under the programme umbrella, this would be a proof of concept for the loyalty industry. Moreover, from the loyalty marketer's perspective, secure transactions can reduce costs associated with points fraud, and resulting savings could be passed down to members in the form of lower redemption thresholds for rewards or higher value benefits. Blockchain looks attractive in this respect given its resistance to decrypting: however, new quantum computers are 10 million times faster than common ones and might crack the codes necessary to make blockchain transactions secure (Higginson, Nadeau and Rajgopal, 2019).

Other issues with loyalty programmes that are more customer-facing – such as storing one's points from several loyalty programmes in one place, keeping track of multiple memberships, redeeming from multiple partners by exchanging tokens for a variety of businesses or rewards – might be addressed with blockchain-like solutions. These issues, however, have been addressed by loyalty coalition operators for decades (see Chapter 2) and are currently managed and solved without blockchain technology. Given current restraints on blockchain scalability (the speed of transaction recording, for example) the solution is not optimal today, and the same result can currently be obtained with other technologies (Burnett, 2018). In fact, according to Burnett, a large loyalty programme would need much more than three transactions recorded per second (the speed of bitcoin), or even more than 15 per second (Ethereum, another cryptocurrency).

Another critical area is the possible clash between the perfectly identifiable transaction ledger that is the core of a blockchain solution and the tightening up of personal data privacy and security rules ushered in by the implementation in 2018 of the General Data Protection Regulation (GDPR) in Europe. Data that is defined by the regulation as sensitive will have to be stored in legacy systems, not in the blockchain.

Let us conclude this chapter with a few correctives. When speaking of the blockchain and loyalty, some authors are not talking about the technology but the cryptocurrencies. They speak of loyalty programmes based on bitcoins or other cryptocurrencies. For example, Shelper (2018, p. 1) defines 'blockchain marketing' as 'rewarding members with cryptocurrency or cryptotokens in exchange for their attention, brand advocacy and data insights, while giving them full control over their personal data which is stored in a secure digital wallet on the blockchain'. We believe that expressions such as 'blockchain marketing' are not a helpful contribution to the literature. Testing to see if cryptocurrencies can work as a loyalty reward should be done in a scientific way.

In other cases, authors writing about the blockchain and loyalty are, in fact, talking about branded currency (see Chapter 2), choosing to embellish the topic with the new and fashionable nomenclature of the blockchain, where in fact it has little or nothing to do with it. The idea of creating a common currency for loyalty programmes *is not new*, as this book makes clear. After all, coalition loyalty programmes that use point collection methods are based on the idea of a more 'liquid' point that *acts as a currency*. There is a substantial difference between a loyalty currency and a cryptocurrency. Loyalty programmes points, tokens or miles are a closed-circuit currency. Consequently, they are not regulated in most countries. If they are converted to a cryptocurrency like bitcoin, the brand or loyalty programme owner will have to become a regulated entity, with all the consequences that ensues. And they will, in all probability, not want this (McIntosh, 2018).

In a nutshell, the blockchain is an infrastructural innovation that will find its place within value chains, even loyalty value chains, once a sound use case is built. We believe that instead of offering cryptocurrencies as rewards, marketers should focus on providing payment solutions that add value for customers, such as the Starbucks wallet. The Starbucks branded currency is not built on the blockchain (yet) but has proved a fun, secure and successful strategy for retention and acquisition.

The revolution in big data and AI is changing the customer experience as we know it. It is creating value not just by making marketing processes more efficient, but by making them supremely effective since they are now being driven by better prediction, automation and innovation. Value creation is the driver of loyalty. And we are just at the beginning.

References

Agrawal, A., Gans, J. and Goldfarb, A. (2018) *Prediction Machines: The Simple Economics of Artificial Intelligence*. Boston, MA: Harvard Business Review Press.

Alibaba Group (2017) 'Alibaba: at Alibaba, artificial intelligence is changing how people shop online'. *MarketScreener*, 5 June. Available at: https://www.marketscreener.com/ALI BABA-GROUP-HOLDING-LTD-17916677/news/Alibaba-At-Alibaba-Artificial-Intelli gence-is-Changing-How-People-Shop-Online-24540779/ (Accessed: 20 January 2019).

Balmat, N. (2018) 'Venteprivée announces the acquisition of Daco, French fashion AI startup'. *Futur404*, 17 October. Available at: https://futur404.com/venteprivee-daco/ (Accessed: 19 January 2019).

Bhattarai, A. (2018) 'The personal stylists who are training the bots to be personal stylists'. *The Washington Post*, 17 August. Available via: https://www.washingtonpost.com (Accessed: 1 January 2019).

Blattberg, R. C., Glazer, R. and Little, J. D. (1994) *The Marketing Information Revolution*. Boston: Harvard Business School Press.

Brennen, S. and Kreiss, D. (2014) 'Digitalization and digitization'. *Culture Digitally*, 8 September. Available at: http://culturedigitally.org/2014/09/digitalization-and-digitization/ (Accessed: 24 January 2019).

Brown, B., Chui, M. and Manyika, J. (2011) 'Are you ready for the era of "big data"?', *McKinsey Quarterly*, 4(1), pp. 24–35.

Burnett, S. (2018) 'Can blockchain reinvigorate loyalty programs?'. *Forbes Magazine*, 11 December. Available at: https://www.forbes.com/sites/forbesagencycouncil/2018/12/11/can-blockchain-reinvigorate-loyalty-programs/ (Accessed: 14 January 2019).

Butterfield, B. (2018) 'See it, search it, shop it: how AI is powering visual search'. *Adobe Blog*, 12 December. Available at: https://theblog.adobe.com/see-it-search-it-shop-it-how-ai-is-powering-visual-search/ (Accessed: 17 January 2019).

Cakebread, C. (2019) 'Hey Siri, what are hearables? A new category of wearable emerges'. *eMarketer*, 9 January. Available at: https://www.emarketer.com/content/hey-siri-what-are-hearables (Accessed: 19 January 2019).

Chou, C. (2018) 'Top tech trends to watch in 2018 from Alibaba scientists'. *Alizila*, 6 February. Available at: https://www.alizila.com/top-tech-trends-to-watch-in-2018/ (Accessed: 19 January 2019).

Chui, M., Manyika J., Miremadi M., Henke, N., Chung, R., Nel, P. and Malhotra, S. (2018) Notes from the AI frontier: Insights from hundreds of use cases. *McKinsey*, April. Available via: http://www.mckinsey.com/ (Accessed: 12 January 2019).

Cohen, M. (2018) 'Blockchain's potential role in multi-partner loyalty'. *LoyaltyOne*, 18 September. Available at: https://www.loyalty.com/home/insights/article-details/blockchain-s-potential-role-in-multi-partner-loyalty (Accessed: 17 January 2019).

Collins, J. (2018) 'Preparing for voice search'. *Planet Retail*, 1 June (updated 6 June). Available (subscribers only) at: www.planetretail.net/NewsAndInsight/Article/164194 (Accessed: 20 January 2019).

Dhanrajani, S. (2018) 'Here are the top 10 AI trends to watch out for in 2019'. *YourStory*, 27 December. Available at: https://yourstory.com/2018/12/top-10-ai-trends-watch-2019/ (Accessed: 20 January 2019).

DeNardis, L. and Raymond, M. (2017) 'The Internet of Things as a global policy frontier'. *UC Davis Law Review*, 51(2), pp. 475–495.

Drucker, P. (2013) *Managing in the Next Society*. 2nd ed. London: Routledge.

Empirica (2018) 'What is blockchain?' 19 March. Available at: https://www.empirica.fi/what-is-blockchain/ (Accessed: 14 January 2019).

Ericson, J. and Wang, S. (2017) 'At Alibaba, artificial intelligence is changing how people shop online'. *Alizila*, 5 June. Available at: https://www.alizila.com/at-alibaba-artificial-intelligence-is-changing-how-people-shop-online/ (Accessed: 5 January 2019).

Gershgorn, D. (2017) 'Stitch Fix is letting algorithms help design new clothes – and they're allegedly flying off the digital racks'. *Quartz*, 16 July. Available at: https://qz.com/1028624/stitch-fix-let-an-algorithm-design-a-new-blouse-and-they-flew-off-the-digital-racks/ (Accessed: 3 January 2019).

Golder, S. A. and Macy, M. W. (2011) 'Diurnal and seasonal mood vary with work, sleep and daylength across diverse cultures'. *Science*, 30 September; 333(6051), pp. 1871–1881.

Handley, L. (2018) 'Alibaba's new A.I. tool can produce thousands of ads a second but it says it won't replace humans'. *CNBC*, 4 July. Available at: https://www.cnbc.com/2018/07/04/alibabas-ai-makes-thousands-of-ads-a-second-but-wont-replace-humans.html (Accessed: 20 January 2019).

Heller, L. (2018) 'Amazon and Snapchat form a powerful partnership'. *Forbes Magazine*, 26 September. Available at: https://www.forbes.com/sites/lauraheller/2018/09/26/amazon-and-snapchat-form-a-powerful-partnership/ (Accessed: 19 January 2019).

Higginson, M., Nadeau, M. C. and Rajgopal, K. (2019) 'Blockchain's Occam problem'. *McKinsey*, January. Available at: https://www.mckinsey.com/industries/financial-services/our-insights/blockchains-occam-problem (Accessed: 19 January 2019).

Hilbert, M. (2012) 'How much information is there in the "information society"?'. *Significance*, 9(4), pp. 8–12.

Hollis, S. (2018) 'The Stitch Fix story: changing the way millions of people dress with data'. *Upsell* (publication of Jilt), 6 August. Available at: https://jilt.com/upsell/stitch-fix-data/ (Accessed: 1 January 2019).

Hvistendahl, M. (2017) 'Inside China's vast new experiment in social ranking'. *Wired*, 14 December. Available at: https://www.wired.com/story/age-of-social-credit (Accessed: 3 January 2019).

Juniper Research (2018) 'Nearly two-thirds of large enterprises currently aiming to deploy blockchain, Juniper finds'. 11 September. Available at: https://www.juniperresearch. com/press/press-releases/nearly-two-thirds-of-large-enterprises-currently (Accessed: 14 January 2019).

Khyade, V. B. and Khyade, R. V. (2018) 'Strengthening role of information and communication technology in global society'. *Management*, 5(2), pp. 42–49.

Kinsella, B. (2018) 'Amazon moves back to top spot for Q3 2018 smart speaker sales – Canalys'. *Voicebot*, 15 November. Available at: https://voicebot.ai/2018/11/15/ama zon-moves-back-to-top-spot-for-q3-2018-smart-speaker-sales-canalys/ (Accessed: 19 January 2019).

Kokoszka, P. (2018) 'Chatbots in retail: nine companies using AI to improve customer experience'. *Retail Insight Network*, 21 August. Available at: https://www.retail-insight-network.com/features/chatbots-in-retail-ai-experience/ (Accessed: 20 January 2019).

Kumar, V., Dixit, A., Javalgi, R. G. and Dass, M. (2016) 'Research framework, strategies, and applications of intelligent agent technologies (IATs) in marketing'. *Journal of the Academy of Marketing Science*, 44(1), pp. 24–45.

Lake, K. (2018) 'Stitch Fix's CEO on selling personal styles to the mass market'. *Harvard Business Review* (May–June), pp. 35–40.

Lupton, D. (2016) *The Quantified Self: A Sociology of Self-Tracking*. New York: John Wiley & Sons.

Mack, C. (2015) 'The multiple lives of Moore's law'. *IEEE Spectrum*, 52(4), pp. 31–31.

Mandelli, A. (2017) *Big Data Marketing*. Milan: EGEA.

Mandelli, A. (2018) *Intelligenza artificiale e marketing: Agenti invisibili, esperienza, valore e business*. Milan: EGEA.

Manyika, J., Chui, M., Brown, B., Bughin, J., Dobbs, R., Roxburgh, C. and Byers, A. H. (2011) 'Big data: the next frontier for innovation, competition, and productivity'. *McKinsey*, May. Available at: https://www.mckinsey.com/business-functions/digital-mckinsey/our-in sights/big-data-the-next-frontier-for-innovation (Accessed: 9 January 2019).

Marr, B. (2018) 'Stitch Fix: the amazing use case of using artificial intelligence in fashion retail'. *Forbes Magazine*, 25 May. Available at: https://www.forbes.com/sites/bernardma rr/2018/05/25/stitch-fix-the-amazing-use-case-of-using-artificial-intelligence-in-fashion-retail/ (Accessed: 2 January 2019).

Mayer-Schönberger, V. and Cukier, K. (2013) *Big Data: A Revolution That Will Transform How We Live, Work and Think*. London: John Murray.

McClelland, A. (2017) 'The difference between artificial intelligence, machine learning, and deep learning'. *Medium*, 4 December. Available at: https://medium.com/iotforall/ the-difference-between-artificial-intelligence-machine-learning-and-deep-learning-3aa67bff 5991 (Accessed: 6 January 2019).

McIntosh, A. (2018) 'Winning coalitions will become marketplaces'. *Loyalty Magazine*, 19 December. Available (subscribers only) via: https://www.loyaltymagazine.com (Accessed: 14 January 2019).

Milano, A. (2018) 'E-Commerce giant Rakuten is launching its own crypto'. *CoinDesk*, 27 February. Available at: https://www.coindesk.com/e-commerce-giant-rakuten-launching-cryptocurrency (Accessed: 7 January 2019).

Negroponte, N. (1995) *Being Digital*. New York: Alfred A. Knopf.

Nilsson, N. J. (2010) *The Quest for Artificial Intelligence: A History of Ideas and Achievements.* Cambridge: Cambridge University Press.

O'Brien, M. (2018) 'Brands and blockchain: How Walmart, Burger King and De Beers are snuggling up to decentralization'. *ClickZ*, 31 January. Available at: https://www.clickz.com/brands-blockchain/209093/ (Accessed: 14 January 2019).

Panetta, K. (2017) 'Gartner top strategic predictions for 2018 and beyond'. *Gartner*, 3 October. Available at: https://www.gartner.com/smarterwithgartner/gartner-top-strategic-predictions-for-2018-and-beyond/ (Accessed: 17 January 2019).

Parbey, C. (2018) '3 content creation AI that can write a story for you'. *Edgy Labs*, 22 November. Available at: https://edgy.app/3-content-creation-ai-that-can-write-a-story-for-you (Accessed: 20 January 2019).

Pariser, E. (2011) *The Filter Bubble: What the Internet is Hiding from You.* London: Penguin.

Pinto, J. (2002) 'The 3 technology laws'. Available at: http://www.jimpinto.com/writings/techlaws.html (Accessed: 3 January 2019).

Planet Retail (2018) 'Zalando builds machine learning based styling assistant'. 1 November. Available (subscribers only) at: https://www.planetretail.net/NewsAndInsight/Article/165853 (Accessed:19 January 2019).

Porter, M. E. and Millar, V. E. (1985) 'How information gives you competitive advantage'. *Harvard Business Review*, July. Available at: https://hbr.org/1985/07/how-information-gives-you-competitive-advantage (Accessed: 2 February 2019).

Ray, S. (2018) 'The difference between blockchains & distributed ledger technology'. *Towards Data Science (Medium)*, 19 February. Available at: https://towardsdatascience.com/the-difference-between-blockchains-distributed-ledger-technology-42715a0fa92 (Accessed: 7 January 2019).

Ricker, T. (2018) 'Walmart launches exclusive personal shopping service that you text'. *The Verge*, 1 June. Available at: https://www.theverge.com/2018/6/1/17416518/jetblack-membership-price-specs-walmart (Accessed: 20 January 2019).

Rouhiainen, L. (2018) *Artificial Intelligence: 101 Things You Must Know Today About Our Future.* Charleston, SC: CreateSpace.

Sachin, S. (2018) 'How does AI work on marketing ads?' *Quora*, 5 September. Available at: https://www.quora.com/How-does-AI-work-on-marketing-ads (Accessed: 20 January 2019).

samim (2015) 'Generating stories about images: recurrent neural network for generating stories about images'. *Medium*, 5 November. Available at: https://medium.com/@samim/generating-stories-about-images-d163ba41e4ed (Accessed: 20 January 2019).

Saon, G. (2016) 'Recent advances in conversational speech recognition'. *IBM*, 28 April. Available at: https://developer.ibm.com/watson/blog/2016/04/28/recent-advances-in-conversational-speech-recognition-2/ (Accessed: 2 February 2019).

Shankar, V. and Carpenter, G. S. (eds) (2012) *Handbook of Marketing Strategy.* Cheltenham: Edward Elgar.

Shelper, P. (2018) *Blockchain Loyalty: Disrupting Loyalty and Reinventing Marketing Using Cryptocurrencies.* Sydney: Loyalty & Reward Company.

Shoham, Y., Perrault, R., Brynjolfsson, E., Clark, J. and LeGassick, C. (2017) *The AI Index 2017 Annual Report.* Available at: http://cdn.aiindex.org/2017-report.pdf (Accessed: 5 January 2019).

Stone, P., Brooks, R., Brynjolfsson, E., Calo, R., Etzioni, O., Hager, G., Hirschberg, J., Kalyanakrishnan, S., Kamar, E., Kraus, S., Leyton-Brown, K., Parkes, D., Press, W., Saxenian, A. L., Shah, J., Tambe, M. and Teller, A. (2016) *"Artificial Intelligence and Life in 2030". One Hundred Year Study on Artificial Intelligence: Report of the 2015–2016 Study Panel, September 2016.* Stanford University. Available at: https://ai100.stanford.edu/2016-report (Accessed: 7 January 2019).

Taylor, H. (2017) 'The future of search will be all about pictures, not keywords, says Pinterest CEO'. *CNBC*, 3 April. Available at: https://www.cnbc.com/2017/04/03/pinterest-ceo-future-of-search.html (Accessed: 19 January 2019).

The Economist (2015) 'Ever more from Moore'. 18 April. Available at: https://www.economist.com/business/2015/04/18/ever-more-from-moore (Accessed: 2 January 2019).

Tiwari, P. (2017) '4 reasons why voice is the future of customer experience'. *Interactions*, 29 November. Available at: https://www.interactions.com/blog/customer-care/4-reasons-voice-future-cx/ (Accessed: 19 January 2019).

Van der Velde, N. (2018) 'A complete guide to speech recognition technology'. *Globalme.com*, last updated 25 October. Available at: https://www.globalme.net/blog/the-present-future-of-speech-recognition (Accessed: 2 February 2019).

Wilson, J. M. (2012) 'Computing, communication, and cognition: three laws that define the internet society: Moore's, Gilder's, and Metcalfe's'. Available at: http://www.jackmwilson.net/Entrepreneurship/Cases/Moores-Meltcalfes-Gilders-Law.pdf (Accessed: 3 January 2019).

Wooldridge, M. (2002) *An Introduction to MultiAgent Systems*. Chichester: John Wiley & Sons.

Wurmser, Y. (2018) 'Visual search 2018: New tools from Pinterest, eBay, Google and Amazon increase accuracy, utility'. *eMarketer*, 26 September. Available at: https://www.emarketer.com/content/visual-search-2018 (Accessed: 17 January 2019).

Yao, M., Jia, M. and Zhou, A. (2018). *Applied Artificial Intelligence: A Handbook for Business Leaders*. Middletown, DE: TOPBOTS.

5

WHAT WE KNOW ABOUT LOYALTY PROGRAMMES

Marco Ieva

What is a loyalty programme?

Loyalty programmes (LPs) started to be adopted in the early 1980s and have gained influence across multiple industries since (Berry, 2013). The majority belong to the retail industry (Colloquy, 2017), and in the United States, companies invest an astonishing $2 billion in them (Taylor et al., 2015). They have been widely studied in academia and are regarded by marketers as a key marketing tool and customer experience touchpoint. Unsurprisingly, there has been no shortage of attempts to define LPs. The American Marketing Association (AMA) defined what it called 'frequent shopper programmes' as 'continuity incentive programmes offered by a retailer to reward customers and encourage repeat business'.[1] Several scholars have identified further features. Bijmolt, Dorotic and Verhoef (2011) pointed out that LPs develop across multiple industries both in business-to-business (B2B) and business-to-consumer (B2C) settings.

Kumar and Reinartz (2018) identified them as marketing processes that reward customers for certain behaviours they undertake with brands, for instance repeat purchases, engagement with the brand assets, and so on. LPs provide consumers with benefits that include tangible rewards and statuses. They provide companies with identifiable advantages such as increasing the likelihood of retaining members and gaining insight on purchases at an individual level. LPs generate switching costs, since members lose value if they decide to switch to another company (Leenheer et al., 2007), and switching costs play a role in reducing customer switching behaviour (Pick and Eisend, 2014). Companies can leverage customer

---

1 Until recently the AMA published this definition in its online dictionary at www.ama. org, but the dictionary now no longer appears on the website. It is, however, a widely known definition and believed to be the first attempt to categorize loyalty programmes.

insight to deploy personalized and targeted marketing activities, such as customized offers (see Breugelmans et al., 2015; Liu, 2007).

That these definitions focus on distinct features points to the fact that LPs are broad marketing initiatives. They include distinct typologies of marketing programmes that differ in many ways. Several terms have been employed to refer to them. Indeed, we could make a long list, on which reward programmes, frequency reward programmes, loyalty cards or schemes, points cards, advantage cards, frequent flyer programmes and frequent shopper programmes would feature, among others (see Bijmolt, Dorotic and Verhoef, 2011). However, in all cases the underlying concept of an LP is that customers enrolled in one are encouraged to maintain or increase their spending with a given company in exchange for some asset – points, coupons, stars, air miles, etc. – that can be converted into products and services. Kumar and Reinartz (2018) identified four distinct goals, all or some of which LPs are designed to accomplish:

- building attitudinal and behavioural loyalty
- generating efficiency profits
- generating effectiveness profits
- achieving value alignment.

Let's take these in turn. Attitudinal loyalty involves a positive customer perception and attitude towards a particular product or service or company, while behavioural loyalty refers to the actions that customers undertake with respect to a product or service. Both are key forms of loyalty and usually correlate – although one does not necessarily imply the other. Efficiency profits are profits resulting from a change in customer purchase behaviour brought about by membership of an LP. Effectiveness profits are medium-term or long-term profits generated by improvements a company makes to a product offering, communication or promotion on the basis of information gathered though the LP. Finally, value alignment refers to the possibility of aligning marketing efforts and related investment with the assessed value of customers targeted by the LP.

Clearly, success in achieving these goals depends on how an LP can influence customer behaviour. Blattberg, Kim and Neslin (2008) identified three key elements of LPs that aim to do this: the points-pressure mechanism, rewarded behaviour and personalized marketing. The points-pressure mechanism influences customers to accelerate their purchases as they draw nearer to gaining a certain reward. The receipt of a programme reward can increase the strength of the relationship between the customer and the company. Personalized marketing involves the delivery of offers and communications tailored to an individual and aimed at triggering an attitudinal and behavioural response, something which we will return to later in this chapter. Scholars have identified four key components of LPs: membership requirements, programme structure, point and reward structure, and programme communication (see Liu and Yang, 2009; Bijmolt, Dorotic and Verhoef, 2011; Breugelmans et al., 2015). This section discusses these components in more detail and reviews the recent literature on each before moving on to address a specific type: the coalition LP.

Membership requirements

Membership requirements refer to the rules that define how customers are to be enrolled in LPs. We can identify two specific aspects: (1) voluntary versus automatic enrolment; (2) open versus closed enrolment. LPs commonly offer voluntary enrolment, meaning customers are asked if they want to join. This leads to self-selection: customers that are enrolled in the LP have chosen to be members and thus probably differ in some meaningful way from customers that have decided not to join. On the one hand, customers who have a positive attitude towards the company might be more inclined to be members of an LP. On the other hand, customers who are sensitive to promotional activities might also be keen to join.

There are other variables to take into account in understanding why customers join an LP. For example, Demoulin and Zidda (2009) and Gómez, Arranz and Cillán (2012) identified several drivers positively or negatively related to the likelihood of completing a voluntary subscription to an LP in a supermarket retail setting: shopping enjoyment, individual desire for privacy, perceived scheme disadvantages, perceived scheme advantages, perceived complexity, distance from the store, and attitudinal and behavioural loyalty. They found that customers who regard shopping as a hedonistic activity are more reluctant to share their personal information with a company, and those who are sceptical about the advantages of an LP (for example, if it has an overly complicated points accrual mechanism or structure) are less likely to subscribe. By contrast, the perceived benefits stemming from subscribing can positively influence the decision to join. Attitudinal and behavioural loyalty is also a factor: the higher the positive attitude towards the retailer, or the amount of time spent with the retailer, the higher the likelihood a customer will join its LP. Customers who live close to the store are also more likely to become LP members, probably a consequence of the convenience of having a store nearby.

Whatever the motivations to join, voluntary enrolment is certainly the most employed enrolment mechanism. In this respect, one of the most frequently used key performance indicators (KPIs) for LPs is the percentage of transactions and turnover that is made only by LP members out of the total number of transactions and amount spent in the store made by all customers. These figures tend to vary depending on the industry. For instance, in Italy, consumer surveys run by the Loyalty Observatory showed that the turnover related to LP members in grocery retailing might reach percentages higher than 80% of the total turnover, while in consumer electronics or in fashion this figure was usually much lower.

Automatic enrolment, which is less commonly deployed, means that customers join an LP upon their first purchase of a given product and service. From that moment the company can automatically track future transactions made by the customer. Unfortunately, there is not much research on the difference in terms of effectiveness of automatic versus voluntary enrolment. The main benefit of automatic enrolment is that it allows companies to track the purchase behaviour of all the customers purchasing at least one product. Hence, no selection bias arises when evaluating the effects of an LP using this enrolment type. However, automatic enrolment can have several downsides. For example, customers may perceive the enrolment mechanism itself as a limitation of their freedom of choice and might then be sceptical of the related advantages of the programme. Moreover, since the customer is to be identified at first purchase, this implies requesting personal information and creating a new customer profile, tasks that can be time-consuming. This process may irritate the occasional customer, and may prevent some from completing the purchase altogether. Finally, the new regulations on data privacy introduced in Europe from May 2018 call for further legal evaluations of the feasibility of automatic enrolment.

The second aspect of enrolment mechanism is the decision to make an LP open to everybody or restricted to customers with certain requirements. The latter are commonly known as closed or 'selective' LPs. Esmark, Noble and Bell (2016) studied the extent to which an open versus closed LP (for a coffee shop) could be more effective in fostering consumer attitudes towards the company such as gratitude, in-group identification and loyalty. Their main findings were as follows. First, open LPs seemed to be more effective in the grocery industry, while closed LPs were more effective in those businesses where the hedonic component plays a stronger role, such as travel services, restaurants and coffee shops. Second, both open and closed LPs contributed to enhancing customer loyalty but in a different manner depending on the stage of the customer relationship: beginning and growth, maturity or decline.

At the beginning and growth stage, there was no difference in the effectiveness of open versus closed LPs. At the maturity stage, both types of LPs were effective in fostering loyalty. Specifically, open LPs positively influenced customer in-group identification (the consumer belief of being consistent with the image of the average programme member). In-group identification, in turn, had a positive effect on loyalty intentions. By contrast, closed LPs influenced gratitude, which arises when a customer feels that the company has adopted a behaviour that leads to advantages for the customer (see Raggio et al., 2013). Gratitude also impacted loyalty intentions. Finally, when the relationship was in the declining stage, closed LPs were more effective at developing in-group identification in customers, thus leading to higher customer loyalty. Therefore, the closed LP was shown to be useful in retaining customers more likely to abandon the company and restoring the quality of the relationship with them.

Customers can join a closed LP by invitation or by paying a membership fee. The membership fee is a lump sum paid at the enrolment stage or a periodical subscription fee that is charged, for instance, every month or year. One of the most famous closed LPs is Amazon Prime, which requires customers to pay a membership fee in order to enrol and enjoy its benefits (e.g. no delivery costs, access to entertainment services, and more, as discussed in Chapter 1). Given that LPs can entail huge investment in terms of money and effort, companies can use the membership fee to help cover their costs and thereby offer more valuable and meaningful benefits to customers. However, a membership fee can discourage some consumers from joining if they perceive the advantages as failing to justify the membership fee or if they are put off by being tied in to an annual paid subscription.

Ashley, Gillespie and Noble (2016) studied the effect of membership fees on consumer perceptions of LPs. Their study found that fee-based LPs were likely to attract consumers who felt committed to the company and were willing to spend with it. They also found that fee-based programmes can increase the revenues of the LP: in addition to the fee received, such LPs are able to elicit a more favourable perception of the programme and, in turn, increase the average customer spend after enrolment. Their findings offer an important lesson in how to increase the likelihood that customers will join a fee-based LP. The answer is related to the interaction between the membership fee and the accrual system. If the membership fee is low, it is better to offer a simple accrual system, one that can be easily understood and keeps the customer focused on the benefits of the programme rather than on price. Where the membership fee is high, increasing the perceived complexity of the accrual system contributes to increasing membership intentions because it triggers a more comprehensive evaluation of the costs and benefits of the programme rather than an evaluation of the fee alone.

Programme structure

Breugelmans et al. (2015) identified two main programme structures: frequency reward and customer tier. Frequency reward programmes assign points based on how much or how frequently a customer spends and rewards are achieved depending on certain point thresholds. Customer tier programmes have a hierarchical structure: customers are classified into tiers according to their purchase behaviour in a previous period (for example, gold, silver and bronze customers) and the classification is typically reviewed every year (see Bijmolt et al., 2018). While frequency reward programmes are employed in settings where purchase occasions tend to be more frequent (for example, in supermarket retailing), customer tier programmes are generally employed in service sectors such as aviation, banking, car rental, and hospitality. This reveals that the type of structure is also clearly linked with the type of business.

Comparing the two programme structures, Kopalle et al. (2012) found that customer tier was more effective than frequency reward in driving loyalty because it continually provides benefits once the customer belongs to a high tier, whereas the frequency reward component displays a short-term impact only. This is due in part to the effect of points pressure, which pushes the consumer to reach a certain threshold to gain a reward, and in part to the effect of receiving the reward itself, which triggers subsequent short-term purchase behaviour. Tier structures have also been found to drive gratitude towards the company (see Steinhoff and Palmatier, 2016), specifically when advancement within the programme hierarchy is earned (see Eggert, Steinhoff and Garnefeld, 2015). It should be noted, however, that these results varied slightly according to the industry of reference and gender of programme members: apparently men were more likely to be engaged in a customer tier programme if their status was made visible to others.

Chaabane and Pez (2017) added yet more insight on this topic. They found that the effectiveness of frequent reward versus customer tier depended on the congruence between the programme and the brand concept. They classified brand concepts as symbolic and functional. Symbolic brands satisfy the needs of self-expression and self-enhancement and are related to the expression of a status – Ferrari is a good example of a symbolic brand. Functional brands, by contrast, are brands that solve practical issues and provide more tangible bene-fits – Chevrolet could be included in this typology. The authors found that symbolic brands perceived a hierarchical LP structure as more congruent with their brand concept and this congruency was reported to lead to increased loyalty to the surveyed companies. However, frequent reward and customer tier were found to be equally congruent with a functional brand concept. These studies thus provide evidence for the superiority of a multi-tier LP in driving loyalty, at least in certain circumstances.

It is, however, worth mentioning what has been referred to in many studies as the dark side of customer tier LPs. The first issue relates to the situation when customers receive endowed – rather than achieved – elevated customer status. If the status is not perceived as a customer personal achievement, consumer scepticism arises. This scepticism might hamper the effectiveness of the status upgrade in driving customer loyalty (see Eggert, Steinhoff and Garnefeld, 2015). Marketers are therefore advised to frame the higher status offered to consumers as a reward for the customer behaviour, leaving to the customer the final decision of whether to change or keep their current status. Moreover, consumer tier demotion – when a consumer, due to a lower spend, is shifted to a lower tier – represents a second key issue. Quite simply, individuals are more sensitive to tier demotions than they are to tier promotions. Tier demotions may thus have a higher negative effect on trust, commitment and loyalty than do the positive effects of tier promotions (see Van Berlo, Bloemer and Blazevic, 2014). According to Ramaseshan and Ouschan (2017), this is more evident for high-status consumers than it is for low-status consumers. To take a hypothetical example, Gold customers that are shifted to a lower tier (Silver) are more likely to display negative reactions in terms of purchase behaviour than Silver customers that are shifted to the lower tier (Bronze). The third issue is more strategical: marketers planning to introduce a customer tier programme should understand that the termination of that programme might ser-iously harm the relationship with those customers accustomed to accessing benefits related to the highest programme tiers (Bijmolt et al., 2018).

Point and reward structure

The main issues, as outlined by Breugelmans et al. (2015), concerning the point and reward structure of an LP revolve around the design of the points accrual system and type of rewards offered in both frequency reward and customer tier programmes. Companies managing LPs can take advantage of what are known as the points-pressure effect and rewarded behaviour effect (see Taylor and Neslin,

2005; Bijmolt et al., 2018). The points-pressure effect occurs when a customer is approaching a certain threshold that triggers a reward and accelerates their purchases in order to gain it more quickly. To elicit this effect, companies must avoid two common mistakes, outlined by Bijmolt et al. (2018) and Drèze and Nunes (2011): (1) setting thresholds that are too easy to reach and consequently demotivate customers; (2) setting thresholds that are too high and thus discourage occasional customers from engaging with the programme. The rewarded behaviour effect occurs when a customer receives the reward and experiences feelings of joy and happiness that reinforce their engagement with the LP and might lead to a positive change in purchase behaviour (Colliander, Söderlund and Szugalski, 2016). Even though this effect appears to be a significant driver of a long-term relationship with customers (according to Taylor and Neslin, 2005), there are some caveats that should not be overlooked: the duration of this effect is short term, from two to seven weeks, and tends to be different depending on the characteristics of the customer and their previous engagement with the LP (see Taylor and Neslin, 2005; Kopalle et al., 2009) .

Timing is critical here. Two issues need to be taken into account: the difference between achieving an immediate versus a delayed reward, and the points expiration policy (that is, the amount of time that members have at their disposal to accrue points in order to achieve a reward). Regarding the former, Roehm and Roehm (2011) found that consumers favoured delayed rewards if those rewards fit with their personal values. Regarding the latter, unredeemed points can become an issue for some companies, which tend to cope with it by introducing points expiration policies. Consumer personal characteristics might help explain the likelihood that a programme member will redeem points or would rather accumulate them. Hwang et al. (2016) found that young consumers were more likely to redeem points compared with older consumers. Moreover, according to their study, high-income consumers were more likely than low-income consumers to redeem points. These results indeed suggest that companies should be willing to differentiate their marketing actions related to points redemption depending on the personal (in this case, socioeconomic and demographic) characteristics of members.

Breugelmans and Liu-Thompkins (2017) found that establishing a points expiration deadline elicited a positive effect on purchase behaviour. However, in their study, this positive impact was identified only for those consumers who displayed a higher degree of flexibility in their purchases. Consumers who tended to buy fewer products with the company offering the LP and who shopped across multiple stores were more flexible in managing their purchases and adapting their behaviour with respect to the points expiration policy. In contrast, those who already spent a significant amount of money with the company were less likely to adapt their purchase behaviour to comply with the expiration policy. Hence, they perceived the expiration policy as a restriction on their flexibility, which for them made the programme less appealing.

As far as the rewards are concerned, there are usually two categories: hard and soft rewards. Arbore and Estes (2013) offered definitions for these terms. Hard rewards are tangible benefits, including, for instance, discounts, free products and monetary incentives. Soft rewards are intangible benefits, mostly psychological, relational or emotional, that include preferential treatment, status visibility, priority check-in and special events. Previous research has found that consumers tend to prefer tangible rewards (see Keh and Lee, 2006). Soft rewards have been found to drive attitudinal loyalty, namely commitment (see Bridson, Evans and Hickman, 2008), whereas tangible rewards contribute to developing higher behavioural loyalty (see Meyer-Waarden, 2015).

Usually, what we observe in practice is that both hard and soft rewards are strictly linked to the core business of the company. For instance, airline industry LPs might offer fast check-in or supermarket retailers might offer coupons on the next purchases in their stores. Meyer-Waarden (2015) found that rewards aligned with the image of the company were more effective in driving loyalty intentions. Another way to make sure that rewards look appealing to consumers is to ensure price inequity (whereby the point price of the reward is higher than the market price) is avoided, especially as far as expensive rewards are concerned. On this point, Danaher, Sajtos and Danaher (2016) found that price inequity was more often perceived for high-priced catalogue items than for low-priced ones. Moreover, the authors found that when price inequality was higher than 10%, the majority of programme members, unsurprisingly, experienced substantial feelings of irritation!

Programme communication

The fourth component, communication, plays a vital role in the management of an LP. First, at a strategic level the LP should be fully integrated in the marketing strategy of a company with all the other touchpoints that the company can directly or indirectly manage or monitor. Second, the effectiveness of an LP might be related to how companies frame their communication of the points-earning mechanism or decide how consumers are going to be informed about their points-balance status (for instance, if automatically or not).

Bonezzi, Brendl and De Angelis (2011) found that when consumers were motivated to reach a given points threshold and were at the beginning of their goal pursuit, they took as a reference their initial state, namely the amount of points already collected. Consumers approaching the end goal, by contrast, took as a reference their desired end state, namely the amount of points they needed to reach. However, individuals in the middle – that is, neither close to the start nor to the end of the goal pursuit process – were demotivated to pursue the final goal. These findings point to the importance of framing messages in an effective way to avoid members remaining stuck in the middle of the goal pursuit process. According to the study of Ku, Yang and Chang (2018), messages that highlight the amount of money that should be spent to achieve a reward or the loss stemming from consumer inaction were more likely to erode intention to redeem the reward. However, this effect occurred only for those individuals who were 'stuck in the middle'. More research is needed in this area to assess how companies can design communications to maximize consumer engagement with their programmes.

What is clear from our discussion in this section is that the four key components of LPs – membership requirements, programme structure, point and reward structure, and programme communications – are not mere trivial aspects but key considerations that any company must take into account when designing a programme. As the body of evidence suggests, deciding whether an LP should be open or selective, include a membership fee or not, adopt a frequency award or customer tier structure, harness the points-pressure or rewarded-behaviour effects, and so on, are all matters that must be considered carefully alongside a myriad of different customer variables and being mindful of the long-term costs and challenges that might arise from having to make alterations or wholescale changes to the programme design. It is imperative too, regardless of how an LP is designed, that its benefits and features are communicated to customers clearly and that programme communication is both integrated into the overarching company marketing strategy and designed to maximize individual customer engagement.

Coalition LPs

Before we move on to assess how LPs achieve the four goals identified by Kumar and Reinartz (2018), it is worthwhile saying something about the coalition model given its distinct characteristics, economic relevance and diffusion. Payback and Nectar are leading examples of this type of programme today, but the concept dates back to the late 1980s (as we discussed in Chapter 2). Coalition LPs are unique in that they seek to bring together a group of different partners, usually active in different sectors, such as the retail and service sectors (see Moore and Sekhon, 2005). They allow members to earn points when shopping at any of the different partners of the programme and usually involve partners that cooperate to create a unified coalition programme and a third non-participating party that manages its operations. As some scholars have noted, there are benefits to both companies and customers in joining a coalition LP (see De Noni, Orsi and Zanderighi, 2014).

For companies:

- It allows them to cross-sell and cooperate to achieve mutual gain by expanding the customer base for customer relationship marketing activities (Dorotic, Bijmolt and Verhoef, 2012).
- Because the costs of introducing and running an LP are shared among partners, the financial burden placed on individual companies is limited (Capizzi and Ferguson, 2005). This is particularly appealing to local and smaller companies.
- Costs are also saved because the company managing the programme has the skills and infrastructure necessary to maximize the usage of the information collected through it and effectively manage the different loyalty marketing activities (Nath, 2005).

- Since a coalition LP enables customers to earn and burn points for purchases across a wide range of product categories, they may be more appealing to some consumers and lead to higher enrolment rates than traditional LPs.

Customers enjoy benefits too:

- They can earn points faster without increasing their spending with a company. Customers don't need to spend more on a single product category to earn more points but can simply switch the same spending on a given category to a different company that is a partner in the programme.
- They can enjoy a wider variety of rewards, which are usually aligned with the business of the companies joining the coalition.

There are, however, significant risks in adopting a coalition LP. First, the programme might lose focus and meaning if too many and diverse partners are included (Kumar and Reinartz, 2018). Second, each partner will bring to the programme a customer base that differs in size, turnover and, more importantly, points-earning patterns. Therefore, it is not a simple task for the company managing the coalition to plan marketing activities and achieve cooperation among partners. On the one hand, the major partners in a coalition LP might invest more in the programme and demand more attention from the company managing it. On the other hand, the minor partners might be unwilling to cooperate if they feel that the programme is not delivering substantial results for their business. While there are coalition programmes that were able to achieve success in Germany and United Kingdom, there is also evidence of unsuccessful coalition LPs, for example the closure of both Nectar in Italy in 2016 and of the American Express coalition programme, Plenti, in the United States in 2018. Schumann, Wünderlich and Evanschitzky (2014) further explored the 'dark side' of coalition LPs by studying the spill-over effect of a service failure for a company that is active in a coalition LP. Their study found that service failure caused by one partner in a coalition LP does not simply impact the other partners. The negative consequences are, in fact, extended to the coalition programme as a whole. If catastrophic, it is hard to see how the programme can recover.

How successful are loyalty programmes?

We've discussed the key features of LPs. But how do they perform in reality? Several studies have attempted to measure this. This section reviews the existing evidence of the performance of LPs in achieving the four goals outlined in the first section. It looks at the influence of LPs on customer loyalty attitudes and behaviours, and thus how they generate efficiency profits from the resulting changes in customer purchase behaviour, before moving on to discuss how they contribute to medium-term and long-term profits and function to pursue value alignment.

Before delving into the literature, it is important to keep in mind, in the case of programmes that adopt voluntary enrolment (the vast majority), that customers self-select: they *choose* to enrol in LPs. It is important to account for this self-selection bias in order to estimate the actual effect LPs have. Otherwise, there is the tangible risk that we overestimate the impact LPs have. Usually, consumers who are more prone towards a given company tend to join its LP. Evidently this is one, but not the only, reason why their behaviour is different from consumers who do not join the programme. Leenheer et al. (2007) highlighted this issue by demonstrating that a methodology that ignores self-selection bias estimates that LPs lead to a 30% increase in share of wallet. When taking into account self-selection bias, that percentage drops dramatically to 4%. One cannot overemphasize the importance of employing sound and proper statistical methods that take bias into account when measuring programme performance.

Influence on attitudinal loyalty

There is a plethora of studies that have focused on the influence of LPs on both attitudinal and behavioural loyalty. But these have tended to analyse the short-term effects of LPs in driving customer attitudes and intentions. Although one of the declared objectives of an LP is to build commitment towards the company offering it, the reality, according to Kumar and Reinartz (2018), is that companies have struggled to develop genuine attitudinal loyalty by means of programme rewards and bonuses alone.

Attitudinal loyalty – often expressed as commitment, satisfaction or positive perceptions, and generally measured by means of consumer surveys – has been regarded by many as a key performance metric and antecedent to behavioural loyalty (see Furinto, Pawitra and Balqiah, 2009; Dorotic, Bijmolt and Verhoef, 2012). It is important because it prevents programme members from switching to other companies that might offer programmes with better perceived benefits (see Hansen, Deitz and Morgan, 2010) and supports a company in retaining customers and driving long-term purchase behaviour effects. Some scholars have argued that LPs might be more effective in building attitudinal loyalty for those customers who already prone to develop a relationship with the company (see Dholakia, 2006; Daams, Gelderman and Schijns, 2008). Others have observed that enhancing how consumers perceive an LP and its rewards might lead to increased attitudinal loyalty to the company (see Demoulin and Zidda, 2008; Furinto, Pawitra and Balqiah, 2009). Moreover, Vesel and Zabkar (2009) found that employees who interact with customers and address their questions about the programme could increase customer satisfaction and commitment, leading, in turn, to increased behavioural loyalty.

Other, more recent studies have focused on how LPs can drive attitudinal loyalty. Stathopoulou and Balabanis (2016) found that members' positive perception of programme benefits led to increased trust and satisfaction, while Kang, Brashear-Alejandro and Groza (2015) discovered that values and benefits were significant antecedents to both company and programme loyalty. Consumer perception of the values and benefits of enrolling in a LP is the key driver of loyalty to that programme. In turn, loyalty to the programme may lead to loyalty to the company through a specific mechanism: the consumer-company identification, in which consumers are attracted by the company brand and begin to identify themselves with it. The LP itself may help to develop, or even initiate, the bond between company and consumer, and this has been shown to contribute to increasing attitudinal loyalty to the company.

Along the same lines, Brashear-Alejandro, Kang and Groza (2016) found that delivering non-monetary incentives to LP members can be a valuable means of driving feelings of identification. Ma, Li and Zhang (2018) studied the effects of LP in service sectors and found both positive and negative consequences for attitudinal loyalty. On the one hand, tangible rewards, preferential treatment and perceived status exerted a positive effect on customer relationship quality. However, perceived status can backfire. Ma, Li and Zhang (2018) found that for gold programme members who had developed a high perception of their status, the joint offering of preferential treatment and tangible rewards led them to develop entitlement behaviours. They started to expect preferential treatment and extra efforts from the company, and such expectations negatively affected satisfaction, profitability and, ultimately, the relationship with the company. Vilches-Montero et al. (2018) found that consumer perceptions of the innovativeness and competitive advantages offered by an LP can drive attachment to it and, in turn, increase store loyalty. This relationship was, again, found to vary depending on gender. For men, the perceived competitive advantages of the programme were significantly related to store loyalty; for women, the perceived innovativeness of the LP was a significant antecedent to store loyalty.

Influence on behavioural loyalty

If an attitudinally loyal customer is someone who perceives a brand, product or programme in a positive way and feels, internally, committed and satisfied with it, a behaviourally loyal customer is someone who takes specific positive actions in respect of that brand, product or programme (e.g. maintaining his purchases or recommending the company/brand to others). The same customer can be one without being the other, and although attitudinal loyalty can be an antecedent to other forms of loyalty (as is argued by many of the aforementioned scholars), it is not necessarily so. So, to move beyond studies that look at how LPs affect customer perceptions and attitudes, we now turn to those that look at how they perform in changing purchase behaviour and influencing customer behavioural loyalty. There is evidence to suggest that LPs may do this over time, if not in the short term. Dorotic, Bijmolt and Verhoef (2012) offered an extensive review of how LPs influence customer behaviour and the remainder of this section seeks to review and update it.

Several early studies were conducted measuring the impact of LPs on purchase behaviour in aggregate terms (e.g. Cigliano et al., 2000) and found that LPs, in the first year of introduction, increased average sales by a percentage ranging from 1%

to 3% in grocery retailing and 5% to 8% in department stores. It is clear that these percentages were also related to the key characteristics of the industry and company in question. For instance, research has found that, when the degree of competitiveness in the market is high and when the number of LPs in the market increases, the aggregate effect of each programme is significantly reduced (see Kopalle and Neslin, 2003; Liu and Yang, 2009). Moreover, other studies have shown that while big brands seem to achieve benefits from introducing an LP because they can count on a big share of customers, small firms launching the LP as a late competitive response seem to encounter a higher risk of failure (see Meyer-Waarden and Benavent, 2006).

When reviewing the effects of LPs on purchase behaviour at the individual customer level, purchase frequency, share of wallet and purchase volume are generally regarded as the relevant KPIs. As we have stated before, LP members displayed a higher spending than non-members in many previous studies (e.g. Meyer-Waarden, 2008). However, when accounting for self-selection, there is evidence to suggest that the positive effects of LPs on purchase behaviour may be limited to short-term loyalty marketing activities only, such as instant reward programmes. Instant reward programmes are short-term programmes that reward consumers upon the act of purchase with small prizes per fixed spending (see Minnema, Bijmolt and Non, 2017). Generally speaking, these rewards are part of a collectable set and encourage customers to come back to the point of sale in order to obtain new rewards that are part of the collection. Some companies also offer rewards to customers if they purchase specific products or brands.

Early studies in this respect showed that instant rewards programmes increased average spending levels by 6% during the promotional period (see Taylor and Neslin, 2005). Minnema, Bijmolt and Non (2017) estimated the substantial effects of instant reward programmes in a grocery retailing setting and found that these initiatives had a positive impact on the frequency of visits to the store but did not affect the number of products bought. This impact was much stronger for customers taking an active part in the reward collection. Moreover, delivering a free gift associated with the purchase of a given product was reported to increase the probability that the involved consumers would choose that brand and was particularly effective when coupled with a price discount.

The evidence on the long-term effects of LPs, and indeed the effectiveness of long-term LPs, is mixed: while some studies report positive effects on purchase behaviour, others display no such effects. Specifically, across grocery retailing, airline services and insurance there is evidence for an increase in purchase frequency and volume and share of wallet driven by LPs (see Verhoef, 2003; Leenheer et al., 2007). The highest effects are reported just after the introduction of the LP. Melnyk and Bijmolt (2015) investigated the effects of introducing and terminating a LP on the likelihood that customers will stay with the company and increase their spending with it. Their study spanned different industries: food, telecommunications, oil, financial services, utilities and retail. The results show that LPs that provided members-only services and special events had a positive effect on loyalty intentions when the programme was first introduced. When the programme was terminated, there was no significant decrease in terms of loyalty intentions, which means that the impact of members-only services and special events were still lasting. Moreover, the authors found that at the introduction stage, programme structure and point and reward structure were key influences on the behaviour of members.

The negative effects of terminating a LP are largely dependent on the competitive environment and how long a customer has been a member of the programme. Many studies have reported a 'ceiling effect' in the impact of LPs depending on the customer segment of reference (see, e.g., Bolton, Kannan and Bramlett, 2000; Lal and Bell, 2003). Heavy buyers tend to have less room to increase their spending as a consequence of the LP because they are already top spenders. Therefore, the effects of the LP might be more visible and significant for customer segments that are low or medium spenders.

Despite this evidence in favour of the effectiveness of LPs, other studies conclude that LPs do not substantially change consumer behaviour (see, e.g., Bellizzi and Bristol, 2004; Meyer-Waarden and Benavent, 2006). The mixed picture reveals the key role played by contextual factors such as customer segments, settings, industries and programme design in the study of LP performance. It is, then, very challenging to provide a definitive answer on the impact of LPs. However, from this updated review of previous studies, several key insights do emerge:

- LPs are related to change in customer attitudes and behaviours, but this change is driven by a complex set of different factors that very often are not under the control of the company.
- The chosen programme structure and reward and points-earning mechanism are key drivers of the impact of LPs.
- Marketers should carefully measure the short-term results of LPs by considering different KPIs and different customer segments to capture the potential heterogeneity of effects.

There is no simple and unique answer to the question of how effective LPs are in influencing attitudinal and behavioural loyalty. This is largely due to the complexity of assessing their performance in terms of variables that are empirically challenging. We believe, rather, that the greater value of LPs lies in their effect on profits and their capacity to provide value alignment opportunities.

Influence on profits and value alignment

Kumar and Reinartz (2018) define effectiveness profits as those profits that companies can achieve by relying on a better knowledge of their customer base through the information gathered by LPs. Utilizing LP-generated data, companies can customize their offer and tailor communications to customers and customer segments. Moreover, they can take informed decisions regarding other aspects, such as assortment, merchandising and promotional strategy, by relying on customer data at an individual level. Hence companies can use LPs at a strategic level to learn about customer preferences and use this actionable data in a way that could result in a win-win situation for both the customer and the company.

Kumar and Reinartz (2018) understand value alignment as the capability to serve each customer by investing monetary and non-monetary efforts that are in line with the value that each customer brings to the company. By following this path, the company ensures that the profits received are aligned with the costs needed to serve any given customer. The risk of value alignment is that each customer might be treated differently. Thus, value alignment is advisable and feasible only when there is high heterogeneity in customer spending and if the characteristics of a given business allow it to implement this kind of differentiation: i.e. customers or customer segments can be distinguished by employing direct and personal means of communication. It is plain, then, that both effectiveness profits and value alignment have several requirements that need to be met if they are to work. It is not easy for any company to achieve these goals and develop a significant competitive advantage.

Studying the effects of LPs on effectiveness profits and value alignment is a challenging task and this explains why there is a lack of academic literature on this topic. To this aim, studies should adopt a long-term approach and track how companies, internally, take advantage of the customer information gathered through the development of an LP. However, the success story of the Tesco Clubcard programme in the 2000s could be considered a good example on how LPs can contribute to generating effectiveness profits and achieving value alignment by leveraging individual customer information. In this respect, Humby, Hunt and Philips (2003) have explained how Tesco achieved outstanding results by relying on customer data to take informed decisions on many different marketing aspects and deliver customized offers to customers.

How are loyalty programmes changing today?

Among practitioners across different countries and industries there is a growing concern regarding the need to innovate LPs. The growth of digital channels and e-commerce has changed the customer journey and empowered consumers in the shopping process. In such an environment, consumers may develop a dimmer view of the benefits of LPs that rely on reward catalogues and plain discounts, which may be in danger of becoming outdated. Breugelmans et al. (2015) identified three new key trends in loyalty marketing associated with the digital transformation:

- the growth of coalition LPs and the need to develop partnerships among players in different industries
- the growth of the mobile channel, which can change the whole experience customers have with an LP
- the rise of intermediaries that can aggregate information on LP membership and compare the terms and conditions of scores of LPs with the click of a button, thus allowing consumers to choose programmes offering them the most value.

Companies across the world are forging other pathways to LP innovation too. LPs are increasingly rewarding non-transactional customer behaviour. Responding to the increased use by both consumers and brands of social media, some LPs are expanding their points-earning mechanisms to include the option of collecting points by sharing or liking brand posts, recommending the brand to other consumers online, or updating their customer profile. For example, Tarte, a New York-based cosmetic and skincare retailer, has begun rewarding customers for publishing user-generated content online. Customers can gain points by posting selfies featuring Tarte products or making video tutorials reviewing their purchases from the retailer (see Peacock, 2018).

Tarte is not the only company innovating its LP. Alibaba's 88 Membership programme (discussed in Chapter 1) is changing how it rewards both spending and engagement. In this respect, it seems to be following evidence from academic literature that supports the introduction of rewards for non-purchasing activities. Indeed, a study by Rehnen et al. (2017) focused on BahnBonus, Deutsche Bahn's loyalty scheme which rewards customers for their engagement in its Facebook community. The authors found that rewarding customer engagement with monetary incentives led to an improved attitude towards the programme and increased loyalty intentions towards the company.

Using monetary incentives to rewards customers for taking specific non-purchase actions is also a key factor in the rise of the referral reward programme. Referral reward programmes (also called 'member get member' programmes) are on the rise. They acquire customers by providing incentives to existing customers to recommend the company to new customers (Jin and Huang, 2014). Orsingher and Wirtz (2018) studied the key drivers of referral reward programme effectiveness and found that the face value of the incentive was a key positive driver of the recommenders' perceived attractiveness of the incentive. The perceived attractiveness of the incentive led, in turn, to higher intention to recommend the company. However, if the face value of the incentive was too high, recommenders were worried about being negatively perceived by their peers and this was shown to hamper the likelihood they would recommend the company to others.

Another way in which LPs are innovating is in the shift to online and mobile channels. Ieva and Ziliani (2017) demonstrated that consumer medium preference for LPs features is heterogenous. In their study, two customer segments displayed an exclusive preference for print or online LPs, while all other segments showed mixed preferences for both print and online LPs elements. Gender, age and affluence were found to explain the medium preference for LPs. Specifically, females preferred print over online but the reverse was true of their male counterparts. Younger customers displayed a stronger preference towards online elements. Low-affluent customers preferred to engage across multiple channels, while high-affluent consumers were more likely to stick with one channel. These results suggest that companies are advised to allow consumers the opportunity to engage with their LPs seamlessly across both online and offline channels. In doing so, consumers are given the choice to engage with the programme through the channel they prefer.

LPs as a customer experience touchpoint

While most of the literature on loyalty marketing has focused on the specific features and effects of LPs, there is a growing stream of studies related to CEM and touchpoints that have considered LPs as an example of the latter (see, e.g., Wind and Hays, 2016). As defined by Duncan and Moriarty (2006), touchpoints are all verbal and non-verbal incidents which an individual perceives and consciously relates to a given firm or brand. We discuss the new literature on touchpoints in greater depth in Chapter 6, but it is relevant to the present discussion to briefly review the findings from those studies that have analysed the role of LPs as a touchpoint among others in a given company's repertoire (e.g. its website, stores and mobile app).

According to Verhoef et al. (2009), LPs have the potential, just like any other touchpoint, to shape the customer experience and thus contribute towards achieving customer satisfaction and loyalty. The question that inevitably arises is to what extent LPs are more or less important than other touchpoints in driving experience and loyalty. Mohd-Ramly and Omar (2017) studied the role of store attributes, including LPs, as antecedents to the customer experience in the retail sector. They hypothesized that customer satisfaction may lead to an improved customer experience. The results from their study show that LPs were the second most important driver of the customer experience after store atmosphere. Though more research is needed to confirm a positive and substantial relationship between LPs and customer experience, Mohd-Ramly and Omar's study is a good indication that an association between the two exists.

In a similar vein, Ieva and Ziliani (2018a; 2018b) and Ziliani and Ieva (2018) focused on the relationship occurring between touchpoint frequency and positivity and loyalty intentions. They measured, by means of a survey, three dimensions of touchpoint interaction: reach, frequency and positivity. Each of these terms requires brief explanation. Touchpoint reach, defined by Romaniuk, Beal and Uncles (2013), is the indication of whether a customer has been exposed or not to a given touchpoint over time. Touchpoint frequency is the frequency of exposure to a given touchpoint over a specific period of time (see Baxendale, Macdonald and Wilson, 2015). Touchpoint positivity is the customer's affective response when encountering a given touchpoint in a period of time (ibid.).

These three variables were measured with reference to any touchpoint (store, website, mobile app, LP, etc.) relevant to the setting of reference. Through this method it was possible to identify the relative role played by LPs – as far as the frequency and positivity of exposure are concerned – in their relationship with loyalty intentions. By means of a segmentation study, Ieva and Ziliani (2018a) found that, in a grocery retail setting, the customer segments displaying higher exposure to all the different touchpoints, including LPs, were positively related to higher loyalty intentions, namely a willingness to disclose private information to the company, a relationship commitment and positive word of mouth. In a study that followed soon after, Ieva and Ziliani (2018b) investigated the relationship between touchpoint reach, frequency and positivity and loyalty intentions, considering around 20 different touchpoints in the mobile service industry. Loyalty intentions were measured including different perspectives: the extent to which a customer intended to say positive things about the provider, to recommend it to others, to consider it as their first choice for mobile services, and to increase their use of its services in the future. Their results showed that being exposed to LPs was positively related to higher loyalty intentions, but that there was no evidence of a relationship between positive affective response to LPs and loyalty intentions.

In another study, Ziliani and Ieva (2018) focused on how touchpoint frequency and positivity were related to relationship commitment and positive word of mouth towards a grocery retailer. The results were completely different from the 2018b study. This time affective response to LPs had a positive and significant relationship with both relationship commitment and positive word of mouth towards the retailer, while frequency of exposure to LPs had no significant relationship with the two outcomes. Thus, this suggests that the role of LPs in terms of frequency and positivity on loyalty intentions is very specific and may change depending on the setting, in this case mobile services versus grocery retailing. The key message for us here, however, is that LPs played a role in influencing loyalty intentions even when their role was considered in the context of a broader, more comprehensive study of all available touchpoints. Of course, it should be highlighted that these three studies did not control for the selection bias occurring with LPs: customers exposed to the LP may have had different characteristics (such as a more positive attitude towards the retailer) than those not exposed to it.

What next for loyalty programmes?

The aim of this chapter has been to review the existing literature on LPs to provide an updated overview of what we currently know about what they are, how they work and what they can achieve. It would be remiss to end this chapter without offering some reflections on potential areas for future research.

First, the design of the point and reward structure is a challenging task that requires many key decisions. Management and marketers, short on time or lacking the resources, often base these decisions on gut instinct rather than sound rational analysis and that is an understandable reality. However, there are several questions for researchers and practitioners alike to consider. The first challenge is how to define the ratio between the amount spent and number of points issued to members, what we have described in this chapter as the points-earning mechanism. Should points be granted for a specific amount spent or for purchasing certain products in certain categories? What is the optimal points-earning mechanism that maximizes engagement and effectiveness in terms of future spending without hurting profits? The second relates to customer tier programmes. What is the best number of tiers? Can more tiers encourage higher spending? What are the optimal thresholds that should be employed to shape each tier? With a higher number of tiers there is also higher risk that consumers experience demotion more frequently, with the related negative consequences.

Second, the impact of digital technology is changing how consumers interact with LPs. Many programmes can be accessed through smartphone apps where customers can check in real time their current point status and request their rewards. They can also glean which purchases or non-purchase actions are required to meet a certain threshold. It would be interesting to understand how digital technology can impact the way customers engage with LPs. Is the online channel capable of boosting interaction? Can the digital channel increase the control customers want to have on their points and programme goals?

Third, members of Generation Z (the post-millennials loosely defined as those born between the mid to late 1990s and 2010) are gaining purchasing power and are emerging as a new and valuable customer segment for companies. Previous studies have shown that age plays a significant role in explaining consumer preference for LPs (see Ieva and Ziliani, 2017). Questions will inevitably arise about the appeal of LPs to this new generation. Will LPs be able to catch the attention of Generation Z? How will the meaning of loyalty differ for this generation? Will the traditional reward catalogue disappear with the rise of digital collections and mobile apps? Should companies adapt their engagement strategies to meet the characteristics of Generation Z?

Fourth, in the new omnichannel scenario there is a greater need to identify consumers across channels and especially at every interaction with any touchpoint. LPs could be very important in tracking consumers any time they encounter the brand. If the consumer is going to identify himself by means of his loyalty card, his personal code, his mobile application or his username and password, companies can recognize him, address his complaint and register his preferences and purchase intentions in a seamless way, provided they can reconcile the information across multiple touchpoints. LPs, then, could become integral to the design of a true omnichannel strategy that enables a company to deliver a seamless customer experience. Indeed, LPs might just be the starting point to involve the customer, track their purchasing and non-purchasing activity, and communicate with them in a personalized way.

There is work to be done then. LPs currently absorb a huge amount of efforts and resources, but they are key marketing tools that gain valuable and actionable customer insight and help drive, in certain circumstances, customer attitudes and behaviours. The world of the consumer is rapidly changing, and given the growth of digital technology and the changes in needs and expectations, companies must now keep pace by monitoring and revising their LPs in a way that responds to new challenges and is consistent with all the other touchpoints that contribute to the customer experience.

References

Arbore, A. and Estes, Z. (2013) 'Loyalty program structure and consumers' perceptions of status: feeling special in a grocery store?'. *Journal of Retailing and Consumer Services*, 20(5), pp. 439–444.

Ashley, C., Gillespie, E. A. and Noble, S. M. (2016) 'The effect of loyalty program fees on program perceptions and engagement'. *Journal of Business Research*, 69(2), pp. 964–973.

Baxendale, S., Macdonald, E. K. and Wilson, H. N. (2015) 'The impact of different touchpoints on brand consideration'. *Journal of Retailing*, 91(2), pp. 235–253.

Bellizzi, J. A. and Bristol, T. (2004) 'An assessment of supermarket loyalty cards in one major US market'. *Journal of Consumer Marketing*, 21(2), pp. 144–154.

Berry, J. (2013) *Bulking up: The 2013 COLLOQUY Loyalty Census*. Colloquy, 25 June. Available at: http://www.totalcustomer.org/2013/06/25/whitepaper-download-2013-colloquy-loyalty-census/ (Accessed: 24 February 2019).

Bijmolt, T. H., Dorotic, M. and Verhoef, P. C. (2011) 'Loyalty programs: generalizations on their adoption, effectiveness and design'. *Foundations and Trends in Marketing*, 5(4), pp. 197–258.

Bijmolt, T. H., Krafft, M., Sese, F. J. and Viswanathan, V. (2018) 'Multi-tier loyalty programs to stimulate customer engagement'. In Palmatier, R. W., Kumar, V. and Harmeling, C. M. (eds), *Customer Engagement Marketing*, Cham: Palgrave Macmillan, pp. 119–139.

Blattberg, R. C., Kim, B. D. and Neslin, S. A. (2008) 'Why database marketing?' In Blattberg, R. C., Kim, B. D. and Neslin, S. A. (eds), *Database Marketing*, New York: Springer, pp. 13–46.

Bolton, R. N., Kannan, P. K. and Bramlett, M. D. (2000) 'Implications of loyalty program membership and service experiences for customer retention and value'. *Journal of the Academy of Marketing Science*, 28(1), pp. 95–108.

Bonezzi, A., Brendl, C. M. and De Angelis, M. (2011) 'Stuck in the middle: the psychophysics of goal pursuit'. *Psychological Science*, 22(5), pp. 607–612.

Brashear-Alejandro, T., Kang, J. and Groza, M. D. (2016) 'Leveraging loyalty programs to build customer–company identification'. *Journal of Business Research*, 69(3), pp. 1190–1198.

Breugelmans, E. and Liu-Thompkins, Y. (2017) 'The effect of loyalty program expiration policy on consumer behavior'. *Marketing Letters*, 28(4), pp. 537–550.

Breugelmans, E., Bijmolt, T. H., Zhang, J., Basso, L. J., Dorotic, M., Kopalle, P., Minnema, A., Mijnlieff, W. J. and Wünderlich, N. V. (2015) 'Advancing research on loyalty programs: a future research agenda'. *Marketing Letters*, 26(2), pp. 127–139.

Bridson, K., Evans, J. and Hickman, M. (2008) 'Assessing the relationship between loyalty program attributes, store satisfaction and store loyalty'. *Journal of Retailing and Consumer Services*, 15(5), pp. 364–374.

Capizzi, M. T. and Ferguson, R. (2005) 'Loyalty trends for the twenty-first century'. *Journal of Consumer Marketing*, 22(2), pp. 72–80.

Chaabane, A. M. and Pez, V. (2017) '"Make me feel special": are hierarchical loyalty programs a panacea for all brands? The role of brand concept'. *Journal of Retailing and Consumer Services*, 38, pp. 108–117.

Cigliano, J., Georgiadis, M., Pleasance, D. and Whalley, S. (2000) 'The price of loyalty'. *McKinsey Quarterly*, 4, pp. 68–77.

Colliander, J., Söderlund, M. and Szugalski, S. (2016) 'Multi-level loyalty program rewards and their effects on top-tier customers and second-tier customers'. *Journal of Consumer Marketing*, 33(3), pp. 162–171.

Colloquy (2017) *Loyalty Census 2017*. 29 June. Available at: https://www.the-cma.org/Contents/Item/Display/327325 (Accessed: 26 February 2019).

Daams, P., Gelderman, K. and Schijns, J. (2008) 'The impact of loyalty programmes in a B-to-B context: results of an experimental design'. *Journal of Targeting, Measurement and Analysis for Marketing*, 16(4), pp. 274–284.

Danaher, P. J., Sajtos, L. and Danaher, T. S. (2016) 'Does the reward match the effort for loyalty program members?'. *Journal of Retailing and Consumer Services*, 32, pp. 23–31.

De Noni, I., Orsi, L. and Zanderighi, L. (2014) 'Coalition loyalty-programme adoption and urban commercial-network effectiveness evaluation'. *International Journal of Retail & Distribution Management*, 42(9), pp. 818–838.

Demoulin, N. T. and Zidda, P. (2008) 'On the impact of loyalty cards on store loyalty: does the customers' satisfaction with the reward scheme matter?'. *Journal of Retailing and Consumer Services*, 15(5), pp. 386–398.

Demoulin, N. T. and Zidda, P. (2009) 'Drivers of customers' adoption and adoption timing of a new loyalty card in the grocery retail market'. *Journal of Retailing*, 85(3), pp. 391–405.

Dholakia, U. M. (2006) 'How customer self-determination influences relational marketing outcomes: evidence from longitudinal field studies'. *Journal of Marketing Research*, 43(1), pp. 109–120.

Dorotic, M., Bijmolt, T. H. and Verhoef, P. C. (2012) 'Loyalty programmes: current knowledge and research directions'. *International Journal of Management Reviews*, 14(3), pp. 217–237.

Drèze, X. and Nunes, J. C. (2011) 'Recurring goals and learning: the impact of successful reward attainment on purchase behavior'. *Journal of Marketing Research*, 48(2), pp. 268–281.

Duncan, T. and Moriarty, S. (2006) 'How integrated marketing communication's "touchpoints" can operationalize the service-dominant logic'. In Lusch, R. F. and Vargo, S. L. (eds), *The Service-Dominant Logic of Marketing: Dialog, Debate, and Directions*, Abingdon: Routledge, pp. 236–249.

Eggert, A., Steinhoff, L. and Garnefeld, I. (2015) 'Managing the bright and dark sides of status endowment in hierarchical loyalty programs'. *Journal of Service Research*, 18(2), pp. 210–228.

Esmark, C. L., Noble, S. M. and Bell, J. E. (2016) 'Open versus selective customer loyalty programmes'. *European Journal of Marketing*, 50(5/6), pp. 770–795.

Furinto, A., Pawitra, T. and Balqiah, T. E. (2009) 'Designing competitive loyalty programs: how types of program affect customer equity'. *Journal of Targeting, Measurement and Analysis for Marketing*, 17(4), pp. 307–319.

Gómez, B. G., Arranz, A. M. G. and Cillán, J. G. (2012) 'Drivers of customer likelihood to join grocery retail loyalty programs: an analysis of reward programs and loyalty cards'. *Journal of Retailing and Consumer Services*, 19(5), pp. 492–500.

Hansen, J. D., Deitz, G. D. and Morgan, R. M. (2010) 'Taxonomy of service-based loyalty program members'. *Journal of Services Marketing*, 24(4), pp. 271–282.

Humby, C., Hunt, T. and Phillips, T. (2003) *Scoring Points: How Tesco is Winning Customer Loyalty*. London: Kogan Press.

Hwang, J. H., Chung, J., Kim, J. W., Lee, D. and Yoo, W. S. (2016) 'Antecedents to loyalty point redemption: implications for customer equity management' *Journal of Business Research*, 69(9), pp. 3731–3739.

Ieva, M. and Ziliani, C. (2017) 'Towards digital loyalty programs: insights from customer medium preference segmentation'. *International Journal of Retail & Distribution Management*, 45(2), pp. 195–210.

Ieva, M. and Ziliani, C. (2018a) 'Mapping touchpoint exposure in retailing: implications for developing an omnichannel customer experience'. *International Journal of Retail & Distribution Management*, 46(3), pp. 304–322.

Ieva, M. and Ziliani, C. (2018b) 'The role of customer experience touchpoints in driving loyalty intentions in services'. *The TQM Journal*, 30(5), pp. 444–457.

Jin, L. and Huang, Y. (2014) 'When giving money does not work: the differential effects of monetary versus in-kind rewards in referral reward programs'. *International Journal of Research in Marketing*, 31(1), pp. 107–116.

Kang, J., Brashear-Alejandro, T. and Groza, M. D. (2015) 'Customer–company identification and the effectiveness of loyalty programs'. *Journal of Business Research*, 68(2), pp. 464–471.

Keh, H. T. and Lee, Y. H. (2006) 'Do reward programs build loyalty for services? The moderating effect of satisfaction on type and timing of rewards'. *Journal of Retailing*, 82(2), pp. 127–136.

Kopalle, P. K. and Neslin, S. A. (2003) 'The economic viability of frequency reward programs in a strategic competitive environment'. *Review of Marketing Science*, 1(1), pp. 1–39.

Kopalle, P., Neslin, S. and Sun, B. (2009) 'A dynamic structural model of the impact of loyalty programs on customer behavior'. In Samu, S., Vaidyanathan, R. and Chakravarti, D. (eds), *AP – Asia-Pacific Advances in Consumer Research*, Vol. 8, Duluth, MN: Association for Consumer Research, pp. 265–266.

Kopalle, P. K., Sun, Y., Neslin, S. A., Sun, B. and Swaminathan, V. (2012) 'The joint sales impact of frequency reward and customer tier components of loyalty programs'. *Marketing Science*, 31(2), pp. 216–235.

Ku, H. H., Yang, P. H. and Chang, C. L. (2018) 'Reminding customers to be loyal: does message framing matter?' *European Journal of Marketing*, 52(3/4), pp. 783–810.

Kumar, V. and Reinartz, W. (2018) 'Loyalty programs: design and effectiveness'. In Kumar, V. and Reinartz, W. (eds), *Customer Relationship Management*, Heidelberg: Springer, pp. 179–205.

Lal, R. and Bell, D. E. (2003) 'The impact of frequent shopper programs in grocery retailing'. *Quantitative Marketing and Economics*, 1(2), pp. 179–202.

Leenheer, J., Van Heerde, H. J., Bijmolt, T. H. and Smidts, A. (2007) 'Do loyalty programs really enhance behavioral loyalty? An empirical analysis accounting for self-selecting members'. *International Journal of Research in Marketing*, 24(1), pp. 31–47.

Liu, Y. (2007) 'The long-term impact of loyalty programs on consumer purchase behavior and loyalty'. *Journal of Marketing*, 71(4), 19–35.

Liu, Y. and Yang, R. (2009) 'Competing loyalty programs: impact of market saturation, market share, and category expandability'. *Journal of Marketing*, 73(1), pp. 93–108.

Ma, B., Li, X. and Zhang, L. (2018) 'The effects of loyalty programs in services: a double-edged sword?' *Journal of Services Marketing*, 32(3), pp. 300–310.

Melnyk, V. and Bijmolt, T. (2015) 'The effects of introducing and terminating loyalty programs'. *European Journal of Marketing*, 49(3/4), pp. 398–419.

Meyer-Waarden, L. (2008) 'The influence of loyalty programme membership on customer purchase behaviour'. *European Journal of Marketing*, 42(1/2), pp. 87–114.

Meyer-Waarden, L. (2015) 'Effects of loyalty program rewards on store loyalty'. *Journal of Retailing and Consumer Services*, 24, pp. 22–32.

Meyer-Waarden, L. and Benavent, C. (2006) 'The impact of loyalty programmes on repeat purchase behaviour'. *Journal of Marketing Management*, 22(1–2), pp. 61–88.

Minnema, A., Bijmolt, T. H. and Non, M. C. (2017) 'The impact of instant reward programs and bonus premiums on consumer purchase behavior'. *International Journal of Research in Marketing*, 34(1), pp. 194–211.

Mohd-Ramly, S. and Omar, N. A. (2017) 'Exploring the influence of store attributes on customer experience and customer engagement'. *International Journal of Retail & Distribution Management*, 45(11), pp. 1138–1158.

Moore, G. and Sekhon, H. (2005) 'Multi-brand loyalty cards: a good idea'. *Journal of Marketing Management*, 21(5–6), pp. 625–640.

Nath, S. (2005) 'Choosing the right loyalty programme'. *European Retail Digest*, 48(3), pp. 53–56.

Orsingher, C. and Wirtz, J. (2018) 'Psychological drivers of referral reward program effectiveness'. *Journal of Services Marketing*, 32(3), pp. 256–268.

Peacock, L. (2018) '10 examples of innovative retail loyalty programs'. *Shopify blog*, 4 September. Available at: https://www.shopify.com/blog/loyalty-program (Accessed: 26 February 2019).

Pick, D. and Eisend, M. (2014) 'Buyers' perceived switching costs and switching: a meta-analytic assessment of their antecedents'. *Journal of the Academy of Marketing Science*, 42(2), pp. 186–204.

Raggio, R. D., Walz, A. M., Godbole, M. B. and Folse, J. A. G. (2013) 'Gratitude in relationship marketing: theoretical development and directions for future research'. *European Journal of Marketing*, 48(1/2), pp. 2–24.

Ramaseshan, B. and Ouschan, R. (2017) 'Investigating status demotion in hierarchical loyalty programs'. *Journal of Services Marketing*, 31(6), pp. 650–661.

Rehnen, L. M., Bartsch, S., Kull, M. and Meyer, A. (2017). 'Exploring the impact of rewarded social media engagement in loyalty programs'. *Journal of Service Management*, 28 (2), pp. 305–328.

Roehm, M. L. and Roehm, H. A. (2011) 'The influence of redemption time frame on responses to incentives'. *Journal of the Academy of Marketing Science*, 39(3), pp. 363–375.

Romaniuk, J., Beal, V. and Uncles, M. (2013) 'Achieving reach in a multi-media environment: how a marketer's first step provides the direction for the second'. *Journal of Advertising Research*, 53(2), pp. 221–230.

Schumann, J. H., Wünderlich, N. V. and Evanschitzky, H. (2014) 'Spillover effects of service failures in coalition loyalty programs: the buffering effect of special treatment benefits'. *Journal of Retailing*, 90(1), pp. 111–118.

Stathopoulou, A. and Balabanis, G. (2016) 'The effects of loyalty programs on customer satisfaction, trust, and loyalty toward high-and low-end fashion retailers'. *Journal of Business Research*, 69(12), pp. 5801–5808.

Steinhoff, L. and Palmatier, R. W. (2016) 'Understanding loyalty program effectiveness: managing target and bystander effects'. *Journal of the Academy of Marketing Science*, 44(1), pp. 88–107.

Taylor, G. A. and Neslin, S. A. (2005) 'The current and future sales impact of a retail frequency reward program'. *Journal of Retailing*, 81(4), pp. 293–305.

Taylor, M., Buvat, J., Nambiar, R., Singh, R. R. and Radhakrishnan, A. (2015) *Fixing the Cracks: Reinventing Loyalty Programs for the Digital Age*. Capgemini, 26 March. Available at: https://www.capgemini.com/resources/fixing-the-cracks-reinventing-loyalty-programs-for-the-digital-age/ (Accessed: 26 February 2019).

Van Berlo, G., Bloemer, J. and Blazevic, V. (2014) 'Customer demotion in hierarchical loyalty programmes'. *The Service Industries Journal*, 34(11), pp. 922–937.

Verhoef, P. C. (2003) 'Understanding the effect of customer relationship management efforts on customer retention and customer share development'. *Journal of Marketing*, 67(4), pp. 30–45.

Verhoef, P. C., Lemon, K. N., Parasuraman, A., Roggeveen, A., Tsiros, M. and Schlesinger, L. A. (2009) 'Customer experience creation: determinants, dynamics and management strategies'. *Journal of Retailing*, 85(1), pp. 31–41.

Vesel, P. and Zabkar, V. (2009) 'Managing customer loyalty through the mediating role of satisfaction in the DIY retail loyalty program'. *Journal of Retailing and Consumer Services*, 16(5), pp. 396–406.

Vilches-Montero, S., Pandit, A., Bravo-Olavarria, R. and Chao, C. W. F. (2018) 'What loyal women (and men) want: the role of gender and loyalty program characteristics in driving store loyalty'. *Journal of Retailing and Consumer Services*, 44, pp. 64–70.

Wind, Y. J. and Hays, C. F. (2016). 'Research implications of the "beyond advertising" paradigm: a model and roadmap for creating value through all media and non-media touchpoints'. *Journal of Advertising Research*, 56(2), pp. 142–158.

Ziliani, C. and Ieva, M. (2018). 'The role of touchpoints in driving loyalty: implications for omnichannel retailing'. *Micro & Macro Marketing*, 27(3), pp. 375–396.

6

MANAGING CUSTOMER EXPERIENCE TO FOSTER CUSTOMER LOYALTY

Marco Ieva

Customer experience as a multidimensional concept

In one of the most important and seminal articles on customer experience, Pine and Gilmore (1998) pointed out that consumers were seeking not just products and services but also experiences. To understand to what extent an experience differs from a service, it is worth recalling the brilliant example provided by these two authors in their article. They referred to an American TV series: *Taxi*. In this sitcom, Iggy, a cab driver, aims to be the best taxi driver in the world. As part of this goal, he transforms the standard taxi ride into a true experience by serving sandwiches and drinks, conducting tours of the city, and singing Frank Sinatra songs. Iggy wants to engage his customers and create a memorable experience that is distinct from the service itself. The taxi service is just the setting for the whole experience. Pine and Gilmore's article on the 'experience economy' was to kickstart a proliferation of studies focusing on customer experience. An emerging concept in the late 1990s, customer experience now plays a key role for practitioners and academics. The proliferation of channels has dramatically increased the number of opportunities for interactions between consumers and companies within the customer journey (Hall and Towers, 2017). This is putting increasing pressure on companies to design and manage the customer experience in a seamless way across multiple channels.

Before we talk about customer experience in a book about loyalty management, it is important to clarify what we mean by it. We deem it necessary to focus on the definition and explanation of this concept by highlighting the different stages of its theoretical development.

Attempts to define it were made by Holbrook and Hirschman (1982), Pine and Gilmore (1998) and Schmitt (1999). These authors focused on the role of emotions and feelings that consumers experience in the whole shopping process and thus adopted an experiential view of consumer behaviour. They pointed out that companies are called to sell personal and memorable experiences rather than simply products and services. Developing entertaining experiences, then, is now seen as a task not confined to the entertainment industry but one to be embraced by companies in different industries. In the contributions to this area that followed (e.g. Addis and Holbrook, 2001; LaSalle and Britton, 2003), the whole consumption process starts to be considered as an experience: the involvement in the experience is recognized to occur at different levels (emotional, cognitive, etc.) and takes place at every interaction between the company and the consumer. Just selling memorable experiences then is not enough. Companies are called to take a further step. They should design and manage the customer experience at every interaction between the company and the customers to match their expectations.

Lipkin (2016) offers a comprehensive classification of the literature in this area by identifying two streams of studies: one regards the customer experience as a subjective experience, the other stresses the contextual and event-specific element of it. In the first stream, customer experience is seen as a subjective experience that occurs due to external stimuli that are capable of influencing how customers perceive a given experience. In this respect, these studies do not see the customer as a passive receiver of external stimuli but take into account the two-way interactions that occur between customers and companies. Within the contextual approach, customer experience is seen as created and co-created through multiple touchpoints. Along this line, Carù and Cova (2015) argue that customers live a continuum of consumption experiences. These experiences can be constructed by the consumer themselves, developed by the company, or co-created by the company and the consumer.

In more recent years, academics have increased their efforts to define customer experience by issuing several definitions that could help to clarify the concept. The most important and widely accepted definitions of customer experience available both in business and academia are:

- 'Customer experience is the internal and subjective response customers have to any direct or indirect contact with a company' (Meyer and Schwager, 2007, p. 2).
- 'Customer experience is comprised of the cognitive, emotional, physical, sensorial, spiritual, and social elements that mark the customer's direct or indirect interaction with (an)other market actor(s)' (De Keyser et al., 2015, p. 23).
- 'Overall, we thus conclude that customer experience is a multidimensional construct focusing on a customer's cognitive, emotional, behavioral, sensorial, and social responses to a firm's offerings during the customer's entire purchase journey' (Lemon and Verhoef, 2016, p. 71).
- 'Customer experience is the evolvement of a person's sensorial, affective, cognitive, relational, and behavioural responses to a firm or brand by living through a journey of touchpoints along pre-purchase, purchase, and post-purchase situations' (Homburg, Jozić, and Kuehnl, 2017, p. 8).

These definitions highlight several key characteristics of the customer experience:

- It is a complex and multidimensional construct that involves multiple components that are cognitive, emotional, behavioural, sensorial and social.
- It is strictly personal in that it might engage each customer differently as far as each level is concerned (e.g. rational, emotional, sensorial, physical).
- Even though it has a strong personal nature, it occurs in social environments; customer experience is therefore shared within institutional and social structures that make its nature as interpersonal.
- It has a temporal dimension based on contact with a whole set of touchpoints that allow customers to encounter a given company; for this reason, it should be seen as a continuum in time, given that relationships with customers are increasingly based on multiple interactions (Klaus et al., 2013).
- It is a dynamic process that cannot be restricted to just the purchase or the service delivery stage; on the contrary, it encompasses the whole customer journey across all the different situations before, during and after the purchase.

The multidimensionality of the customer experience is a key conclusion coming from all the presented definitions (Bonfanti, 2018). Customer experience has indeed a multidimensional structure composed of elementary components (Gentile, Spiller and Noci, 2007). Moreover, the customer experience can be intended as a general and broad concept. However, it could also specifically refer to particular aspects of a company offering, such as a brand (e.g. Brakus, Schmitt and Zarantonello, 2009) or the store (Verhoef et al., 2009; Bustamante and Rubio, 2017) or website or the service offer.

Constructs of customer experience

Within the area of customer experience, academic studies have focused on four key constructs: brand experience, retail (or in-store) customer experience, online customer experience and service experience.

Brand experience

The definition of brand experience starts from the consideration that consumers encounter various specific brand-related stimuli, namely brand-identifying colours, brand shapes, slogans, mascots and brand characters. These elements are strongly related the brand identity (e.g. logo), its packaging, and marketing communications (e.g. advertisements, websites) and can be associated with all the environments and situations where the brand is marketed or sold (e.g. stores, events). Thus, Brakus, Schmitt and Zarantonello (2009, p. 53) conceptualize brand experience as: 'subjective, internal consumer responses (sensations, feelings, and cognitions) and behavioural responses evoked by brand-related stimuli that are part of a brand's design and identity, packaging, communications, and environments'. They posit that brand experience consists of four separate, though related, dimensions: sensory, affective, intellectual and behavioural. Brand experiences are thought to vary in intensity, in valence and in time: they can be strong or weak, positive or negative, long or very short.

Retail customer experience

In the retailing context, customer experiences specifically stem from the interaction with the different elements of the retail mix (i.e. price experience, promotion experience). This in-store experience arises from both elements that are under (e.g. merchandising) and outside (e.g. influence from peers) the control of the retailer. The in-store/retail customer experience specifically takes into account the cognitive, emotional, social and physical responses to a service that results from the customer shopping visit to the physical retail store (Bustamante and Rubio, 2017).

Online customer experience

The third key area that has been studied with reference to the customer experience is the online context. This distinction stems from the consideration that online shoppers are not just shoppers but visitors and actual users of a technological system (Cho and Park, 2001). For this reason, academics have specifically studied the experience in the online environment and developed a specific construct, namely the online customer experience or online shopping experience. Klaus et al. (2013, p. 445) define the online customer experience as the customers' 'mental perception of interactions with a company's value proposition online. These mental perceptions in turn drive a set of outcomes, namely benefits, emotions, judgments (including perceived value) and intentions'. Rose et al. (2012) specifically develop a concept of online customer experience as a psychological state – in the form of a subjective response to the digital assets of the retailer. Specifically, the customer undertakes a cognitive and affective processing of information stemming from the website. Trevinal and Stenger (2014, p. 324) define the online shopping experience as 'a holistic and subjective process resulting from interactions between consumers, shopping practices (including tools and routines) and the online environment (e.g. shopping websites, online consumer reviews, and social media)'. They highlight the complexity of this type of customer experience, given that online shoppers interact in both online and offline contexts (in a specific place, time, with or without a companion's presence …).

Service experience

In the service domain, service experience is a key construct in understanding value creation and has to do with the consumption of experiences rather than goods (Jain, Aagja and Bagdare, 2017). According to Jaakkola, Helkkula and Aarikka-Stenroos

(2015), service experience involves dynamic, experiential and relational activities and interactions. It is important to distinguish between customer experience and service experience, since they are often used to refer to the same concept. As highlighted by Bustamante and Rubio (2017), customer experience and service experience should not be used interchangeably; while service experience is limited to the subject who is actually experiencing the service, customer experience includes all the direct and indirect interactions occurring between the customer and the entity that is providing the experience.

Brand experience, retail (in-store) customer experience, online customer experience and service experience reveal the need for both practitioners and academics to take into account the contextual factors that help to define and shape the customer experience.

Dimensions of customer experience

In the studies on the different types of customer experience, there are similarities and differences in how they identify its dimensions. Presented below is a summary of the six dimensions of customer experience that have been identified by the main studies on the topic: cognitive, emotional, social, sensorial, physical and lifestyle. These dimensions are also referred to as strategic experiential modules (Schmitt, 1999). Customer experience is conceptualized as the 'sum' of cognitions, feelings, sensations, and social and physical responses triggered by an experience provider.

Cognitive dimension

The cognitive dimension of the customer experience (some authors refer to this dimension as intellectual) has to do with all the cognitive efforts occurring during the experience. For instance, while a customer is in the store, he or she might be involved in thinking about the displayed assortment or about how a given product could be used to achieve a given outcome. Cognition is defined as the ability to process information acquired from what individuals perceive and learn and from their subjective characteristics (Bustamante and Rubio, 2017). Scholars claim that cognition is the first state of the customer experience occurring before the affective response, because cognition primarily processes acquired knowledge (Da Silva and Syed Alwi, 2006). The cognitive dimension of the customer experience has to do with all the mental responses to the brand or store stimuli that involve customers (Schmitt, 1999). To clarify, mental responses are basically thoughts, ideas, or memories, among others (Bustamante and Rubio, 2017). The creativity or the problem-solving skills of the customer could be stimulated by the offering of a given brand and retailer, leading to an increase in their attention to, for example, the product quality and the displayed information. Positive thoughts and memories could be elicited when in contact with a given product, brand or store. In turn, these cognitive responses are supposed to lead to strong, enduring attitudes towards the object if the stimulus has sufficiently persuasive content (Wright, 1973).

Emotional dimension

The affective or emotional component relates to the generation of emotions and moods within the affective system. The affective system can be defined as a 'valenced feeling state', that includes emotions and moods as key elements (Richins, 1997). There is a difference between emotions and moods: the former is related to stimuli that elicit them and are usually stronger, while moods tend not to be linked with a specific stimulus and are lower in intensity (Erevelles, 1998). With reference to the customer experience, the affective dimension largely involves emotions rather than moods given that the experience is created by responses to stimuli, specifically touchpoints (Bustamante and Rubio, 2017). Emotions are mental states arising as a consequence of cognitive evaluations of events or thoughts and are usually associated with physical reactions, such as facial expressions or body movements (Cacioppo and Gardner, 1999). We can refer to emotions such as interest, joy, surprise, sadness, anger and disgust. Emotions are very powerful drivers of behaviour and they have the potential to influence how individuals process information.

Why are they so important to the customer experience? Marketing stimuli have the potential to drive consumers to feel emotions that shape affective experiences (Bustamante and Rubio, 2017). Positive affective experiences can then have a positive impact on multiple customer behaviours that are key for companies, such as positive word of mouth, intention to re-patronize a store and willingness to pay more. Emotions can also be negative and can negatively influence the development of positive experiences and the related customer behaviours. This is why when considering the affective dimension of customer experience both positive and negative emotions should be taken into account (Fornerino, Helme-Guizon and Gotteland, 2006).

Social dimension

The social (or relational) dimension of the customer experience is gaining increasing relevance due to the growth of social media and the proliferation of touchpoints that allow consumers to interact not only with the company but also with each other. The social component has to do with the extent of human interaction that takes place in online and offline environments and to the social identity of an individual and his or her linkage to a specific group of people (Brun et al., 2017; Bustamante and Rubio, 2017). In this respect, it is believed that the social context – which involves the whole set of interactions and relationships among people – of the experience is relevant to influence how consumers live this experience. Two key elements shape the social dimension of the customer experience: consumers-to-consumers and employees-to-consumers interactions. Companies are willing to leverage the social aspects of the experience by encouraging consumers to consume products together, to feel a part of a community that shares not only the products but the values and ideals that are related to those products. Moreover, previous research has shown that peer observation is a very influential touchpoint in retailing (Baxendale, Macdonald and Wilson, 2015). Hence, the social context is not only capable of providing an 'augmented' experience but also of directly influencing how the experience takes place. In the offline environment, the retail store is a natural drive of human interactions: shoppers meet sales assistants and other shoppers and social relationships are built (Hu and Jasper, 2006). As far as the online environment is concerned, social media, messenger applications such as WhatsApp and Telegram and online customer support such as live chats are key drivers of online human interactions.

Sensorial dimension

The sensorial component of the customer experience is related to how external stimuli affect the senses of consumers (Gentile, Spiller and Noci, 2007). Hence, it has to do with the perception of experience through the senses: sight, hearing, touch, taste and smell (Brun et al., 2017). Different means could be employed to enhance the sensorial dimension of the customer experience. The usage of a particular smell, the control of light and music in the store, the design and the images employed in the development of a website could all elicit a sensory response in consumers. This could have an impact on how consumers perceive their experience with the brand or in the store.

Physical dimension

The physical (or pragmatic/behavioural) component was identified by Bustamante and Rubio (2017) when studying the in-store customer experience as a physiological response to environmental stimuli in the store. This response is intended as a state of comfort or lack of comfort that is elicited by the environment. This is a dimension that is specific to the in-store customer experience and that could be assimilated, to a certain extent, to the pragmatic/behavioural dimension that has been identified when conceptualizing customer experience in general terms (Bustamante and Rubio, 2017). As a matter of fact, the pragmatic/behavioural component has to do with all the physical acts that characterize a given experience. Gentile, Spiller and Noci (2007) highlight that this specific dimension should not be considered as usability, because it does not simply refer to the usage of a product after the purchase. This component embraces all the actions undertaken at the different stages of the customer journey. As Brun et al. (2017) point out, there is no consensus among scholars on the measurement of this dimension. According to Brun et al. there are two main issues that hamper it. First, this dimension is very hard to capture in some industries such as banking where customers do not engage in particular behaviours. Second, the measures employed to identify the behavioural dimension might not only be related to the experience itself. For instance, reviewing many times the bank account has been employed as one indicator to measure the behavioural dimension of the customer experience in banking. However, this type of behaviour is also strongly correlated with consumer perceived risk.

Lifestyle dimension

The lifestyle dimension has been identified by Gentile, Spiller and Noci (2007) and further developed by Trevinal and Stenger (2014). These authors conceptualize it as the summary of values and beliefs that become manifest by behaving in a certain consistent manner, hence by consistently adopting a lifestyle. Trevinal and Stenger (2014) found in their qualitative study that this component is largely evident across three key elements: shopping orientation (that could be hedonistic/utilitarian), the daily routines that are associated with online shopping, and individual values, such as privacy concerns and political issues, that are related to shopping choices. This component has not been studied and quantitatively measured in further studies. We could argue that scholars might find it challenging to capture the specific characteristics of this dimension, given that expressing a lifestyle is something that might include, for instance, sensorial, physical and cognitive aspects of the customer experience.

Understanding these dimensions and how they differ offers the possibility of measuring the customer experience and making it actionable for marketers. The development of a proper measure of customer experience is the concern of the next section.

Measuring customer experience

Measuring customer experience has been regarded both as a pressing marketing issue (Verhoef et al., 2009) and a very challenging task in marketing research for academics and practitioners (Lemon and Verhoef, 2016; Flacandji and Krey, in press). Despite the challenge, measuring something is the first step towards managing it. Companies that are able to measure and identify strengths and weaknesses of the customer experience that they deliver can change how they design and implement it. Palmer (2010) already predicted that measuring customer experience would be a key but complex issue for academics.

Lemon and Verhoef (2016) provide a rich description of the key challenges and metrics that have been adopted in marketing in the last 20 years by researchers and managers to try to tackle this challenge. By updating their valuable work with the most recent developments in customer experience measurement, we could summarize the different available measures of customer experience in four segments:

- customer feedback metrics
- service experience quality
- measures based on strategic experiential modules
- shopping experience memory scale.

By employing these metrics, managers can measure customer experience at different levels. First, customer experience could be measured with reference to the most recent experience of the customer or as a summary of multiple experiences that occur in a given period of time. Second, customer experience could be measured with reference to a specific touchpoint (e.g. the experience with the customer service), with an environment (e.g. the in-store customer experience) or with the set of touchpoints encountered in different environments. Depending on the needs of the company, measures can be customized and results interpreted accordingly.

All four groups of metrics have something in common: they are based on surveys of customers and not on behavioural data or other sources. This, of course, carries both advantages and limitations. The survey allows companies to extract more detailed information on the customer experience and to discover the drivers of a given behaviour. However, running a survey involves taking many decisions that can significantly influence the final results: the sampling, the wording of questions, the channel employed to administer the survey, the means undertaken to address the non-response and response biases – not to even mention the risk that the engaged respondents fill in the survey without paying attention to the questions just to achieve the reward related to survey completion. And this is in line with recent criticism that has arisen around the usage of panels of respondents such as Amazon MTurk (Ford, 2017). Hence, despite the following discussion on which metric is more appropriate to represent and summarize the customer experience, the methodological rigour adopted to administer any survey is critical to a successful measurement. A good expression summarizing this point is a wisdom known among many researchers: doing research is more a matter of bias management. Thus paying attention to reducing biases in research should be the first concern when running a survey. Now that the reader is sufficiently worried about the potential influence of researchers on results, let us review in detail the different categories of metrics!

Customer feedback metrics

Customer feedback metrics are measures that aim to capture how customers perceive a part of the whole experience with the company or a brief summary of the whole experience (Lemon and Verhoef, 2016). Just to make it clear, the two most popular metrics in this category are customer satisfaction and net promoter score, which we discussed in Chapter 1. One relevant difference between them is that, according to Zeithaml et al. (2006), net promoter score is more suitable to measuring future behaviour, whereas satisfaction is oriented towards measuring past behaviour as far as the relationship with the company is concerned. We could, rather, see these metrics as a proxy for customer experience measures rather than true ones.

The reader might justifiably ask, then, why customer satisfaction and net promoter scores are employed at all. The answer lies in the fact that these two metrics are quite simple; both are generated from answers given by respondents and analysed by companies. Moreover, even if we are to consider them proxies for true measurement, there is evidence of a significant, if small (according to some reported cases), correlation between these two metrics and firm revenue growth and other financial metrics (see, e.g., Reichheld, 2003; Keiningham et al., 2007; Van Doorn, Leeflang and Tijs, 2013). Hence, we could assume that an increase in customer satisfaction or in the net promoter score might be somehow related to an increase, for instance, in revenues. Intuitively, this has a certain appeal to marketers who are maybe obliged to rely on such simple metrics rather than look for more complex and insightful alternatives.

Service experience quality

The second group of metrics refers to the service experience quality metrics that have been developed in recent years, starting with the work of Parasuraman, Zeithaml and Berry (1988) and Zeithaml, Berry and Parasuraman (1996) and progressing to the measures developed by Klaus and Maklan (2012) and Klaus et al. (2013). In this respect, it is important to stress, as highlighted by Bustamante and Rubio (2017), that this group of measures has been developed by researchers in the domain of services marketing who tend to consider customer experience and service experience as interchangeable concepts. Moreover, all these measures are multi-item scales.

The service quality measure (SERVQUAL), developed by Parasuraman and his colleagues, is a reliable and multidimensional measure that has been employed as a proxy for customer experience. Its importance and relevance can be understood just by looking at the citation metrics of the article that launched this measure in 1988. According to Google Scholar, more than 30,000 academic and non-academic works have cited it in 30 years. The SERVQUAL was developed to measure perceived quality, which is the overall consumer evaluation of an entity in terms of excellence or superiority (Parasuraman, Zeithaml and Berry, 1988).

It is a multidimensional scale, given that it measures perceived quality across five different dimensions: reliability, assurance, tangibles, empathy and responsiveness. SERVQUAL is employed to provide an evaluation of the perceived quality of a service both at the level of each of these five service dimensions and at the overall level, across them all. The five dimensions can be explained as follows:

- tangibles: the perceived quality of physical facilities, equipment and appearance of personnel
- reliability: the extent to which the company is capable of performing the service in a precise and reliable manner
- responsiveness: the extent to which the company is available and willing to support customers and provide help promptly
- assurance: the ability of the company, through their staff, to show knowledge and friendliness and to develop trust in its customers
- empathy: the extent to which the company is able to devote personal and careful attention to each customer to express caring with respect to his or her needs.

It is evident that this measure is not capable of capturing the full meaning of the customer experience nor measuring each of the customer experience dimensions. However, this is indeed a good starting point towards the assessment of the quality of the service experienced by customers.

As a matter of fact, starting from the concept of service quality, Klaus and Maklan (2012) have adopted a measurement of customer experience that is based on how customers perceive or subjectively judge the components of the service experience, namely service experience quality. In this respect, service experience quality is considered as an updated formulation of the traditional service quality concept. In their conceptualization, Klaus and Maklan (2012) argue that specific and concrete service attributes are the drivers of perceptual attributes. These perceptual attributes, which are consumer evaluations of the service, are the elements that define the four customer experience quality dimensions: product experience, outcome focus, moments of truth and peace of mind. The dimensions can be described as follows:

- Product experience could be considered the extent to which the customer perceives that they have multiple options to choose from and that they can compare offers. In this respect, the authors are referring to the customer's feeling of choosing what they prefer at any stage of the shopping process. Moreover, this dimension also involves the feeling of being under the ongoing care of the company that makes the whole shopping experience very easy and smooth.
- Outcome focus has to do with the orientation that customers have to stick with the same company in order to get the desired results rather than look for offerings from competitors or question the quality of the offering of the current provider.
- Moments of truth refer to the extent to which the customer perceives that the company was flexible and caring enough to meet their needs and to manage service failures or critical requests in the proper manner. This dimension also includes the perceived risk felt by customers during these interactions, namely the perceived risk that is related to a service failure or to a pain point.
- Finally, peace of mind involves the evaluation of all the interactions between the customer and the service provider, taking into consideration all the stages of the customer journey. This dimension is more related to the emotional aspects of the experience with the service provider and the creation of a relational bond between customer and company.

Klaus and Maklan incorporate these four dimensions in the final scale, which they call the customer experience quality (EXQ) scale and which they adopt as a general measure of customer experience in further works (e.g. Klaus and Maklan, 2013). The EXQ scale is based on the customer point of view, captures the value of a company offer when it is experienced by the customer, encompasses the stages before and after the service delivery and considers behavioural and intentional measures (Klaus et al, 2013). Despite these strengths, Klaus et al. do point to the limitation of EXQ, which is its limited empirical validation, and develop the scale further in the banking context. This last work results in quite a change to the EXQ scale. Four dimensions become three: brand experience (not to be confused with that developed by Brakus et al.), service (provider) experience and post-purchase experience. These three new dimensions can be described thus:

- Brand experience involves how the customer perceives the brand and all the elements that are employed to take a decision in the pre-purchase stage of the customer journey.
- Service (provider) experience is associated with the customer–company interaction; specifically, in the case of the banking industry, it has to do with the bank branch, the staff and the specifics of the banking service that is provided. This dimension is related to accessibility, how the service delivery works, evaluation of the personal interactions undertaken and the setting of service delivery.
- Post-purchase/consumption experience is related to the part of the experience that follows service delivery, such as the development of the relationship with the company, the attachment to the company and service recovery situations.

This review of the development and further validation of the EXQ scale in its different versions leads us to formulate several considerations:

- In terms of actionability, the EXQ could indeed be appealing to practitioners and even easy to interpret for customers, given that each dimension is related to concrete situations in the experience with the service provider.
- The EXQ might have some issues in terms of generalizability, given that it seems more appropriate to measure the experience in services rather than the customer experience in other contexts.
- The four dimensions identified by the scale seem not to be in line with the generally employed conceptualization of the customer experience as a multi-dimensional construct that involves cognitive, affective, sensorial, social and behavioural dimensions; this is, of course, due to the different theoretical background on which the scale relies.

Despite its limitations (outlined too by Lemon and Verhoef, 2016), the EXQ has been recently employed as a measure of the customer experience, namely by Roy (2018), thus proving to still be an actionable option for both scholars and practitioners. In the final section, 'Customer experience and customer loyalty', we will describe in detail the implications of the results from Roy's study.

Measures based on strategic experiential modules

The third group of customer experience metrics has been developed in alignment with the conceptual framework of Schmitt (1999) that identifies strategic experiential modules. In this respect, customer experience is seen as the mixture of cognitions, feelings, and sensorial, social and physical responses driven by the provider of the experience (Bustamante and Rubio, 2017). Therefore, these measures seem more in line with the conceptual framework of customer experience that has attracted the most attention and support among scholars. This typology of scales seeks to capture the result of a continuum of multiple experiences that occur throughout a series of interactions between the consumer and the stimuli that are somewhat related to the company. Hence, the respondent is supposed to recall what he or she has stored in their long-term memory.

In this area, we can find different types of measures of customer experience that are related to the setting where the experience takes place or that attempt to measure the experience with a specific entity, for instance a brand or store. In this respect, we can identify several strategic experiential modules scales:

- brand experience scale, as developed by Brakus, Schmitt and Zarantonello (2009)
- in-store/retail customer experience scale, as developed by Bustamante and Rubio (2017) (while some previous scales exist, they could be considered the first to attempt it in this domain)
- general customer experience scales applied to specific contexts such as retailing, retail banking or travelling; Brun et al. (2017) and Srivastava and Kaul (2016) provide some examples of scales developed from the work of Schmitt (1999), Gentile, Spiller and Noci (2007) and Brakus, Schmitt and Zarantonello (2009).

According to Brakus, Schmitt and Zarantonello (2009), the brand experience scale aims to measure four experience dimensions – sense, feel, think and act. In their conceptualization, brand-related stimuli such as colour, shape, design, slogans and brand characters have the potential to impact one or multiple experience dimensions at the same time. The 12 items of the scale, in the view of the authors, measure the extent, namely the intensity, to which the respondent has lived an experience with a brand along the sensory, affective, intellectual or behavioural dimensions. Is the experience emotionally intense? Does it trigger the customer to think? Does it drive their senses? How far does the experience with the brand invite the customer to act or to complete certain actions due to brand-related stimuli? Moreover, it is worth highlighting that this scale is not aimed at capturing the outcomes of just one cross-sectional incident with the brand but measures the experience stemming from a series of multiple interactions between the customer and all the different brand-related stimuli.

This scale, then, could be useful to managers and practitioners willing to assess the extent a brand is able to involve its customers and to understand the impact that the experience with a given brand might have on other consumer attitudes, such as brand personality, satisfaction and loyalty.

The in-store/retail customer experience scale developed by Bustamante and Rubio (2017) aims to capture the specific experience lived by the customer in the physical store. The authors of the scale conceptualize the in-store customer experience as a subjective internal response to all the elements that are part of the physical environment of the store. Among these responses, interaction with other customers or with store associates is also included as an important part of the experience. One key characteristic of this scale is that it considers all the physical and sensorial responses to the store stimuli as part of one unique dimension. Hence, the physical dimension of the experience is not disentangled from the sensorial one. While previous scales in this area (e.g. Bagdare and Jain, 2013) take into account only the affective dimensions of the retail experience or adapt the brand experience scale to the store environment (e.g. Srivastava and Kaul, 2016), this measure is based on a full theoretical development of the in-store customer experience that has been empirically tested by the authors. The scale goes beyond the hedonic side of the experience and measures the cognitive, affective, physical and social dimensions. This measure is then different from other scales in this area and aims to capture the mental responses to the in-store stimuli, the emotions aroused by the environment, the extent of social interaction occurring between the customer and store associates or other customers and, finally, the physiological responses to the interaction with different retail stimuli. As a result, the in-store customer experience includes 15 items in total. It represents an important tool for retailers to evaluate how good they are at delivering a successful in-store customer experience and to understand the extent to which a positive experience can be translated into loyalty or purchase behaviour.

The generic customer experience scale of Brun et al. (2017) is designed based on the theoretical works of Schmitt and Gentile et al. and developed based on Brakus's brand experience scale. Specifically, this scale aims to capture the whole experience of a customer with a given company, regardless of the environment or channel where the experience takes place. The scale includes both the positive and negative affective dimensions and distinguishes between the sensorial and the behavioural dimensions. It includes 21 items measuring the cognitive, positive affective, negative affective, sensorial, social and behavioural dimensions. While its general scope might be considered an advantage, a related disadvantage is its low flexibility in measuring customer experiences that occur in specific contexts. For this reason, researchers who aim to measure the experience customers have with a brand or store are advised to employ instead the scales formulated by Brakus, Schmitt and Zarantonello (2009) and Bustamante and Rubio (2017) respectively.

Shopping experience memory scale

Last but not least, academic research has seen the recent development of the shopping experience memory scale, which aims to capture the memory of the shopping experience, specifically the extent to which the customer is able to recall the experience, the extent to which a given experience is memorable. The authors of this scale (Flacandji and Krey, in press) agree with the view of Kahneman (2011) that customers are willing to repeat an experience lived in the past exclusively because of the memory that is associated with that past experience. Flacandji and Krey have developed a scale that is based on theory and empirical evidence to capture customers' memories that are related to the consumption experience. This scale has been specifically developed for the retail context and involves 14 items measuring four different main dimensions: attraction, structure, affect, social.

Attraction captures the capability of the retail environment and the products to attract the customer; hence to what extent the customer perceives the experience as appealing. Structure measures the key elements of the memory of the experience, such as its vividness, accessibility and coherence; it assesses how far the customer is able to recall the details and temporal sequence of the experience. Affect refers to all the emotions felt when recalling the experience; for example, has the experience elicited positive feelings and a general feeling of comfort? The social dimension captures whether the recalled experience has a social meaning; recalling the experience might lead the consumer to perceive himself as an important part of a group or to have something valuable to share with others. Given that this is an emerging scale, it would be interesting to see to what extent this scale can explain customer loyalty or loyalty attitudes in general compared to the strategic experiential modules scales.

To summarize, some further considerations are needed to put all these scales into context. Academics and practitioners are currently working to improve the measurement of customer experience, such a complex construct. We have reviewed different approaches that stem from different theoretical perspectives and goals. While the service experience quality and the strategic experiential modules scales have been increasingly adopted by academics in retailing and consumer services, customer feedback metrics are still widely employed by practitioners in industry. However, given the importance of the concept of 'memorable experiences', the shopping memory scale might be employed in the future to understand if the memory of the experience is actually the key driver to measure. Despite this attention to measuring customer experience, two issues remain unaddressed. How can companies manage the customer experience, and what is its effect on customer attitudes and behaviours? We will tackle these two topics in the following paragraphs.

Customer experience management and touchpoints

To develop and manage the customer experience, practitioners have in recent years started to adopt a new managerial framework that has taken the name of CEM (Homburg, Jozić and Kuehnl, 2017). Since the 2000s, the recognition of customer experience has led to companies seeing its management as an increasingly important activity. Puccinelli et al. (2009) and Grewal, Levy and Kumar (2009) have fostered the relevance for companies to design and manage the customer experience, while Palmer (2010) has argued the need for a concrete meaning of CEM beyond the hype initially associated with the term. A clear and well-defined framework of CEM was, until very recently, still missing. As a matter of fact, while the concept of customer experience was taking a well-defined shape, CEM was still an emerging managerial practice rather than a well-structured strategic approach.

Homburg, Jozić and Kuehnl (2017) have addressed this gap. Their influential work has helped define the key characteristics of CEM. The CEM framework is a firm-wide management approach to designing customer experience. The final goal of CEM is achieving long-term customer loyalty by designing and continually renewing touchpoint journeys (Homburg, Jozić and Kuehnl, 2017). Organizations that are able to properly manage the customer experience are more likely to obtain gains such as higher employee satisfaction, customer satisfaction and, more importantly, higher revenues (Rawson, Duncan and Jones, 2013; McColl-Kennedy et al., in press).

At this point the reader might ask what the difference is between CRM and CEM, given that both approaches share the final goal of achieving long-term customer loyalty. It's a valid question. CRM is regarded as a data-driven process that implies planning, implementing and monitoring the set of relationships occurring with customers (Payne and Frow, 2005). CRM is involved with collecting data on customers to react to purchasing behaviour patterns with marketing actions. The focus of the second approach, then, is more oriented towards the analysis of the customer to implement specific actions that are aimed at specific goals.

Dimensions of customer experience management

CEM is conceptualized by Homburg, Jozić and Kuehnl (2017) as a managerial framework that is oriented towards managing the customer experience by adopting an active and not reactive approach. Specifically, CEM involves three main dimensions: cultural mindset, strategic direction and capabilities. All three dimensions refer to the cultural orientation towards customer experience, the strategy to shape it and the firm's capabilities to adapt and renew the designed experiences. Let us, drawing on Homburg et al., clarify each one in turn.

Cultural mindset

Cultural mindset involves three main elements that a company should recognize in its DNA: achieving an ongoing commitment throughout the organization towards the creation of experiences at each touchpoint; understanding that touchpoint journeys across pre-purchase, purchase and post-purchase stages are key factors that should be considered in daily decision-making; cooperating with company partners with a goal to aligning the different touchpoints that the customer encounters in the same shopping situation. In this regard, the company needs to take into account the customer experience and the related touchpoints in every decision that is going to affect the customer. Thus a key element in CEM is the focus on touchpoints. As a matter of fact, strategic direction and firm capabilities are specifically concerned with managing touchpoints.

Strategic direction

Strategic direction refers to all the strategies that aim to maximize the coordination among touchpoints in order to provide a seamless experience that is flexible depending on the situation but that develops throughout all the different touchpoints. To this aim, four elements are key:

- achieving a thematic cohesion of touchpoints in line with the brand image developed by the company and its related elements (thematic cohesion of touchpoints)
- ensuring the consistency of all touchpoints in delivering experiences that are thematically linked to the brand (consistency of touchpoints)
- improving the link between situations where the customer is exposed to certain touchpoints and the features of each touchpoint that is present in that situation (context sensitivity of touchpoints)
- integrating all touchpoints across online and offline channels to deliver an omnichannel customer experience that prevent customers from perceiving barriers and differences across channels (connectivity of touchpoints).

Capabilities

Finally, a firm's capabilities refer to the extent to which it is able to perform a series of ongoing activities to manage touchpoints. Specifically:

- planning customer journeys around its touchpoints and assigning requirements across company functions on how to address the different moments and places of these journeys (touchpoint journey design)
- assigning priorities in terms of monetary, human and time resources to a given set of touchpoints in a flexible manner based on data collected through the different touchpoints (touchpoint prioritization)
- coordinating the set of touchpoints by reflecting on what the touchpoint journey orientation within the company is (touchpoint journey monitoring)
- developing and checking key performance indicators for each touchpoint with the goal of renewing existing touchpoint journeys or developing new ones (touchpoint adaptation).

Establishing the cultural mindset, strategic direction and capabilities towards customer experience enables a company to regard the customer experience as the core concept of the company strategy with the final goal of fostering long-lasting customer loyalty.

Role of touchpoints

In reviewing Homburg et al.'s conceptualization of CEM, we can quickly see that the set of touchpoints available to a company is the very playground in which customer experience is designed. More, we might follow Jain, Aagja and Bagdare (2017) and say that touchpoints are in fact the determinants of the customer experience. It is thus also worth reviewing the main studies that have dealt with the role of touchpoints in delivering a successful customer experience.

Touchpoints can be defined as the verbal and non-verbal incidents that any person perceives and relates to a firm or a brand (Duncan and Moriarty, 2006). Hence, they should be regarded as an episode of direct or indirect encounter with a firm (Lemon and Verhoef, 2016). From this definition we can understand that the concept of touchpoint is much broader than other related concepts that have been employed in the past, such as media or channel. Already we are faced with a definitional challenge: what should be considered a touchpoint and what not? This is one of the most difficult decisions to make when adopting a touchpoint perspective. To find a solution, we should look to the evidence from previous studies in this domain.

Previous studies on the topic, such as Baxendale, Macdonald and Wilson (2015), do not mention specific criteria based on which touchpoints should be selected, aggregated or disentangled. Some studies, to cope with the overwhelming variety of touchpoints, have decided to disregard those that reach only a low number of customers (e.g. Romaniuk, Beal and Uncles, 2013). Others employ specific lists of touchpoints that are worth considering depending on the type of setting or interest (e.g. Zahay et al., 2004; Romaniuk, Beal and Uncles, 2013; Li and Kannan, 2014; Baxendale, Macdonald and Wilson, 2015; Wind and Hays, 2016; Hallikainen, Alamäki and Laukkanen, in press; Ieva and Ziliani, 2018a; Ieva and Ziliani, 2018b; McColl-Kennedy et al., in press; Wagner, Schramm-Klein and Steinmann, in press). For instance, in retail settings the touchpoints that have been identified include traditional media, in-store, telephone, salesforce, catalogues, loyalty programmes, mobile apps, email, word of mouth, and so forth. Therefore, touchpoints are not restricted to a specific domain but can be physical, digital or even personal interactions, such as a friend or a shop assistant who recommends a particular brand (Voorhees et al., 2017).

Classifying touchpoints

To handle the explosion in the last few decades of touchpoints, scholars have attempted to provide classifications to help group them into different categories. For example, Lemon and Verhoef (2016) have classified touchpoints based on who is responsible for managing any given one: brand-owned, partner-owned, customer-owned and social/external. Touchpoints are defined as brand-owned if the company itself is managing them: for example, a loyalty programme or a product. Partner-owned touchpoints are managed by the company and a partner, such as another company (e.g. coalition loyalty programmes) or a service provider (e.g. a digital agency that is in charge of the social media communications of the company). Customer-owned touchpoints are those that cannot be influenced by the company since they are under the full disposal of the customer. Examples include a customer deciding her preferred method of payment among those available or a customer producing user-generated content about a given brand. Finally, the social/external touchpoints are those occurring in social contexts: peer observation, as shown by Baxendale, Macdonald and Wilson (2015), is a very influential touchpoint. A typical situation is when we are seated in a restaurant and we see what the person sat at the next table is eating. Or we spot a nice car while we are driving home from work.

Lemon and Verhoef's classification is indeed very clear and it is important to have an organizing framework to understand and utilize touchpoints. However, as the authors recognize, this classification has to cope with the variety and dynamics of business situations, where the difference between brand-owned touchpoints and partner-owned touchpoints or between customer-owned and social touchpoints might be not so well-defined. In the first case, the best example might be a loyalty programme: every decision on the touchpoint is taken by the company, but the programme might rely on the IT platform of a technology provider (the partner) and a system error might influence the performance of that touchpoint and the related customer experience, and thus harm the company. Hence, in this case, what is conceptually a brand-owned touchpoint could, in fact, be considered partner-owned. In the second case, a review on TripAdvisor by a customer about his positive experience in a hotel is, at first at least, a customer-owned touchpoint – it cannot be influenced by the hotel owner. However, when the review is shared and seen by other customers it becomes a social touchpoint too – it could influence the choice of other customers.

Another classification, proposed by Manser Payne, Peltier and Barger (2017), differentiates between personal versus non-personal touchpoints: to what extent is there a human component in a given interaction with a customer? This classification is worth highlighting because it could be increasingly important in the future given that companies are likely to increase the adoption of digital assistants and chatbots. In this respect, it would be interesting to understand whether personal touchpoints are more or equally effective than non-personal touchpoints. Answering this question will lead to a shift in the investment that companies devote to technology versus human staff. Sometimes, in the same customer journey, a customer will interact first with a chatbot, which then links the customer to a person in charge of customer service who might be better equipped to fix the issue.

Other studies have distinguished between firm-initiated and customer-initiated touchpoints (e.g. Anderl, Burnkrant and Unnava, 2016). Here the point is to distinguish among touchpoints depending on who is starting the interaction: has the company contacted the customer? Or has the customer visited or interacted with the company's webpage, or sent them an email? Classifying touchpoints is indeed a tricky business but it is important for marketers to clarify the key characteristics and categories of the touch-points they manage daily. Moreover, specific classifications and labels have been proposed with reference to digital touchpoints. Straker, Wrigley and Rosemann (2015) have classified digital touchpoints into four different categories: functional touchpoints, social touchpoints, corporate touchpoints and community touchpoints. Email and websites are examples of functional touchpoints and their purpose is to provide diversion, functionality and interaction. Social touchpoints include social media, where the key feature is the extent of interaction that they allow. Corporate touchpoints aim to achieve customer feedback: FAQs, customer feedback forms, and the like. Finally, community touchpoints have in common a strong cohesion among users: blogs are, for instance, included in this category.

Assessing touchpoints

Studies have been undertaken to assess the role of touchpoints, specifically in the business-to-consumer (B2C) setting. The key considered variables in this domain are the reach, frequency and positivity of exposure to touchpoints.

Reach

Reach has to do with the fact that a given customer has been exposed or not exposed to a given touchpoint. Why is achieving reach important? The capability of addressing the right customer segment with the right touchpoint is key for media placement (Romaniuk, Beal and Uncles, 2013). In this regard, studies on touchpoint reach have found that the extent to which brand users versus brand non-users are able to recall touchpoint exposure significantly differs. Specifically:

- Brand users are more likely to recall having been exposed to the advertising of the brand (Vaughan, Beal and Romaniuk, 2016).
- TV advertising, gift packs, in-store displays/promotions and outdoor advertisements reach average brand users (Romaniuk, Beal and Uncles, 2013).
- Social media and word of mouth have been found to reach heavy brand users (Romaniuk, Beal and Uncles, 2013).

Frequency

As far as the frequency of exposure to touchpoints is concerned, studies have focused on its relationship with loyalty intentions and its impact on brand attitudes. Ieva and Ziliani (2018a) have segmented consumers based on frequency of exposure to touchpoints in a retail setting. They found that consumers can be largely segmented based on the intensity of the exposure to all the touchpoints rather than based on the exposure to a given set of specific touchpoints. Moreover, the exposure is significantly and positively related to loyalty intentions: more loyal customers tend to encounter more frequently their main retailer through all the different touchpoints. Ieva and Ziliani (2018b) also studied the relationship between frequency of exposure and loyalty intentions in a mobile services setting. They found that the higher the willingness to recommend the company and to stay as a long-term customer, the higher the likelihood of recalling exposure to certain touchpoints, such as the store, the website, email, mobile app, word of mouth and loyalty programmes.

Frequency of exposure also impacts brand attitudes (Campbell and Keller, 2003) and brand consideration changes (Baxendale, Macdonald and Wilson, 2015). Specifically, Baxendale, Macdonald and Wilson (2015) have conducted a study on brand touchpoints in four consumer categories: electrical goods, technological products, mobile handsets and soft drinks. Their study found that frequency of exposure to brand advertising, peer observation, in-store communications and retailer advertising has a positive effect on brand consideration: higher frequency of touchpoint exposure (expressed by a natural log decay) increases the likelihood that consumers will consider that brand in their consideration set.

Positivity

It should be clarified that positivity is the valence of the affective response to a touchpoint (Baxendale, Macdonald and Wilson, 2015). Previous studies have found that positivity drives spending and repeat purchase intentions (Arnold and Reynolds, 2009) and that it is positively correlated with satisfaction (Westbrook and Oliver, 1991) and commitment (Ahluwalia, Burnkrant and Unnava, 2000). Why is positivity so important? How a customer lives the experience with a given touchpoint in affective terms is actually embodied in how they evaluate that touchpoint and this evaluation is believed to influence brand-related cognitions that will occur in the future (Baumeister et al., 2007). Affective responses have been recently found to impact loyalty intentions (Ou and Verhoef, 2017; Ieva and Ziliani 2018b). Baxendale, Macdonald and Wilson (2015) have also discovered positive effects on brand consideration of all touchpoints they considered (traditional earned, such as editorial and news coverage, brand advertising, word of mouth, peer observation, in-store communications and retailer advertising). Specifically, Ieva and Ziliani (2018b), in the mobile services setting, have found that touchpoint positivity stemming from the interactions with customer service, mobile messaging, provider website, TV and cinema advertising, the physical store, mobile apps, word of mouth and provider store associates is positively related to customer loyalty.

Prioritizing touchpoints

As we can see, the findings on touchpoint reach, frequency and positivity in the B2C setting support the view that touchpoints differ in their relationship with consumer attitudes, such as loyalty intentions. Thus companies should prioritize touchpoints depending on their effects on consumer attitudes. Digital touchpoints and touchpoints in B2B settings have also attracted specific attention. As far as the role of digital touchpoints is concerned, Hallikainen, Alamäki and Laukkanen (in press) have identified a broad range of segments in terms of their preferences for digital touchpoints. For instance, their segmentation has found anti-digital consumers (people who do not like digital touchpoints) but also digital enthusiasts (consumers that are keen on using new touchpoints and channels as soon as they are available to the public). Wagner, Schramm-Klein and Steinmann, (in press) have shed light on the role of touchpoints in the online environment in influencing how channels are evaluated. Specifically, they found that the type of digital touchpoint through which consumers interact and its level of development affect how the online channel is perceived.

As far as touchpoints are concerned, the B2B context has certainly received less attention compared with B2C. In this domain, McColl-Kennedy et al. (in press) have developed a six-step framework of analysis that employs text-mining techniques to identify critical touchpoints in B2B customer journeys. On data collected over the course of a year through surveys, they deploy text-mining analytics to identify touchpoints that are effective, not effective or should be improved. Research on CEM and touchpoints is currently in the developing stage and more is needed in this area and on related specific issues. We will provide a more complete research agenda in Chapter 10.

Customer experience and customer loyalty

This last section aims to provide empirical evidence in favour of one of the main assumptions of this chapter: a better customer experience can increase customer loyalty. This is also the reason why we are addressing the topic of customer experience in this book. We see it as the latest stage in the 'evolution' of loyalty management. There is indeed wide consensus that customer experience is a driver of customer loyalty (Jain, Aagja and Bagdare, 2017). The intuitive idea behind this relationship is that having a positive customer experience contributes to further develop the relationship between the customer and the company, thus leading to higher customer loyalty in the long run. This consideration is assumed to be valid in different B2B and B2C contexts, in different industries and for different types of customers. Below we are going to briefly review the main results from the most recent studies concerning the relationship between customer experience measures with customer loyalty measures. First, we present their findings on the relationship between EXQ and customer loyalty. Second, we show the results from previous research on the relationship between the customer experience scale and strategic experiential modules and customer loyalty. By comparing these two streams of studies we can draw relevant and robust conclusions on the role of customer experience in driving long-term customer loyalty.

EXQ and customer loyalty

Klaus and Maklan (2013) and Klaus et al. (2013) have studied the relationship between customer experience measured by means of the EXQ scale and a series of constructs that are employed as measures of customer loyalty or as proxies for it: customer satisfaction, loyalty intentions and word of mouth. The contexts of reference where these relationships have been studied are as follows: mortgages, fuel and service stations, retail banking and luxury goods. Both studies consistently show that the customer experience is significantly and positively related to customer satisfaction, loyalty intentions and word of mouth. Roy (2018) takes a step further by measuring how the effect of customer experience on loyalty intentions (and satisfaction and word of mouth) changes when considering the following: a hedonic (e.g. restaurant) versus utilitarian (e.g. banking) service and first-time versus regular customers. Roy takes a longitudinal perspective, thus observing changes occurring over time. Results show that the positive impact of customer experience on customer loyalty is significant in both utilitarian and hedonic settings. However, it is stronger in the case of the hedonic setting than the utilitarian one. This means that customer experience seems to matter more for settings where the affective component has a predominant role and less in settings that are more concerned with rationality. A second result of the study regards the estimation of customer experience effects for a first-time customer. Specifically, results show that for a first-time customer, their experience has a positive effect on customer satisfaction but no effect on customer loyalty and word of mouth. This means that customer satisfaction is the most immediate outcome of customer experience, while loyalty and word of mouth can be influenced only with a continuum of multiple experiences. In fact, findings from the same study show that the impact of customer experience on customer loyalty, satisfaction and word of mouth increases with time. Specifically, if the first-time customer is then converted into a regular customer, the impact of customer experience on customer loyalty is stronger. According to Roy, these results are in line with the theoretical argument of consumer attitude formation over time. In the first experience, the customer is only capable of developing satisfaction as an immediate attitude if the experience is positive. However, with the occurrence of multiple subsequent experiences, the learning process undertaken by the customer leads to the development of attitudinal and behaviour loyalty. These findings have key implications for managers in terms of the attention that should be paid to first-time customers versus regular customers.

Strategic experiential modules and customer loyalty

The stream of studies adopting measurement scales based on strategic experiential modules (e.g. cognitive, affective) has tested the role of customer experience or its related constructs, such as brand experience and in-store customer experience, on customer loyalty and customer satisfaction. Within this stream of studies, research has also tried to capture, where possible, not only the overall effect of customer experience, but also the effect of each dimension of customer experience on customer loyalty.

Impact of customer experience on customer loyalty

Brun et al. (2017) have studied the impact of each customer experience dimension on customer loyalty and how the type of channel investigated, whether online or offline, moderates this effect. Their study was conducted in the banking and travel industries. Results show that, on average, the cognitive and social dimensions have a positive impact on customer loyalty, whereas the negative affective and behavioural dimensions have a negative effect. No overall impact was found to stem from the sensorial or positive affective dimensions. Moreover, these results tend to vary slightly depending on the channel considered (e.g. the bank branch or travel agency versus online travel agency or home banking), whether online or offline, and on the considered industry, whether banking or travel. For instance, the social dimension has a stronger effect on loyalty in the offline environment than online for both banking and travel, while the cognitive dimension has a stronger effect online for banking and offline for travel. Srivastava and Kaul (2016) have estimated the effect of customer experience on share of wallet, attitudinal and behavioural loyalty. Their study finds that customer experience has a positive and significant effect on attitudinal and behavioural loyalty but no effect on share of wallet.

Impact of brand experience on customer loyalty

Brakus, Schmitt and Zarantonello (2009) have studied six different categories of product brands, such as computers, cars, drinking water, sneakers, clothes and newspapers. They found that brand experience has a positive and significant effect on customer satisfaction and, through customer satisfaction, on loyalty. The rationale behind this result is strictly linked with the true nature of an experience: given that a brand involves the senses and elicits good feelings, customers (who are, after all, humans and seek stimuli that produce gratification) might want to receive such stimuli again. This result is then in line with the results on the effect of the general customer experience construct on loyalty.

Impact of in-store experience on customer loyalty

Bustamante and Rubio (2017) have estimated the effect of the in-store customer experience on satisfaction with the retail store and customer loyalty – specifically store loyalty – in a fashion retail context. Their study shows that the customer experience lived in the store has a positive effect on satisfaction and store loyalty and that a positive in-store customer experience is a key driver of the customer relationship with the retailer.

Implications

Let us summarize. Studies on the relationship between customer experience and loyalty (or related variables) seem to point consistently to one conclusion: living a positive customer experience leads one to develop loyalty towards the provider of that experience. This holds for the general concept of customer experience and for experiences that occur in retail stores, and with brands or across different channels. The first managerial implication of these results is straightforward: managers should not ignore or undervalue the customer experience. Customer experience is not a vague or empty concept. It is what customers live across all the different touchpoints they encounter, in multiple environments, with brands and retailers. To foster customer loyalty, it is important to leverage customer experience. The interplay between customer experience and customer loyalty has consistent empirical evidence.

However, this should only be considered a starting point. There are still many research questions that remain unanswered in this area. For instance, is there a dimension that is more effective than others in developing customer loyalty? What are the key determinants; that is, the key touchpoints that can influence the different dimensions of the customer experience? And there is a final challenge. What is the effect of delivering a successful customer experience on the spending of customers? To be blunt, how many euros or dollars is it worth spending on improving the customer experience? We will try to answer these questions in the last chapter of this book, which is concerned with future issues in the domains of loyalty management and customer experience.

References

Addis, M. and Holbrook, M. B. (2001) 'On the conceptual link between mass customisation and experiential consumption: an explosion of subjectivity'. *Journal of Consumer Behaviour: An International Research Review*, 1(1), pp. 50–66.

Ahluwalia, R., Burnkrant, R. E. and Unnava, H. R. (2000) 'Consumer response to negative publicity: the moderating role of commitment'. *Journal of Marketing Research*, 37(2), pp. 203–214.

Anderl, E., Schumann, J. H. and Kunz, W. (2016) 'Helping firms reduce complexity in multichannel online data: a new taxonomy-based approach for customer journeys'. *Journal of Retailing*, 92(2), pp. 185–203.

Arnold, M. J. and Reynolds, K. E. (2009) 'Affect and retail shopping behavior: understanding the role of mood regulation and regulatory focus'. *Journal of Retailing*, 85(3), pp. 308–320.

Bagdare, S. and Jain, R. (2013) 'Measuring retail customer experience'. *International Journal of Retail & Distribution Management*, 41(10), pp. 790–804.

Baumeister, R. F., Vohs, K. D., DeWall, C. N. and Zhang, L. (2007) 'How Emotion shapes behavior: feedback, anticipation, and reflection, rather than direct causation'. *Personality and Social Psychology Review*, 11, pp. 167–203.

Baxendale, S., Macdonald, E. K. and Wilson, H. N. (2015) 'The impact of different touchpoints on brand consideration'. *Journal of Retailing*, 91(2), pp. 235–253.

Bonfanti, A. (2018) *Customer shopping experience: Le sfide del retail tra spazio fisico e digitale.* Turin: Giappichelli.

Brakus, J. J., Schmitt, B. H. and Zarantonello, L. (2009) 'Brand experience: what is it? How is it measured? Does it affect loyalty?'. *Journal of Marketing*, 73(3), pp. 52–68.

Brun, I., Rajaobelina, L., Ricard, L. and Berthiaume, B. (2017) 'Impact of customer experience on loyalty: a multichannel examination'. *The Service Industries Journal*, 37(5–6), pp. 317–340.

Bustamante, J. C. and Rubio, N. (2017) 'Measuring customer experience in physical retail environments'. *Journal of Service Management*, 28(5), pp. 884–913.

Cacioppo, J. T. and Gardner, W. L. (1999) 'Emotion'. *Annual Review of Psychology*, 50(1), 191–214.

Campbell, M. C. and Keller, K. L. (2003) 'Brand familiarity and advertising repetition effects'. *Journal of Consumer Research*, 30(2), pp. 292–304.

Carù, A. and Cova, B. (2015) 'Co-creating the collective service experience'. *Journal of Service Management*, 26(2), pp. 276–294.

Cho, N. and Park, S. (2001) 'Development of electronic commerce user-consumer satisfaction index (ECUSI) for Internet shopping'. *Industrial Management & Data Systems*, 101(8), pp. 400–406.

Da Silva, V. R. and Syed Alwi, F. S. (2006) 'Cognitive, affective attributes and conative, behavioural responses in retail corporate branding'. *Journal of Product & Brand Management*, 15(5), pp. 293–305.

De Keyser, A., Lemon, K. N., Klaus, P. and Keiningham, T. L. (2015) 'A framework for understanding and managing the customer experience'. Marketing Science Institute Working Paper, No. 15–121. Cambridge, MA: Marketing Science Institute.

Duncan, T. and Moriarty, S. (2006) 'How integrated marketing communication's "touch-points" can operationalize the service-dominant logic'. In Lusch, R. F. and Vargo, S. L. (eds), *The Service-Dominant Logic of Marketing: Dialog, Debate, and Directions.* Abingdon: Routledge, pp. 236–249.

Erevelles, S. (1998) 'The role of affect in marketing'. *Journal of Business Research*, 42(3), pp. 199–215.

Flacandji, M. and Krey, N. (in press) 'Remembering shopping experiences: the shopping experience memory scale'. *Journal of Business Research*.

Ford, J. B. (2017) 'Amazon's Mechanical Turk: a comment'. *Journal of Advertising*, 46(1), pp. 156–158.

Fornerino, M., Helme-Guizon, A. and Gotteland, D. (2006) 'Mesurer l'immersion dans une expérience de consommation: premiers développements'. Paper presented at Actes du XXIIème Colloque international de l'Association Française du Marketing, 11 and 12 May, Nantes.

Gentile, C., Spiller, N. and Noci, G. (2007) 'How to sustain the customer experience: an overview of experience components that co-create value with the customer'. *European Management Journal*, 25(5), pp. 395–410.

Grewal, D., Levy, M. and Kumar, V. (2009) 'Customer experience management in retailing: an organizing framework'. *Journal of Retailing*, 85(1), pp. 1–14.

Hall, A. and Towers, N. (2017) 'Understanding how millennial shoppers decide what to buy: digitally connected unseen journeys'. *International Journal of Retail & Distribution Management*, 45(5), pp. 498–517.

Hallikainen, H., Alamäki, A. and Laukkanen, T. (in press) 'Individual preferences of digital touchpoints: a latent class analysis'. *Journal of Retailing and Consumer Services*.

Holbrook, M. B. and Hirschman, E. C. (1982) 'The experiential aspects of consumption: consumer fantasies, feelings, and fun'. *Journal of Consumer Research*, 9(2), pp. 132–140.

Homburg, C., Jozić, D. and Kuehnl, C. (2017) 'Customer experience management: toward implementing an evolving marketing concept'. *Journal of the Academy of Marketing Science*, 45(3), pp. 377–401.

Hu, H. and Jasper, C. R. (2006) 'Social cues in the store environment and their impact on store image'. *International Journal of Retail & Distribution Management*, 34(1), pp. 25–48.

Ieva, M. and Ziliani, C. (2018a) 'Mapping touchpoint exposure in retailing: implications for developing an omnichannel customer experience'. *International Journal of Retail & Distribution Management*, 46(3), pp. 304–322.

Ieva, M. and Ziliani, C. (2018b) 'The role of customer experience touchpoints in driving loyalty intentions in services'. *TQM Journal*, 30(5), pp. 444–457.

Jaakkola, E., Helkkula, A. and Aarikka-Stenroos, L. (2015) 'Service experience co-creation: conceptualization, implications, and future research directions'. *Journal of Service Management*, 26(2), pp. 182–205.

Jain, R., Aagja, J. and Bagdare, S. (2017) 'Customer experience: a review and research agenda'. *Journal of Service Theory and Practice*, 27(3), pp. 642–662.

Kahneman, D. (2011) *Thinking Fast and Slow*. New York: Farrar Straus and Giroux.

Keiningham, T. L., Cooil, B., Aksoy, L., Andreassen, T. W. and Weiner, J. (2007) 'The value of different customer satisfaction and loyalty metrics in predicting customer retention, recommendation, and share-of-wallet'. *Managing Service Quality: An International Journal*, 17(4), pp. 361–384.

Klaus, P. and Maklan, S. (2012) 'EXQ: a multiple-item scale for assessing service experience'. *Journal of Service Management*, 23(1), pp. 5–33.

Klaus, P. P. and Maklan, S. (2013) 'Towards a better measure of customer experience'. *International Journal of Market Research*, 55(2), pp. 227–246.

Klaus, P., Gorgoglione, M., Buonamassa, D., Panniello, U. and Nguyen, B. (2013) 'Are you providing the "right" customer experience? The case of Banca Popolare di Bari'. *International Journal of Bank Marketing*, 31(7), pp. 506–528.

LaSalle, D. and Britton, T. A. (2003) *Priceless: Turning Ordinary Products into Extraordinary Experiences*. Boston, MA: Harvard Business School Press.

Lemon, K. N. and Verhoef, P. C. (2016) 'Understanding customer experience throughout the customer journey'. *Journal of Marketing*, 80(6), pp. 69–96.

Li, H. and Kannan, P. K. (2014) 'Attributing conversions in a multichannel online marketing environment: an empirical model and a field experiment'. *Journal of Marketing Research*, 51(1), pp. 40–56.

Lipkin, M. (2016) 'Customer experience formation in today's service landscape'. *Journal of Service Management*, 27(5), pp. 678–703.

Manser Payne, E., Peltier, J. W. and Barger, V. A. (2017) 'Omni-channel marketing, integrated marketing communications and consumer engagement: a research agenda'. *Journal of Research in Interactive Marketing*, 11(2), pp. 185–197.

McColl-Kennedy, J. R., Zaki, M., Lemon, K. N., Urmetzer, F. and Neely, A. (in press) 'Gaining customer experience insights that matter'. *Journal of Service Research*.

Meyer, C. and Schwager, A. (2007) 'Customer experience'. *Harvard Business Review*, 85(2), pp. 116–126.

Ou, Y. C. and Verhoef, P. C. (2017) 'The impact of positive and negative emotions on loyalty intentions and their interactions with customer equity drivers'. *Journal of Business Research*, 80, pp. 106–115.

Palmer, A. (2010) 'Customer experience management: a critical review of an emerging idea'. *Journal of Services Marketing*, 24(3), pp. 196–208.

Parasuraman, A., Zeithaml, V. A. and Berry, L. L. (1988) 'Servqual: a multiple-item scale for measuring consumer perceptions of service quality'. *Journal of Retailing*, 64(1), pp. 12–40.

Payne, A. and Frow, P. (2005) 'A strategic framework for customer relationship management'. *Journal of Marketing*, 69(4), pp. 167–176.

Pine, B. J. and Gilmore, J. H. (1998) 'Welcome to the experience economy'. *Harvard Business Review*, 76, pp. 97–105.

Puccinelli, N. M., Goodstein, R. C., Grewal, D., Price, R., Raghubir, P. and Stewart, D. (2009) 'Customer experience management in retailing: understanding the buying process'. *Journal of Retailing*, 85(1), pp. 15–30.

Rawson, A., Duncan, E. and Jones, C. (2013) 'The truth about customer experience'. *Harvard Business Review*, 91(9), pp. 90–98.

Reichheld, F. F. (2003) 'The one number you need to grow'. *Harvard Business Review*, 81(12), pp. 46–55.

Richins, M. L. (1997) 'Measuring emotions in the consumption experience'. *Journal of Consumer Research*, 24(2), pp. 127–146.

Romaniuk, J., Beal, V. and Uncles, M. (2013) 'Achieving reach in a multi-media environment: how a marketer's first step provides the direction for the second'. *Journal of Advertising Research*, 53(2), pp. 221–230.

Rose, S., Clark, M., Samouel, P. and Hair, N. (2012) 'Online customer experience in e-retailing: an empirical model of antecedents and outcomes'. *Journal of Retailing*, 88(2), pp. 308–322.

Roy, S. (2018) 'Effects of customer experience across service types, customer types and time'. *Journal of Services Marketing*, 32(4), 400–413.

Schmitt, B. (1999) 'Experiential marketing'. *Journal of Marketing Management*, 15(1–3), pp. 53–67.

Srivastava, M. and Kaul, D. (2016) 'Exploring the link between customer experience–loyalty–consumer spend'. *Journal of Retailing and Consumer Services*, 31, pp. 277–286.

Straker, K., Wrigley, C. and Rosemann, M. (2015) 'Typologies and touchpoints: designing multi-channel digital strategies'. *Journal of Research in Interactive Marketing*, 9(2), pp. 110–128.

Trevinal, A. M. and Stenger, T. (2014) 'Toward a conceptualization of the online shopping experience'. *Journal of Retailing and Consumer Services*, 21(3), pp. 314–326.

Van Doorn, J., Leeflang, P. S. and Tijs, M. (2013) 'Satisfaction as a predictor of future performance: a replication'. *International Journal of Research in Marketing*, 30(3), pp. 314–318.

Vaughan, K., Beal, V. and Romaniuk, J. (2016) 'Can brand users really remember advertising more than nonusers? Testing an empirical generalization across six advertising awareness measures'. *Journal of Advertising Research*, 56(3), pp. 311–320.

Verhoef, P. C., Lemon, K. N., Parasuraman, A., Roggeveen, A., Tsiros, M. and Schlesinger, L. A. (2009) 'Customer experience creation: determinants, dynamics and management strategies'. *Journal of Retailing*, 85(1), pp. 31–41.

Voorhees, C. M., Fombelle, P. W., Gregoire, Y., Bone, S., Gustafsson, A., Sousa, R. and Walkowiak, T. (2017) 'Service encounters, experiences and the customer journey: defining the field and a call to expand our lens'. *Journal of Business Research*, 79, pp. 269–280.

Wagner, G., Schramm-Klein, H. and Steinmann, S. (in press) 'Online retailing across e-channels and e-channel touchpoints: empirical studies of consumer behavior in the multichannel e-commerce environment'. *Journal of Business Research*.

Westbrook, R. A. and Oliver, R. L. (1991) 'The dimensionality of consumption emotion patterns and consumer satisfaction'. *Journal of Consumer Research*, 18(1), pp. 84–91.

Wind, Y. J. and Hays, C. F. (2016) 'Research implications of the "beyond advertising" paradigm: a model and roadmap for creating value through all media and non-media touchpoints'. *Journal of Advertising Research*, 56(2), pp. 142–158.

Wright, P. L. (1973) 'The cognitive processes mediating acceptance of advertising'. *Journal of Marketing Research*, 10(1), pp. 53–62.

Zahay, D., Peltier, J., Schultz, D. E. and Griffin, A. (2004), 'The role of transactional versus relational data in IMC programs: Bringing customer data together'. *Journal of Advertising Research*, 44(1), pp. 3–18.

Zeithaml, V. A., Berry, L. L. and Parasuraman, A. (1996) 'The behavioral consequences of service quality'. *Journal of Marketing*, 60(2), pp. 31–46.

Zeithaml, V. A., Bolton, R. N., Deighton, J., Keiningham, T. L., Lemon, K. N. and Petersen, J. A. (2006) 'Forward-looking focus: can firms have adaptive foresight?'. *Journal of Service Research*, 9(2), pp. 168–183.

7

USING CUSTOMER INSIGHT IN RETAIL MANAGEMENT

Michela Giacomini and Miriam Panico[1]

Customer insight

Behind every sales dollar there is a customer

Everybody needs to buy food on a regular basis, and when they do so they leave with retailers millions of data points through their transactions[1]. More information still is available when one uses a loyalty card because the retailer can easily track the history, habits and needs of every customer. The availability and processability of such a wealth of data is the reason why customer insight has found such fertile ground within the retail industry, and why customer analytics has increased and evolved massively in the last three decades, enjoying the proliferation of data sources (online, offline and third-party) and increasingly sophisticated models with which to utilize them. Here we retrace the steps of the customer insight evolution by presenting the types of analysis that retailers usually employ.

Customer insight in the retail industry starts with the basic view of business performance as being a combination of stores and products and then adds various dimensions of customer behaviour, such as frequency, recency, spend, acquisition and retention, each being behavioural aspects of the customer experience (as discussed in Chapter 6). A simple example is the decomposition analysis of key performance indicators (KPIs), whereby analysts try to decompose the effects of sales performance (see Figure 7.1) and demonstrate that every shift in sales is due to a change in customer behaviour.[2]

1   The contributors of this guest chapter are with dunnhumby, a distinguished partner of the Loyalty Observatory over the years.
2   Figures in this chapter have been reproduced with minor amendment with the permission of dunnhumby.

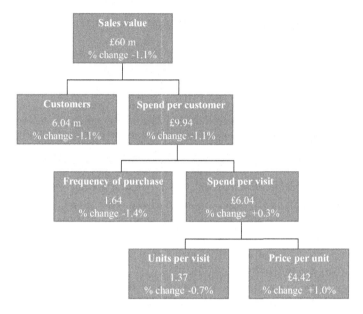

FIGURE 7.1 Decomposition analysis

In the past, these data referred to in-store behaviour only. Today, of course, a multichannel or purely online retailer wants to better understand its customers and the differences between online, offline and cross-shopping customer behaviour. Customers shopping cross-channel are actually more valuable to retailers, as is illustrated in Figure 7.2, which presents the spend per customer by customer group of an anonymized European retailer. It has therefore become fundamental to increase sales for bricks-and-mortar and multichannel

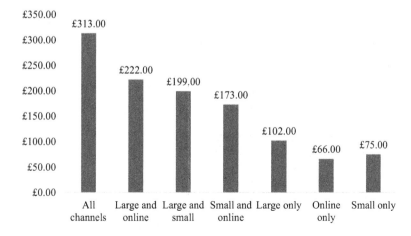

FIGURE 7.2 Spend per customer by customer group

retailers to understand the characteristics and needs of this group in order to move more customers online.

Sometimes, however, customer KPIs and decomposition analysis are not enough to get to the root cause of business performance, as changes may affect only a portion of the customer base. Hence the need for more specific analysis. Retailers can then further break down customers into different segments. A retailer might start with a simple demographic segmentation of customers – for example, by splitting their customer base by age and affluence. Age and income data can be obtained from national census data or from customer surveys. Sometimes just knowing a customer's postal address can give a good indication or whether this customer is old or young, wealthy or poor. The retailer can then try to understand its customers by studying their shopping behaviour, for instance, their level of loyalty or price sensitivity. A simple way to understand a customer's loyalty is to look at their frequency of visit and their spend per week (Figure 7.3): customers who spend and visit more are considered more engaged than those that don't.

The segmentation can become even more sophisticated by looking at the 'categories coverage': a customer who spends a lot but purchases only in two or three categories (e.g. pasta, frozen meals, fresh produce) is very likely to complete her shopping at other retail stores and therefore cannot be considered loyal. Another example of behavioural segmentation, as already mentioned, is price sensitivity. By looking at the type of products purchased over time, this segmentation aims to understand if customers are looking for price or rather for quality. The approach is to identify within one category low-end priced products (usually the so-called 'entry prices', cheaper than the rest of the category) and high-end priced products (the premium ones, most expensive in the category and usually of higher quality) and understand for every customer the balance of these products in their baskets. A customer with a high proportion of low-end products is generally called 'price-sensitive', while a customer with a high proportion of high-end products is 'up-market'. A customer with a good balance between the two is considered 'mid-

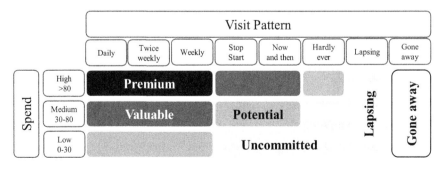

FIGURE 7.3 Customer shopping habits – a proxy for loyalty

market'. Despite being considered rudimentary today, these segmentations can drive recommendations and actions for customer relationship management (CRM), pricing and assortment.

For example, retailers use these to:

- drive the frequency and spend of non-loyal customers through personalized offers
- reward and retain the most valuable customers
- retain and attract more customers by improving the pricing perception through better prices or more adequate assortment (particularly if a store has few loyal customers and a high proportion of price-sensitive customers).

And the list of examples could go on.

For retailers who aspire to know their customers better, customer insight enables the bespoke clustering of customers using a mix of demographic and shopping data, often informed by detailed attitudinal research on customer motivations. Each further division of the customer base helps uncover more detail on how a retailer is performing for different segments of the marketplace. This further step in segmentation might be a lifestyle segmentation to identify macro-groups of customers with similar behaviours, needs and motivations, or something more specific like a health segmentation to identify micro-groups of customers with similar dietary habits (i.e. organic, vegan, sporty, etc.). Figure 7.4 presents an example of lifestyle

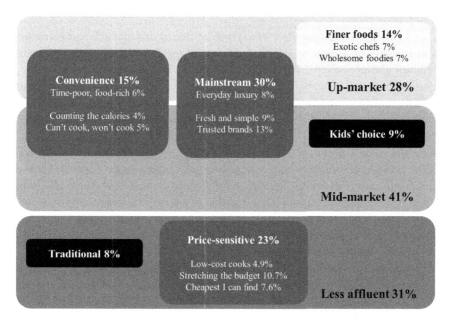

FIGURE 7.4 Example of lifestyle segmentation

segmentation and demonstrates how the split into groups is correlated with customers' price sensitivity.

From clusters to personalization

To help retailers grow, all this understanding and analysis needs to trigger two important questions: 'why is this happening?' and 'what should I do about it?' And in today's multichannel world, responding is even more complex because customers are continuously exposed to multiple stimuli and therefore there is ever more and variegated data. Retailers' understanding must be quick, in real time and at the customer level. Answering these questions involves delving into the customer shopping journey (that we see as composed of the phases we call discover → shop → buy → reflect) and understanding the journey of every customer.

Looking at the customer journey, the questions a retailer wants an answer to become even more numerous.

1. To begin with, how do customers think about a retailer? What does its brand stand for? On what occasions would a customer shop at a particular store? How does the customer look for information about products?
2. How does the customer shop? Online or in-store? When? Where? Why?
3. What do they purchase? How do they pay? Are they collecting points or using a coupon?
4. And then, what are their thoughts after the purchase? Are they sharing the experience with friends or online? Will they shop here again?

A sophisticated customer-led retailer will be able to map the different behaviours and engage with customers during each stage of their shopping journey through a relevant and personalized experience. This means that each customer is offered a personalized path to higher levels of engagement via relevant communication and offers at each step – even more relevant when the engagement happens in real time while shopping online. For example, a customer might be notified at the checkout phase if the product that she usually buys in a given time cycle has been missed or forgotten. The algorithm identifies that it is time to be repurchased. We will see a clear example of customer engagement later on in this chapter ('Step 2: Strategic price and promo analysis'). Equally, if there seems to be a problem at the 'shop' stage of the shopping journey (either online or offline), customer insight can help diagnose the barriers. This can be achieved by using statistical models that help to analyse the dynamics within the purchasing process such as looking at the way customers choose what products to pick up, but factoring in other influencing elements such as the importance of promotions, the exposure to communication and so forth. Once a retailer has built and validated robust models of how customers calculate the attractiveness of their brand and how they decide to buy different products in different circumstances, it is a relatively short step to prescribing smart changes to optimize for profitable sales growth. Understanding customer behaviour through the shopping journey will allow retailers and brands to respond to customers' needs in a more relevant way and, as a result, improve perception, which is anyway a long-term investment.

From past understanding to future forecasting

No retailer would put their strategies entirely in the hands of automated decision-making tools. However, scenario-forecasting category management tools and self-learning targeting algorithms show the extent to which the close integration of customer insight and retail management has become a modern reality. Scenario-forecasting tools allow managers to build 'what if' scenarios; for example, what's the effect of changing the prices of certain products? What happens to the sales of other products in the same category? Is there any cannibalization effect? And what happens to a certain customer group or to total performance? These kinds of forecasting and optimization models allow the retailer to take conscious and targeted decisions for pricing, promotions, assortment and space. Self-learning targeting algorithms are even more sophisticated, providing an automated diagnosis of the performance and the reasons behind it. There is no longer an analyst running hundreds of deep dives to identify the reason for poor performance; the machine automatically diagnoses the effect of multiple factors and detects and isolates the relevant ones.

From customer insight to capability/level management

We generally say that a company is customer-focused when customer insights are not just responding to quick ad hoc questions in order to understand and fix specific issues (a tactical approach) but when insights are regularly built to drive business decisions and strategic plans, to manage marketing and commercial levers in a customer-oriented way. Unfortunately, some retailers buy insights reporting or tools just to use the data, without having a clear understanding of where they are today, what they need, what they want to get out of the data or if they have the right resources or the right company culture. This behaviour can lead to ineffectual decisions. That's why we always recommend that our partners start from an assessment of capability, to *assess a retailer's existing sophistication in planning and execution* in any business area – from data, through loyalty and CRM, to pricing, promotions, assortment and so on. Such an approach explores the current tensions and practices in a detailed manner in order to identify *opportunities to progress along the capability ladder* at the right pace, taking into account business and customer needs and organizational readiness. This assessment generally gives an indication of where the retailer is for all business areas on:

- Strategic planning: the extent to which the actual planning aligns and supports the strategic objectives of the business.
- Process and governance: the presence and extent of established and embedded processes and adherence to them.

- People and integration: the specific roles, functions and structures within the organization, and centres of power.
- Customer understanding and data: the integration of data and customer insight into decision-making.
- Tools and reporting: the existence and use of supporting tools on delivering improved insight, planning and execution.
- Supplier collaboration: ways of working with suppliers.

Understanding at what level the retailer sits for each of these levers is the most important starting point to understanding how to grow and make the most of insights and data.

Figure 7.5 demonstrates the significance of the promotional lever. A retailer that doesn't use customer data but is driven only by the previous year's actions or trading experience is at the lowest level. The first data that are usually collected are competitive indexes as well as competitor information such as promotions they are running and how. These data can be used to set some promotional rules or identify competitive promotional prices (e.g. prices should never be 5% higher than that of the main competitors). Only 20% of retailers use customer data to build better promotions or understand which products attract more customers and how customers behave when exposed to certain promotions (building 'what if' scenarios). The number of retailers that adopt even more sophisticated customer analysis is very limited and below 1%. Before using new customer data or building new tools, a retailer needs to know where it is in this journey and where it wants to go.

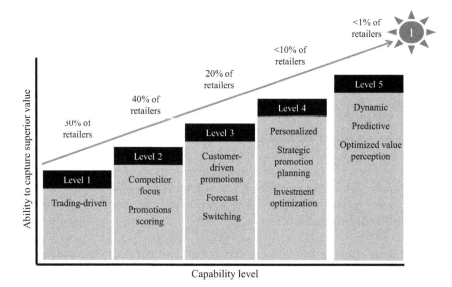

FIGURE 7.5 A retailer's capability levels

As we said before, we recommend that our partners start from an assessment of their capabilities to understand the *existing sophistication of planning and execution* in any business area. Retailers could be at different stages in any area. Some retailers, for instance, are pretty advanced in using data for their loyalty and CRM programmes but still only take trading-driven decisions on pricing, promotions and assortment. It's important to run an assessment that allows retailers to focus on the levers that are most relevant to driving the loyalty of their target customers – and this is generally best understood through customer research.

Category management

Category management is a very important business approach: finding out what the customer wants will help retailers provide a better offer and shopping experience in every category. With the right category management in place, the customer receives the right assortment offering with optimal prices at the right placement in stores. We have demonstrated that successful category management should be customer-oriented, which means driven by customer insight rather than by old habits or intuition, in order to have a clear understanding of what customers want (Ruttenberg, 2016). However, it should also consider the financials and strategic decisions already taken by the company and be operationally manageable. This evolution in category management is what we call category leadership. The typical questions that a retailer should ask are listed in Figure 7.6 and most can be answered using data insights.

Improvements in category management represent a huge source of benefit to retailers: by applying an evolved, customer-centric category management approach, retailers' sales in the category can increase by more than 3%.

CUSTOMER	FINANCIAL	STRATEGIC	OPERATIONAL
How can I focus on what is really important to customers in each category?	Which categories should I be investing in more – and less?	How can I make the customer's experience in categories reflect the strategic choices we make as a business?	How do I ensure my teams focus on activities that will really grow my categories, rather than trying to do everything everywhere?
How can I prioritize the categories most likely to drive customers to my stores?	How do I prioritize categories that are good for my bottom line?	How can I ensure all the resources at my disposal are aligned to my strategic priorities?	What targets should I set for each of my marketing levers?
How can I merchandise my categories more effectively for customers?	How can I get greater return on investment on all my category activities?		How can I get the best support from my suppliers and ensure we are aligned?

FIGURE 7.6 Key questions for successful category management

Category roles

One of the first questions to ask is always: how can I prioritize the categories most likely to drive customers to my stores? Retail is a highly competitive environment; unsurprisingly, we would all like to be the best at everything – but we can't afford to be. We have to make choices. Making tough choices is at the heart of successful category management. Some categories and some marketing levers are more important in driving sustainable growth than others. The challenge is knowing how to identify those categories, so you can make choices about where to invest.

Strategic choices can be taken when building category roles to identify groups of categories that may have the same strategic function for the retailer. Category roles will be useful for answering data-driven questions like: 'which categories are most important – both to the business and to my customers – and why?' Answering this question enables the definition of roles for each category.

In Figure 7.7 the 'importance to customer' is a composite score, built using customers' KPIs like sales and frequency of purchase within the category. But it can also be enhanced using market research information, asking customers how much they value and how they shop in any specific category. The 'importance to retailer' is also a composite score and is based on performance versus the previous year and versus the market, where performance is generally calculated comparing this year's sales and margin versus those of the previous year. The matrix in Figure 7.7 will help the retailer to understand where the company needs to develop, win, control or protect. Business actions will be formalized according to the category roles, such as investing in the right levers (such as pricing, promotions and assortment) for the different categories or recovering some margin from those defined as

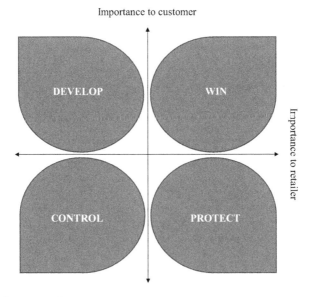

FIGURE 7.7 Category roles map

'control' in the category roles map. Now, this may sound like an obvious approach to managing categories, but it never fails to surprise us just how many retailers are still operating in silos with different categories being managed in isolation and out of sync with the overall objectives of the business. As the retail climate gets more and more challenging, the effective use of resources within category management will be essential for retailers to do well.

Every retailer has four resources they can spend on their categories:

- Money – how much should we invest in pricing, promotions or communications activity to drive the category?
- Time – how much should we allocate to managing and reviewing categories?
- People – who should we dedicate to managing which categories and what are the priorities?
- Space – how much should be allocated to different categories in-store?

Every category is in competition for these resources. How they are optimally allocated should depend on the category's priority and this should be intrinsically linked to the overall strategy for the business. More analysis will be required to understand what the right action is for every category: for instance, is it pricing, promotions or assortment? Examples of the analysis required to take business decisions will be illustrated in the paragraphs that follow.

Customer-oriented assortment

Assortment is an important business lever to consider when reviewing a category. It responds to the question above about resources in space: how much should be allocated to different categories in-store? Here is an example of how tough category choices were implemented to drive strategic change within one large European retailer through a rationalization of ranges. To make the shopping experience easier for customers, this retailer wanted to simplify assortment and reduce range across all food categories in-store, removing duplication whilst retaining market-leading products. In some categories, the range was reduced by up to 30%. By focusing on customer metrics rather than just commercial metrics, this retailer was able to identify and protect the products most important to customers (not necessarily the best-selling lines but those key to driving customer traffic and creating cross-selling opportunities, with low cannibalization of other products). With a 2% average uplift in sales, 1.4% volume growth and improved availability, the results were extremely positive for both retailer and customers. The smaller range and increased space in-store for remaining lines resulted in improved customer satisfaction. Paradoxically, the reduction in choice actually made it easier for customers to find what they were looking for, adding speed, ease and convenience to the overall shopping experience. This was a tough decision to make but ultimately the right one.

At the base of the described example there are analyses such as customer decision trees built using the substitutability index, that we explain below. A customer decision tree is a data-driven hierarchical clustering approach which provides a model for how shoppers make decisions about which products to purchase in a category and identifies the criteria they use to evaluate those products. Substitutability is an index which indicates how customers substitute products in their basket and is derived from looking at all customers' historical baskets. Let's take an example based on mayonnaise and assume that a retailer sells two brands (A and B) of 500-gram bottles. If product A is out of stock and customers who usually buy that product move to product B, then it means that the two products are substitutable. If product A is on promotion, and customers who usually buy that product move to product B, again it means that they are substitutable. If instead, customers don't switch it means that the products represent different needs and are not substitutable. In this case, basket analysis is more important than other research because, as we have seen from experience, what customers say is sometimes very different from what customers do.

In Figure 7.8 you can see a simple example of a customer decision tree for the oral care category. The tree shows how customers shop within the oral care category: a toothbrush and toothpaste are two separate needs, and a customer will never substitute a toothbrush with toothpaste! At a deeper level we understand that when a customer looks for a sensitive toothpaste, he or she will look for a specific brand. If a customer loves Brand 1, any product within that brand will be fine with them, while Brand 3 lovers will look for either paste or gel. Brand 3 gel is, therefore, a specific need, and the retailer should guarantee assortment coverage of Brand 3 gel in all its stores, including small ones. It's very interesting to notice that every retailer, or even

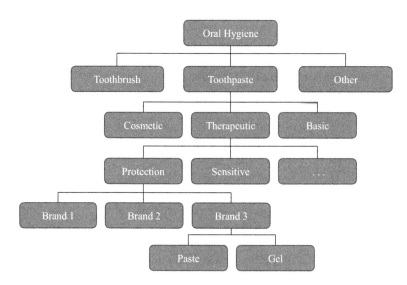

FIGURE 7.8 Example of a customer decision tree

every format within one retailer, could have different customer decision trees because their shoppers, and therefore their needs, will be different.

Customer-oriented assortment means identifying the best products to cover all customer needs and new needs may lead to unexpected new assortment opportunities that aren't being addressed. The best products are usually associated with business KPIs, such as sales combined with customers' KPIs, frequency of purchase and spend per customer. When running a category review, a retailer should try to keep in its assortment the most important products for customers and remove the less important ones, but cover all the needs available – in all its stores' clusters, even the smallest local ones. It is important to note, however, that using customer data alone provides an internal view only, certainly more insightful than it has ever been before but still missing the gap analysis that market data can provide. For a proper range to be defined, retailers can gain a great deal from analysing competitors' data and sales. In e-commerce, there is less of a space issue, but it's still important to propose the products that are more appealing to customers to guarantee a complete coverage of needs and a positive shopping experience. It's also fair to say that even for e-commerce, no warehouse in the world could store all the products available on the market.

Space optimization

Another important business lever that responds to the space question is the layout of stores and the space allocated to every single category. Of course, this is more relevant to physical stores. Retailers must deliver a positive shopping experience that drives high performance. But sometimes managing multiple formats, store size and, as a consequence, layouts, can be very challenging. There are many tools on the market which provide space optimization, as well as planogram or layout recommendations. At the base of these sophisticated tools there is again data and customer insight, linked to information about the physical dimensions of products and space in stores. Analysis will support retailers to answer questions like what are the most important categories for customers that should have more space? What are the categories that sell more when they get more space? What's the right order of products and categories in the stores' aisles?

Space optimization analysis is based on elasticity models (Figure 7.9): all historical sales, coupled with information about the space available, must be collected and analysed to understand if an increase or decrease of space has led to a change in sales. More elastic categories will have more space than less elastic ones. The analysis and algorithms are quite complex because there are always space constraints to be respected: the sum of all the categories' space should be the same of the space available in-store. On top of this, the shape and size of the products within each category should be considered because some categories (like water in Italy, for instance) may come in big six-bottle packs and require a minimum space that is quite large, compared to other categories like spices that, again in Italy, take very little space. The analysis will provide the recommended space per category.

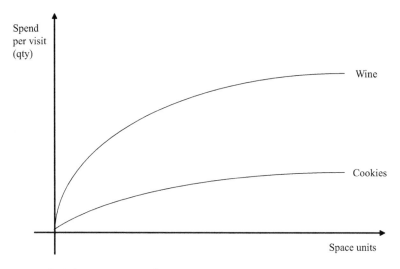

FIGURE 7.9 Elasticity curves examples

Category adjacencies, which means categories that should have an adjacent position in the layout for an eased customer shopping experience, can be identified using simple analyses such as the basket analysis mentioned earlier to identify products that are usually purchased together by customers. An example in the Italian market could be pasta with tomato sauce or oil; this indicates that the three categories should be possibly in close proximity or sequence within the store.

Value for customers

Another critical resource investment point is money: how much should we invest in the category to drive customers' value perception? Every customer perceives a certain value for the products or services they want to buy, which is the gain that the customer will receive versus the price they can pay. Retailers generally want to understand what the average value perception of their customers is to be able to improve their offer and, as a consequence, increase loyalty and attract new customers. There are several analyses that can be run and many tools that can be purchased to understand and optimize the value for customers, from simple descriptive analyses to very sophisticated optimization and simulation tools. However, there is not a standard and fixed process: a retailer should adopt the solutions which better respond to its maturity level and its objectives, as already discussed. Figure 7.10

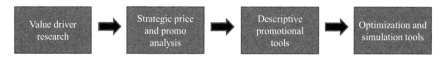

FIGURE 7.10 Retailer journey to improve customers' value perception

shows a simple example of a retailer's journey towards understanding what drives its customers' perception of value.

Step 1: Value driver research

A retailer who wants to analyse the value for customers should start by finding out what customers think about the existing offer (Ciancio, 2017). Understanding if a customer thinks the retailer is cheap or expensive is usually quite simple but identifying the drivers for value perception is far from it. Certainly, regular prices and promotions play a big role, but these are not the only factors. We all know, for instance, that communication is very important. A clear flyer with rounded and highlighted discounts or signage on the shop floor announcing promotional offers can condition customer perception and behaviour. Assortment is important as well: retailers proposing several 'entry prices' or fantasy brands can be perceived as cheap, while those offering only premium products can be perceived as expensive. Perception is then conditioned significantly by the actual offers of competitors in the area. Overall, we say that there are seven levers driving price perception (Figure 7.11).

A retailer who wants to prioritize actions for its business plan should start by understanding which levers are diving the price perception of its customers.

FIGURE 7.11 Drivers of price perception

Step 2: Strategic price and promo analysis

Pricing and promotion are usually the most important levers to determine value perception. Understanding how customers react to the changes in prices and promotions is fundamental to building the right value proposition, which can lead to better perception and therefore higher customer purchases. As pricing and promotion are part of the same 'ecosystem' just presented, we believe that they should be analysed and understood together in order to build integrated plans. Here is a list of questions that should be answered when building an integrated pricing and promotion plan:

- What are the important products for customers?
- How many price-sensitive customers shop in the stores and what products are important to them?
- How do customers react to price changes?

To answer these questions, retailers need to deploy some of the customer insights we discussed earlier in the chapter.

1. The first step is building measures of price sensitivity, which means identifying customers that prefer purchasing cheaper items, like entry prices, fantasy brands or private labels. Price-sensitive customers are generally more perceptive and reactive.
2. The second step is building composite rankings to identify the most important products for customers, based on simple KPIs like customer penetration (percentage of customers buying the product), customer penetration for price-sensitive customers (or for other target customers groups such as loyals), sales or quantity of products, and so forth. We might call the composite ranking 'importance to customers'.
3. The final step is building measures of price elasticity. Price elasticity expresses how much sales can change as a consequence of price variation. Accurate price elasticity estimates are usually built using a long history (usually at least two years, to account for seasonal variation) and looking at all the possible price variations, including price and promotional changes. As we have already explained, we believe it's very important to keep the two levers together to understand customer reactions to all possible changes.

This type of analysis can result in a very simple matrix that can lead to important strategic decisions (Figure 7.12).

In the Hi-Lo corner, we find products with high price elasticity but low importance to customers. The strategy for these products is to regularly run strong promotions and partially recover margins by increasing the regular price. For products in the Hybrid corner, both prices and promotions are very important and therefore these products should have a very competitive regular price and be promoted regularly with competitive promotional prices. Products in the EDV (everyday value) corner are instead

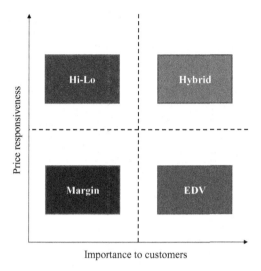

FIGURE 7.12 Matrix for taking strategic decisions based on price and promo analysis

good candidates for an everyday-low-price regime with very good prices but a lack of promotions; promotions are not elastic and therefore do not generate more sales. Finally, products in the Margin area are ideal candidates to recover margins in both levers. This type of matrix is normally used to provide strategic category guidelines to buyers and category managers.

Step 3: Descriptive promotional tools

Category managers also need to understand the performance of previous offers and this usually happens through simple promotional reports that contain descriptive sales and customer KPIs, like the report presented in Tables 7.1 and 7.2. This report

TABLE 7.1 Example of promotional report with customer KPIs (part one)

Product	Category	Discount (%)	Promo-tional price	Reach (basket penetration)	Loyal customers reach	New customers attracted
AAA	Soya sauces	30%–40%	185	0.3%	32%	48%
BBB	Refinery sugar	0%–10%	36	0.6%	29%	67%
CCC	Weighted candies	30%–40%	423	0.2%	37%	5%
DDD	Drinking water	50%–60%	34	0.9%	24%	13%
EEE	Low-alcohol beverages	0%–10%	51	0.4%	23%	7%
FFF	Mineral water	30%–40%	25	0.3%	33%	7%
GGG	Drinking water	30%–40%	51	0%	31%	3%

TABLE 7.2 Example of promotional report with customer KPIs (part two)

Product	Category	Promotional sales	Cannibalized sales within the category	Incremental sales	Recommendation
AAA	Soya sauces	605,510	−17,171	568,438	Strongly recommended
BBB	Refinery sugar	543,580	−12,851	156,108	Acceptable
CCC	Weighted candies	611,385	−71,634	518,697	Avoid
DDD	Drinking water	296,867	−44,773	180,757	Strongly recommended
EEE	Low-alcohol beverages	617,310	−222,717	331,922	Avoid
FFF	Mineral water	260,392	−102,635	142,435	Avoid
GGG	Drinking water	300,674	−88,480	130,212	Recommended

includes some exemplary KPIs; however, a retailer could tailor the report adding other KPIs or building different views, like summary tables, trend charts or multidimensional interactive views.

These kinds of reports are usually refreshed after every promotional campaign in order to provide real-time information to buyers and category managers. Whatever the view or the visualization tool is, it's important to understand how customers react to promotions to identify good promotions or drop bad ones. In Tables 7.1 and 7.2, for instance, we can see that important customer KPIs include:

- Reach: what proportion of all customers shopping purchase the product?
- New customers attracted: of all customers who buy into the offer, how many are new to the category? Or for the store?
- Incremental sales for the category: the difference between observed sales and expected sales (forecasted as if the product was not in promotion) can be considered incremental sales. And these are generally sales coming from existing customers buying more products or new customers attracted by the promotion.
- Cannibalization indicates how customers are switching between products. That is, if Coca-Cola is on promotion, what happens to the sales of other cola products? Again, this is built by forecasting sales for all the products in the category when Coca-Cola is not on promotion and comparing the result to what happens to Pepsi or other cola products when Coca-Cola is on promotion.

This kind of analysis is very useful and allows retailers to cut the tails of bad promotions and improve the overall performance of the promotional periods through improved sales and margin.

Step 4: Optimization and simulation tools

Retailers who have very good historical data, dedicated and skilled resources and a considerable budget can think about purchasing an optimization tool. Advanced tools embed very sophisticated science in forecasting and optimization, which can support simulation scenarios. Where it is feasible, we recommend buying such a tool since building algorithms from scratch would take even numerous expert analysts considerable time (definitely more than a year!). This kind of tool eliminates guesswork from pricing by introducing a superior rule-based pricing engine that can determine the appropriate pricing based on a range of targets. Pricing rules can be automatically managed across thousands of products and categories. Pricing usually includes:

- minimum and maximum gross margin rules
- brand rules to ensure budget brand products are priced lower than premium brand products
- product size rules to maintain the price per unit of measurement (e.g. price per litre) within product families (e.g. different sizes of Coke Zero)
- product importance rules to allow different rules to be applied to the products most and least important to the retailer's customers
- competitor product rules to help maintain a retailer's price position against individual competitor products.

Optimization functionalities enable retailers to reach specific objectives in respect of the defined rules, such as:

1. maximize the performance of each category in line with the role assigned to it by the retailer (i.e. maximize profit in a profit-driver category)
2. meet the budgetary needs of each category (i.e. quarterly and half-year budgets on revenue, margin and profit)
3. maximize the performance of a category with a focus on target customers.

Finally, these tools provide extensive simulation capabilities so that category managers and analysts can create and compare many different scenarios: what happens if we run a specific promotion in a certain period? What happens if we drop the regular prices by 5% in the everyday-low-price line? What happens if we change some promotional mechanics? And so on. Simulations use forecasting science to provide the estimated scenario. The best underlying customer demand models incorporate both promotion and non-promotion data to provide the retail industry with the best possible forecasting accuracy. Throughout our experience, we have been able to reach very high levels of accuracy. Figure 7.13 provides an example of forecasting accuracy for some categories' revenues.

This signals a great revolution for retailers. They can finally take very informed, customer-oriented and effective decisions.

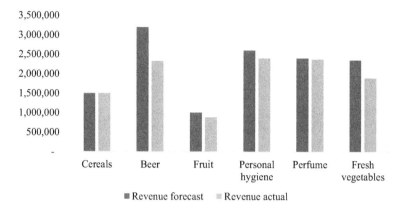

FIGURE 7.13 Example of forecasting accuracy by category

From insight to activation

In this third section we discuss an important strategic marketing lever to connect, influence and establish a durable relationship with customers, in which
insights play a fundamental role: 'customer engagement'. Any single interaction
with a customer can be defined as a form of customer engagement. Therefore,
by 'customer engagement strategy' we mean any form of customer loyalty
programme, lifecycle marketing, CRM or digital experience programme. We
explain how the knowledge gained from customer-driven insights can help the
business to understand customer behaviours, needs, motivations, preferences and
interactions that can be used to make better decisions and to personalize the
customer experience. Some of the most common client concerns and questions
we help to solve relate to whether or not to have a loyalty programme or
whether to change it or embed digital experiences. We believe marketers must
think beyond the scope of their questions and demonstrate loyalty to their
customers with propositions that put their needs first in every interaction with
the company. Successful companies in this space are rewarded by customers not
only with purchases but with their attention, positive word of mouth and long-
term preferences for the brand.

Delivering stand-out customer engagement propositions requires a deep knowledge
of customer wants and needs, an understanding of business goals and objectives and an
approach proven to work. Our approach to helping businesses with customer engagement strategies is called the 'insight to activation process'. It is a roadmap composed of
three macro steps:

1. insights definition
2. engagement strategy development
3. activation plan.

Insights definition

Before embarking on any loyalty programme, CRM strategy or any form of engaging interaction, it is fundamental to gain a deep understanding of the business and its customers. We start from an assessment of current business strategy and objectives to ensure that whatever direction the business wants to go in there is a clear connection with its overarching vision. For example, we run stakeholder interviews across the business to ask key business functions where they believe the business is versus where it wants to go. We then proceed with an analysis of the market context to understand and identify any gaps in where its competitors are and what they are doing in terms of customer engagement. We explore what sort of loyalty propositions are popular and successful in the market, or for example if there are any innovative schemes that are covering emerging customer needs, and where the business we are helping sits in this respect.

Once we have gained this contextual knowledge, it is then possible to run an analytical study of customers' behaviour, their needs and their unique characteristics that will complete the overall picture. We believe that a combination of different analyses and different levels of detail can help to support customer engagement at scale. We frequently see companies invest large amounts of money in expensive market research that does not lead to actionable insights because it does not also take into account actual customer behaviour. Therefore, through a combination of insight layers we can work to understand:

- what customers need and value, in order to understand where to focus investment across the shopping stages/mindsets: discover → shop → buy → reflect
- the customer DNA (see below), to create a customer language and identify unique characteristics
- the customers' current value, their potential one, and winnable potential. One example is measuring how customers spend and visit but also in how many categories they shop. This means identifying and understanding the loyal customers and predicting those that have high potential to become loyal, reduce their loyalty or who are at a high risk of defection.

Let us look at the first two points in more depth since they are significative inputs in understanding customers and giving shape to customer engagement strategies. The first point, understanding customer needs, is a crucial step in shaping a customer engagement strategy. At dunnhumby we approach this with an in-depth and action-oriented package of insights-generating activities that incorporate qualitative research, customer-needs mapping, and behavioural analysis to describe how to better engage customers to increase their frequency, spend, engagement and preference for the brand. We investigate what customers are looking for in a great shopping experience and describe how well every competitor within the market is doing to meet these expectations. By fusing the attitudes collected with traditional marketing research with real customer behaviour (by analysing loyalty card and transactional data), we are able to put the customer at the heart of the strategy definition, define where to play and identify areas to build propositions. This work allows our partners to build a customer engagement contact plan which delivers actions that respond to the identified needs of customers and therefore reduce any risks that might come from ignoring those needs. For example, starting from the fundamental human and emotional needs of customers, such as the desire to be in control and be recognized, we ask if those needs are being fulfilled in the specific retail context and how this differs by individual. Once those needs have been established, we measure how well the retailer is currently satisfying those needs. Moreover, we look at how those needs evolve along the four mindsets/stages of the shopping journey (discover → shop → buy → reflect). Whilst the shopping journey may look linear, customers can jump between mindsets during their shopping journey. With this insight, we can create actionable output in the form of needs-based propositions for priority customer groups and demonstrate how these can support the retailer's initiatives. Similarly, understanding customer DNA is another important phase of research we conduct to better understand customers, their motivations and what attracts them to the brand. Figure 7.14 presents a case study of a French retailer that illustrates how we do this at dunnhumby.

Only by connecting and combining the different layers of insights can we gather the right set of inputs to help businesses to understand where the opportunities are, which groups of customers to invest in and which propositions to develop to best meet the needs of these priority customers whilst delivering against business objectives.

Engagement strategy development

With the insight work completed, it is then possible to move on to the development of an engagement strategy. The insight inputs drive the creation of a final assessment

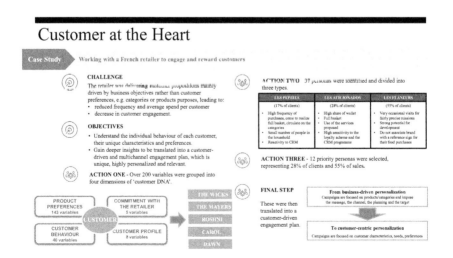

FIGURE 7.14 Case study 1: Customer at the heart

that defines the existing and potential future customer experience. They enable our consultants to validate business requirements by cross-checking business objectives with customer objectives to ensure that both are met and confirming that what the business wants to do responds to the needs of the customer. It is then possible to elaborate some viable options for customer engagement propositions (e.g. programmes to avoid customers from lapsing) which we then workshop with the business. This drives the definition of the characteristics of the customer engagement propositions and, through a customer lens, establishes the customer's reasons to believe in the programme and the designed customer experience. How the programme is structured will determine what it will cost and expected returns.

The development of an engagement strategy proceeds with diagnosis, definition and design:

1. Diagnosis work, which looks at:

   a The current 'as is' programme and touchpoints to be validated against customer and business needs through the results of the insight work.

   b The current competencies (capabilities), evaluated across technology, operations, people, processes, governance and channels to determine if they meet the future orientation. We want to answer questions such as: what technical infrastructure, data and software integration is available?

   c A review of industry benchmarks, case studies and any other relevant research to input in the proposition development; that is, we perform an analysis of competitors to benchmark the business propositions versus the key competitors.

2. Definition work, which looks at:

   a The vision and the proposition to deliver against customer needs and business objectives. This work outlines the future customer experience vision, showing what a customer would experience compared to the present day. For example, we live the experience to see what it feels like for a customer against given customer experience pillars, which means ensuring that what we are developing makes the experience for the customer accessible, relevant, trustable and easy. These are the four key elements that come out again and again over the last 30 years of dunnhumby's customer research and studies on engagement strategies.

   b The development of a 'to be' strategy: the communication approach and any commercialization strategy aimed at involving external partners or suppliers to participate in the programme. We look at the level of personalization, the required data, content, technology, and so on. We develop a strategy and capability roadmap showing the data, science, propositions, technology, resources and organization structure phased over time to realize the vision and opportunities.

    c   The creation of a business case to quantify the financial opportunities in terms of customer potential, campaign uplifts, reach and return on investment (ROI) for a combination of activities.

3.   Design work, which looks at:

    a   The design of the potential future customer experience with a contact strategy, touchpoints, and mechanics across the journey. This means planning the 'who gets what' proposition, the message, the offer, the treatment and the where (channels) and when (timing) across a range of always-on, planned, tactical and triggered communications.

The case study in Figure 7.15 is an example of the work completed for a Canadian retailer where the above described steps were applied.

Activation plan

With the insight and engagement strategy stages complete, this third and final phase of the 'insight to activation' process involves execution, evaluation and optimization, which in turn, activates the feedback loop again to better adjust and evolve any proposition or activity to the customer.

Execution

This is a very sensitive phase, in that often even a brilliant programme or proposition could fail if not supported and communicated properly across the business and to customers. We strongly believe in and support the development of a plan for launching the programme with customers and employees, ensuring the processes are in place to deliver a seamless experience. Again, customer insight plays a fundamental role in this planning

FIGURE 7.15 Case study 2: Customer loyalty design

stage before the programme or proposition goes live in the market – in the development of the right content to use when briefing communication agencies on understanding what customers should think, feel and do; in briefing the company headquarters, stores and employees through trainings; in communicating the programme to suppliers, pre-launching to staff and possibly trialling it with selected groups of customers.

Evaluation

Insights continue to feed into the process through the measurement of the impact of the customer engagement activities. This enables improvements and makes the investment accountable to the business. This is when the business needs to identify the key questions it needs answers to, such as:

1. How much incremental revenue was generated from the campaign?
2. What was the ROI of CRM or digital campaigns?
3. Which customers are most engaged in the CRM and digital channels?
4. What channels, customer segments or tactics are driving the greatest margin and sales uplift?

This process involves the definition of customer and business KPIs to evaluate and the creation of reports reflecting that. Figure 7.16 gives an example of our approach to measurement.

As Figure 7.16 shows, our approach to evaluation is developed across five key elements:

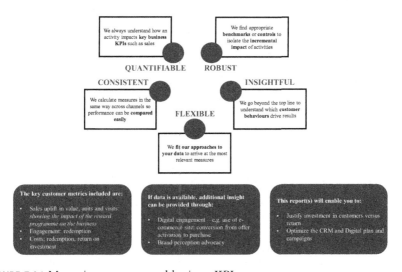

FIGURE 7.16 Measuring customer and business KPIs

- Quantifiable: any customer engagement activity is defined with a set of measurable metrics (KPIs). Therefore, after the execution of the activity, we evaluate the impact for any agreed KPI; for example, the number of sales generated, level of customer participation, and so on.
- Robust: often customer engagement activities run on top of mass commercial plans, during seasonal periods or otherwise can be influenced by several external factors. To evaluate impact by isolating those aspects we find appropriate benchmarks and statistical control groups that allow us to measure the isolated effect of the activity. For example, in an email campaign to a selected group of customers, we remove a small group of control customers (with the exact same profile as those contacted), who will not receive any communication. In this way, we can then measure if there is a sales uplift by comparing the behaviour of the two groups in the campaign and non-campaign (or pre-campaign) period.
- Consistent: this means that measures are calculated in the same way across all the channels that are used as part of the programme so that a comparison of results can be carried out.
- Insightful: the evaluation is not only focused on sales results, which is the end goal; we also look at the components that have driven that result; in particular, the different customer behaviours that have driven it, linking it up with the plan of actions that was activated.
- Flexible: the approach must be flexible and adapt to the business's available data to find the best evaluation solutions (e.g. there might be customer data points that are fundamental to gain a clear view of customer behaviour but that are not available to the business, such as the single customer view which allows one to identify the same customer across the different touchpoints).

Optimization

The evaluation is also very important to optimize future activities. Optimization is possible only after the following steps:

- quantification of the ROI of the programme to drive incremental investment
- repetition of the activities that drive the greatest ROI
- focus on the most valuable shoppers within the programme
- understand how different channels and messages affect the programme engagement
- ROI and long-term shopper value
- test and learn hypotheses through experimental design and evaluation. For example, it is important to test what the right number is of consecutive communications to the different groups of customers, since a loyal customer would have a different approach compared with a less loyal customer, where the frequency of purchase is definitely lower. Another example could be testing a different subject in an email campaign to see which is more effective at driving email-open rates.

Change management

All retailers have a lot of customer and transaction data. Deciding to analyse the data is a big step change but not enough for a company to become data-driven and customer-oriented. We have seen many examples of retailers analysing the data but not taking actions from the insights gained; or again, retailers building impressive plans but not implementing the decisions taken; or lastly, companies who have tried to implement data-driven plans but don't know anything about the level of compliance in-store or about the results achieved. To become data-driven and customer-oriented, every company needs a change management programme which includes the following five steps:

1. use data to better understand customers' needs
2. create and embed a common customer language
3. align people, processes and systems
4. engage 'the army of your people'
5. show tangible change in-store and online.

It is worth noting that most companies do only the first step. Indeed, the first step encompasses everything we have described in this chapter: analyse and understand customer data. In the rest of this chapter, we will describe the steps that follow it.

Create and embed a common customer language

Bringing customer-first to life requires a common language about customers, starting with understanding shopping habits and terms such as price sensitivity, store segments, lifestyles, customer communications, customer promises, and so forth. The challenge is to speak the language to as many people in your organization as often as possible. A good place to start is with a customer-focused purpose and vision. The purpose establishes what a retailer stands for, what its identity is, why and for whom it exists. A retailer should express this both to customers and to employees. The vision should be based on an authoritative knowledge of customers and the market: who the most loyal customers are; their behaviours and preferences; how the company competes to attract and retain them. This should guide decision-making at all levels. One important element of a common customer language is the notion of 'customer promises' – a concept which aims to focus an organization on delivering a consistent customer experience every day from every part of the business. By unifying what really matters to customers into a simple set of commitments, customer promises are measures of how effectively a brand delivers on its brand promises.

Practically speaking, customer promises help to:

• identify opportunities to become closer to the customer and to create a customer-first mindset within your business
• provide a structure for a customer strategy to ensure that all functions and roles can consistently prioritize and take action in ways that are most valuable to customers

- anchor the common customer language in a way that is easy to understand across business functions
- unite all employees (at all levels) to practise customer-first initiatives.

Customer promises should be:

1. priorities that are important to customers, in the voice and language of the customer
2. data-led, based on structured research from the customer up (rather than top-down from management)
3. benchmarked to allow the measurement of progress over time.

Through the customer promises, customers themselves tell businesses where they should start, and what good looks like when they deliver it.

For example, Tesco uses the following promises to make its 'Every little helps' slogan explicit to customers:

- The aisles are clear
- I can get what I want
- The prices are good
- I don't queue
- The staff are great.

Align people, processes and systems

Bringing customer-first to life and inspiring people to do their best for customers will require changes to supporting structures and processes within a company. Of all the steps, this one presents the greatest challenge: to align the business systems around the customer and the data. Customer-first organizations display a single-minded focus on loyal customers – growing this segment and increasing their lifetime value. They set up systems to retain and grow customer loyalty over time. They track, measure and report on customer initiatives such as customer promises or customer-focused KPIs. They implement a process that aligns the customer with strategic plans and reviews, using the customer's perspective as a filter through which to evaluate future plans. Measuring results is a very important step in order to monitor if data-based processes are happening and if they are having an impact on customers. Only through the analysis, understanding and usage of the results can the process last and improve over time.

Becoming customer-first means investing resources in:

1. capabilities to analyse customer behaviour, segment customers and create personalized communications
2. measurement of projects results
3. capabilities that enable organizational change
4. training programmes for employees

5.   performance measures aligned with customer-first initiatives
6.   recognition and rewards for employees who put the strategy into action.

This long-term view transcends the traditional retail instinct to make decisions based on current market trends without considering the lasting impact that these choices – such as matching competitor prices or other 'me too' tactics – may have on customer relationships. The reality is that the best relationships are nurtured. This requires time and investment. By focusing on long-term relationships with loyal customers, retailers can build a path to growth with them at the centre.

Engage 'the army of your people'

All the stakeholders in the company need to be informed, aligned, engaged and inspired. We have seen examples of companies in which the CEO was pushing for the change but middle management was not aligned and had different KPIs. The result? Change didn't happen. At the same time, if middle management believes in customer data but the board of directors don't understand or believe in it, they are unlikely to sign off and fund important projects that use it. Everybody needs to be on-board.

At its best, a customer-first approach is executed in such a deep way that customers can feel a difference in their experience. Winning buy-in through the hearts and minds of staff – from the top executive to the employee who stocks the shelves – builds an incredibly powerful army necessary to deliver the strategy. Sadly, most organizations give front-line employees – the faces of their company – very little trust and authority. Customer-first organizations give front-line employees broad authority to resolve customer needs and extend that power to satisfy customers to most members of staff, in some form. They take advantage of their people to deliver what their most loyal customers want. They invest in training to give employees the tools they need and the permission to use them. They share data to make everyone in the company aware of what is important to customers, tailoring the information to be used by people according to their roles (see Table 7.3). Behaviour change in organizations doesn't happen overnight. Employees have to be engaged via training which teaches examples of good customer judgment. Senior management must be upskilled in leadership behaviours of empathy, dignity and respect for both employees and customers. Aligned behaviours should be rewarded. Everyone in the business should understand they have 'ownership' of the customer.

TABLE 7.3 Example of change in employees' KPIs

Before	After
Executive compensation is tied exclusively to sales and margin	Customer KPIs contribute 33% to compensation bonuses
Merchandising team target is % margin	Target driving $ margin and/or profit
Assortment rationalized to drive % margin by category	Optimized to drive visits and sales of entire store
Pricing strategy focuses on competitiveness	Focus on price perception

Show tangible change in-store and online

Customer data may be used to operate loyalty programmes but there is less evidence that this data is being used to support changes in the shopping experience. Ranging, assortment, layouts, pricing, promotions, customer service – all these elements that make up the shopping experience should be informed by data from loyal customers to ensure that the retailer is delivering what its best customers seek. And as we said above, after execution, all projects should be measured to find out answers to the important questions the business must ask: 'Did it happen? Did it work?' The first question is about compliance. Very often, decisions are taken at the centre but not implemented properly: the centre, for instance, may recommend a new planogram for a certain category but this may be implemented only in a few stores; new prices rules may be introduced and formalized but category managers may try to bypass some of them to recover margin. Compliance is more automated and more measurable online but very often a real challenge in-store, particularly for cooperative or franchising businesses where the centre has less ownership and control. Measuring compliance is fundamental to confirming that change is happening in-store. Then, of course, there is the measurement of KPIs (sales, customer penetration, items per customer) to understand if it worked for the benefit of customers and of the retailer.

To conclude this chapter, then, it is clear to us that efforts to build customer loyalty and grow sales often fail to produce meaningful results for three key reasons:

1. First, loyalty is not about customers being loyal to the retailer – it's about the retailer acting loyally to its customers.
2. Loyalty is not just a programme – it's an approach that puts the customer first in all the decisions a retailer makes.
3. Loyalty is not just about CRM – it's about the store and how the retailer interacts with its customers.

By inviting, listening and responding to customer feedback, retailers can earn the emotional loyalty of their customers. They feel that the retailer cares about them and their needs. Such actions place the customer in the role of a strategic partner. They can share their perspectives and create a two-way conversation. And retailers can embed this idea in their customer interactions to further deepen the relationship.

References

Ciancio, D. (2017) *5 Steps to Becoming a Customer-First Business*. London: dunnhumby.

Ruttenberg, R. (2016) *Re-inventing Category Management – Driving Growth with Category Leadership*. London: dunnhumby.

8

LOYALTY IN THE OMNICHANNEL ENVIRONMENT

Cristina Ziliani and Marco Ieva

The loyalty-oriented organization

Customer loyalty is the declared goal of marketing strategies today: corporate presentations and annual reports invariably mention the firm's commitment to retention. However, beyond public declarations, *how does a company change when it truly commits to building loyalty?* We at the Loyalty Observatory have tried for many years to answer this question by analysing a variety of aspects related to a firms' adoption of a customer relationship orientation. Since 2012,[1] we have witnessed several changes that have taken place within companies in Italy which we interpret as signs of an advancing loyalty culture. This section describes those changes. We hope the evidence presented will inspire academic research and feedback from practitioners.

Relationship orientation

In academic literature, a company's customer relationship orientation is measured by means of the customer relationship orientation scale (see Jayachandran et al.,

1 The Loyalty Observatory conducted an online survey between June and September 2018 on 'The Market for Loyalty Management Products and Services' among vendors and brands in Italy, retrieving over 500 responses. Three hundred and sixty-three valid questionnaires were analysed, 196 completed by vendors of loyalty management products and services and 167 by brands in sectors such as retail, FMCG and other services that purchase said products and services from vendors. This chapter presents the results from this survey and discusses them in light of previous work conducted by the Observatory, specifically surveys carried out in Italy in 2017 on omnichannel loyalty, 2016 on CEM, 2015 on CRM and 2012 on the state of loyalty management. The 2012 survey is available (in Italian) online: see Osservatorio Fedeltà UniPR (2012). The 2015, 2016 and 2017 surveys are the subjects of white papers (in Italian) available at the Observatory website www.osservatoriofedelta.it. The 2018 survey and the 2019 international study (see note 2) are discussed in this book for the first time.

2005). This scale reflects the cultural propensity of an organization to undertake customer relationship management (CRM), and, in view of the evolution of loyalty management towards CRM that we have discussed in this book, we consider it particularly useful for reflecting the cultural alignment of an organization with its loyalty management goals. The scale captures four aspects: (1) the level of priority assigned to retaining customers by the company; (2) the actions targeting employees in order to encourage them to focus on customer relationships; (3) the fact that customer relationships are considered a valuable asset; (4) senior management's commitment to emphasizing the importance of customer relationships. These items are measured on a scale of 1 to 7.

We employed this scale in the 2012 and 2018 surveys. The mean value of the surveyed organizations' customer relationship orientation was 5 and 6 respectively. Despite the limitations inherent in the samples of the two surveys, it is probably a sign that a relationship culture is, on the whole, advancing. However, the reality is composed of very different patterns. For example, in 2018 one company out of four scored below 5, and differences existed across different industries.

Dedicated function for loyalty

A second aspect of loyalty orientation we studied was how companies assign responsibility internally for the deployment of retention strategies. To organize for retention, firms might introduce to their organizational structure a specific function that champions loyalty strategies. Alternatively, they might consider loyalty an overarching goal for the organization with no specific function in charge. Interestingly, a correlation appears to exist between loyalty orientation and the organizational solution designed by the company. We discovered that when a specific function devoted to loyalty is present, the firm tends to score higher along the relationship orientation scale dimensions. This emerged consistently in our 2012 and 2018 surveys. It seems, therefore, that in order to manage loyalty effectively, a dedicated function is an appropriate solution. However, in 2018, only one firm out of three chose this option, representing no change from the 2012 survey. Marked differences did persist among industries: a function dedicated to loyalty was most common in services and retail, but it was an exception in manufacturing.

Use of loyalty metrics

The third feature of a firm's loyalty orientation is the use of loyalty metrics to control the performance of marketing efforts to achieve retention. In the 2018 survey, only half of the surveyed companies systematically evaluated the performance of their loyalty strategies: no change from 2012. Understandably, the systematic use of loyalty metrics was associated with the presence of a loyalty-dedicated function within a firm's structure. The use of metrics differed across industries: two companies out of three in services and supermarket retailing used them, whereas only one in three in manufacturing did so. For those companies that did use metrics to evaluate retention strategies, a variety of solutions emerged, the most popular of which are not really loyalty measures per se (Figure 8.1).

The most cited metric was sales, hardly a measure of retention, while a 'proper' loyalty metric such as retention rate was calculated by only half of the surveyed firms. Other well-known measures such as customer lifetime value and RFM (recency, frequency, monetary) value were even less frequent. As mentioned in Chapter 1, different industries traditionally favour some metrics over others: for example, brand awareness is central for manufacturers of consumer goods but almost non-existent elsewhere, and the reverse is true of customer satisfaction, which is common in retail and other services. Again, we found that a correlation existed between the frequent use of loyalty metrics and the existence of a dedicated loyalty function within the organization: 65% of firms with a loyalty function and 45% of firms without one monitored loyalty metrics – a significant difference.

Investment in loyalty management and CRM

How far a firm invests in loyalty management is another significant indicator of its loyalty orientation. While absolute values are hardly significant, as they differ greatly across industry and company size, it is interesting to consider the relative weight of loyalty marketing expenditure on the total marketing budget. In our 2018 survey, approximately half (47%) of the marketing budget was invested in retention activities. There has been steady progress over the years, as our recurrent surveys on this subject testify: for example, with specific reference to companies in the retail industry, this percentage was 30%, 36% and 43% respectively in 2011, 2012 and 2018.

FIGURE 8.1 Adoption of loyalty metrics

Retention strategies, however, come in different forms. As we described in Chapter 2, loyalty strategies coincided with loyalty programmes 30 years ago – that is, with 'mass, undifferentiated marketing efforts' – and gradually shifted to segmented and personalized activities as CRM came to dominate the scene. We can observe such an evolution of loyalty management in the relative weight of investment in undifferentiated versus targeted retention activities. We asked respondents to account for the relative weight of the two categories of retention activities on the marketing budget. In the 2018 survey, firms invested on average 26% of their marketing budget in undifferentiated loyalty-building activities and 21% for targeted ones (making up the aforementioned 47% of the marketing budget). The retail sector is the best evidence of the shift to CRM activities. Here, targeted loyalty activities have scaled up from one-eighth of the loyalty budget in 2011 to one-third in 2014 to half in 2018 – although it should be noted that these are average values across the industry. Cluster analyses conducted over the period consistently depict a varied landscape in which three groups of retail firms can be identified: laggards, which invest in loyalty programmes but not in CRM; pioneers, which dedicate a major part of their budget to personalized actions; and an intermediate group which invests in both types of loyalty activities. A similar tripolar situation can be found in other industries too.

Data collection, integration and sharing

As loyalty management turns into CRM, and more recently, CEM, a key feature of loyalty-oriented organizations now is the systematic collection of individual customer data. These days, the vast majority of companies have some form of customer database (90% in the 2018 survey). Companies no longer differ insofar as they all collect data, but do diverge in terms of what types of customer data they maintain in their databases, how far they integrate, or are able to, data from various sources and touchpoints, and how far they share it within their organization across departments and hierarchical levels. A company's proficiency in these things is not sufficient to infer its success at managing loyalty. But they are necessary conditions for any retention orientation: without a cross-channel and integrated – at least, partially – view of the customer, the benefits of loyalty cannot be reaped in full.

We found that, across industries, customer databases contained six categories of data on average. Demographics, geo-demographics, transactional data and loyalty programme participation data were the most common, while companies still struggled to align offline and online customer behaviour. In fact, customer profiles were enriched with website visits and online navigation information only in 38% of cases, and 26% reported the inclusion of customers' social media information. We believe that with more firms resorting to new types of vendors in the market for loyalty management services – such as digital agencies, digital engagement and word-of-mouth platforms, discussed in the final section of this chapter – there will be progress made towards a more integrated picture of customer behaviour across touchpoints.

A firm's capacity for information integration can be measured by employing the corresponding part of the scale cited by Jayachandran et al. (2005). It measures multiple aspects, specifically: the firm's ability (a) to integrate information from customer-facing functions (e.g. marketing, sales and customer services); (b) to integrate information from different communication channels and touchpoints (e.g. email, website, telephone and personal contact); (c) to integrate internal customer information with external sources; (d) to merge information collected from various sources for each customer. We employed the scale in two surveys – 2016 and 2018 – and, with the caution dictated by the partial overlap of the two samples, we can say that we saw progress, with the exception of the integration of internal and external sources. Progress will also be dictated by the priority that firms today assign to the tracking of their customers via a digital ID (or digital loyalty card) across online and offline touchpoints. With consumers now encountering, over the course of three months, an average of ten touchpoints for their main supermarket, seven for their main bank and eight for their mobile phone service provider, integration is challenging as well as needed (Osservatorio Fedeltà, 2017).

For customer information to turn into insight that, in turn, fertilizes loyalty management and CEM, we not only need information capture and integration but also access; that is, dissemination throughout the company to the relevant employees and decision-makers. In 2016 we conducted a survey that included an analysis of this phenomenon by means of an adapted version of the information access scale presented by Jayachandran et al. (2005): one firm out of ten declared that customer insight (derived from touchpoints) circulated across different functions and different hierarchical levels. When filtered for the services industry, the proportion was one company out of five.

Loyalty programmes and other tools

Loyalty management tools such as loyalty programmes and customer clubs are no longer the main indicator of a firm's loyalty orientation. However, any loyalty strategy employs tools of some sort. We recurrently survey marketers on the loyalty tools they use and ask them to assess their performance. Marketers responded to our 2018 survey by pointing at loyalty programmes as the most effective loyalty management tool, especially points-based or cashback ones. Coupons received the same high rating. If we consider that previous research the Observatory ran on the Nielsen consumer panel testified that loyalty programmes and coupons have the highest penetration within the customer base, we better understand marketers' perception of their effectiveness (Osservatorio Fedeltà, 2017). Tangible goods employed as rewards for retention activities also rated highly on effectiveness. Print, however, was surpassed by digital: direct emailing (DEM) scored higher than direct mail and customer magazines. Top-rated loyalty tools differed by sector: fast-moving consumer goods (FMCG) manufacturers preferred coupons, then special events and DEM, while supermarkets saw loyalty programmes and coupons as the best options, and non-food retail favoured loyalty programmes, DEM and coupons.

Loyalty programmes are adopted by 62% of Italian firms according to our 2018 survey, a figure that is in line with findings from the Observatory's 2019 international analysis of the top 100 brands which found that:[2]

- 66% of brands had a loyalty programme (81% of retail brands, 46% of other brands)
- 85% of programmes were the stand-alone type, described in Chapter 2 (80% retail, 90% other)
- 86% were multichannel, i.e. employed more than one type of media for customer interaction (92% retail, 79% other)
- 64% were points-based (61% retail, 68% other)
- 52% included a means of payment (54% retail, 37% other)
- 38% offered in-app offers and coupons
- 8% were fee-based.

In general, loyalty programmes worldwide increasingly reward customers for non-shopping behaviours such as sharing or commenting on brand-related content on social media. They reward customers for taking surveys and sharing information that ultimately enables the brand to obtain richer insight. Loyalty activities personalize the customer experience at various touchpoints by means of data collected from the customer's previous activities.

Italian loyalty programmes are still lagging behind in terms of these last features. When asked about the future directions of their loyalty strategy, however, nearly 50% of companies surveyed in 2018 declared they will make changes to their

---

2 Desk research was conducted on the top 50 retailers in the world (source: Deloitte's Global Powers of Retailing 2018) and top 50 brands (source: Interbrand's Best Global Brands 2018). The sample was complemented with seven notable loyalty programme cases drawn from industry sources: Colloquy Loyalty Census 2017, eMarketer, Total Retail, HH Global, CMO Council, Bond and Codebroker. After excluding cases where an insufficient information had been collected, 90 companies and their loyalty programmes formed the final object of analysis. We are deeply grateful to Jessica Borsi, a junior researcher with the Observatory in 2018, who performed the data collection and analysis. We alone are responsible for mistakes and omissions. The complete list of companies follows (ordered as per the two mentioned rankings). (1) Retail: Walmart, Costco, Kroger, Lidl, Walgreens, Amazon, Home Depot, Aldi, Carrefour, CVS Specialty, Tesco, Aeon, Target, Stop & Shop, Lowe's, Metro Cash & Carry, Safeway, Auchan, Edeka, 7-Eleven, Coles, Rewe, Woolworths, Géant Casino, Centre Leclerc, Best Buy, IKEA, JD.com, Publix, Real Canadian Superstore, Sainsbury's, T.K. Maxx, Intermarché, Apple, Sephora, Rite Aid, Macy's, Zara, MM Migros, Lotte Department Store, H-E-B, H&M, Coop, Suning, Kmart, Dollar General, Mercadona, Morrisons, Dollar Tree, Super U. (2) Brands: Apple, Google, Amazon, Microsoft, Coca-Cola, Samsung, Toyota, Mercedes-Benz, Facebook, McDonald's, Intel, IBM, BMW, Disney, Cisco, GE, Nike, Louis Vuitton, Oracle, Honda, SAP, Pepsi, Chanel, American Express, Zara, J.P. Morgan, IKEA, Gillette, UPS, H&M, Pampers, Hermès, Budweiser, Accenture, Ford, Hyundai, Nescafé, eBay, Gucci, Nissan, Volkswagen, Audi, Philips, Goldman Sachs, Citi, HSBC, AXA, L'Oréal, Allianz, Adidas. Additional Cases: Sephora, Nordstrom, Hilton Honors, Starbucks, Panera Bread, American Airlines, Delta.

loyalty strategy in the direction of improving the customer experience, by means of more personalization and customer recognition across touchpoints. One in three said they will invest to make better customer insight available across the organization. Our analysis of this point – how firms evolve their loyalty management to embrace CEM across touchpoints – provides the subject of the next section.

CEM in the omnichannel environment

From 1980 to the end of the twentieth century, managing loyalty basically meant running a loyalty programme. Since 2000, companies have turned to the 'invisible' advantages of loyalty schemes – the insight they unlock and its use for targeted marketing activities. In a word, loyalty management turned into CRM. Companies in Italy today still seem to be busy transforming their loyalty management approach into CRM. This is consistent with our findings from 2015, when an Observatory study on the state of CRM in the country showed that only 30% of firms regarded themselves as advanced in the implementation of CRM (Osservatorio Fedeltà, 2016).[3] The new frontiers of technology for loyalty are of still limited interest to managers. Content marketing, content automation, chatbots, video and text analytics are among the applications of artificial intelligence (AI) that can bring personalization to loyalty-building marketing activities and impact the customer experience. However, as recently as 2018, only a handful of Italian companies seemed aware of this: Figure 8.2 presents the loyalty management technologies that brands were most interested in at the time.[4]

Despite these statistics, we believe that in 2019 we are entering a new phase in which loyalty management is identified with the design and management of a quality customer experience. For a brand today, making a customer loyal means, first of all, ensuring they encounter it along their journey across a variety of touchpoints, from those that are well established such as the physical store to those that have only recently been developed and made widely available such as digital wallets and chatbots. What we know from the literature (see Jain, Aagja and Bagdare, 2017) is that when an encounter with the brand is relevant, engaging, personalized, consistent with the stage of the journey or personal situation of the customer, when it contributes to a simple, convenient and

---

3   The study employed the CRM processes evaluation scale by Reinartz, Krafft and Hoyer (2004), which requires respondents to rate on a scale from 1 to 7 their agreement with a comprehensive list of 39 statements that cover the eight broad areas CRM is concerned with: prospecting, acquisition, current customer measurement, retention, cross-selling and upselling, reactivation, referral, termination. A cluster analysis run on respondents retrieved two groups: CRM best-in-class (around 30% of the sample) and laggards (70%). See Osservatorio Fedeltà (2015).

4   We adopted the classification of technologies for loyalty presented in the first Loyalty360 study on the 'State of the Loyalty Industry'. See https://loyalty360.org/content-gallery/loyalty360-research/loyalty-landscape for the 2019 edition of the study. At the time of writing, the previous edition was no longer available online.

Percentage of companies interested in loyalty tool

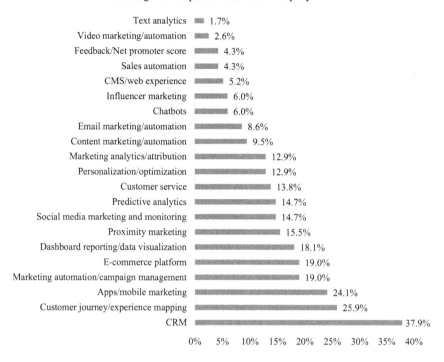

FIGURE 8.2 Tools and technologies for loyalty of interest to marketers in Italy

pleasant journey, saves effort, solves a problem or pain point, then this may turn into a quality experience that will, in turn, make the customer loyal.

Managing loyalty today ought to coincide with managing the customer experience. The CEM framework has been proposed as a firm-wide management approach to designing the customer experience with the final goal of achieving long-term customer loyalty by designing and continually renewing touchpoint journeys (Homburg, Jozić and Kuehnl, 2017) This, in turn, takes the form of designing (or redesigning) touchpoints in a way that maximizes the coordination among them, in order to provide a seamless experience that is flexible depending on the situation. Thematic cohesion, consistency, context sensitivity and connectivity of touchpoints all contribute to the goal. The focus on touchpoints is therefore central to the cultural mindset for CEM: specifically, the orientation should be one that focuses on the understanding that touchpoint journeys across pre-purchase, purchase and post-purchase stages are key factors that should be considered in decision-making. This also entails that in order to align touchpoints and provide a seamless experience, cooperation with partners is necessary, in that many touchpoints are not directly owned and controlled by the brand itself, but by third parties. Brands need to accept that other players – many of them new – have a meaningful role to play in their customers' shopping journeys. One only need consider the role of aggregators and comparison platforms in the journeys of customers purchasing travel deals or hotel rooms, or eating in restaurants. Or the promotional intermediaries we described in Chapter 2: flash sales websites, group deals, cashback apps, payment wallets – they all impact upon the user's experience of brands. Similarly, loyalty programmes are powerful touchpoints that can reach wide segments of the population.

Customer journeys have become increasingly complex and develop across dozens of different online and offline touchpoints. We mentioned earlier that our research has shown, for example, that over three months, the average customer is exposed to eight different touchpoints for his telephone service provider, seven for his bank and ten for his supermarket (Osservatorio Fedeltà, 2017). Brands need to map their customer journeys in order to design interventions appropriately. Without such mapping, it is hard to see how they can effectively leverage the benefits touchpoints have to offer in enhancing the customer experience and helping to create loyal customers.

Creating a seamless experience is not the only approach to developing a differentiated, quality customer experience. The characteristics of the majority of today's consumers – well-informed, always online, time-poor, attention-limited, used to endless choice, and demanding of the best quality or service at the best price – are driving brands to try and win their preferences by curating shopping experiences that are relevant, engaging, personalized, easy, convenient and responsive to their requests. Most of these strategies – from curating and presenting an assortment of products designed on customer specific preferences such as is the case with Stitch Fix, to reacting to customer requests 24/7 at any touchpoint by picking up the dialogue from where it had left off in the previous interaction – are all based on the availability of a 360-degree picture of that customer, available through channels and actionable at all times. In other words, curating a quality experience today increasingly entails connecting one or more channels in such a way that the customer does not experience the existence of different channels at all, but lives a single, unified experience with the company. This is where CEM meets omnichannel management.

Omnichannel management has been defined as 'the synergetic management of the numerous available channels and customer touchpoints, in such a way that the customer experience across channels and the performance over channels is optimized' (Verhoef, Kannan, and Inman, 2015, p. 176). Companies are developing services and solutions to 'weave' channels together for customers: such services take the form, for example, of click & collect, digital loyalty cards, shopping baskets and wish lists available through channels. Think also of the possibility to click & reserve online an appointment in store for personal shopping assistance, or to have access to your complete purchase history – online and offline – via a tablet in store or by logging in to your personal area on the brand website, not to mention services that are becoming commonplace such as returning in-store purchases made online or checking online the in-store availability of a specific product and reserving it for inspection for a period of time.

Huré, Picot-Coupey and Michaud-Trévinal (2017) have compiled an exhaustive list of what they call 'interweaving' solutions, aimed at linking physical and digital touchpoints in order to provide a seamless experience to customers. With specific attention to retailing, an industry that faces major opportunities and challenges as far as omnichannel is concerned, they identified 15 interweaving solutions that can be grouped in two categories: 'web/mobile-to-store', if they encourage the online customer to proceed to the physical touchpoint (the store), and 'store-to-web/mobile' if they drive in-store visitors to the brand's online touchpoints. They are displayed in Tables 8.1 and 8.2.

Our 2019 analysis of the top 100 international brands' loyalty strategies showed that, as far as the above interweaving solutions are concerned:

- 83% offer a store locator feature on their websites
- 75% enable persistent shopping basket
- 67% have wish list features
- 55% offer click & collect service
- 29% allow stock availability check
- 20% have load-to-card or load-to-account coupons and offers
- 9% allow online appointment setting (e.g. Walgreens, Sephora, Macy's, BMW, HSBC, Nordstrom)
- 4% allow click & reserve (only Walmart, Kmart and Nordstrom).

In 2017 we conducted research to gauge the level of interest of Italian brands in these solutions, specifically how they rated them for their loyalty-building potential and how far they had been able to implement them. We repeated the analysis in 2018. Among the surveyed companies in 2017, 43% rated 'drive-to-store' omnichannel solutions (Table 8.1) as very important for loyalty, but only 20% thought the same of 'drive-to-web' solutions (Table 8.2).

Beyond the above average results, however, a cluster analysis of respondents in 2017 outlined three groups of companies. The largest cluster was labelled 'drive-to-store' (55% of the sample). These firms felt the need to adopt omnichannel solutions for loyalty. Nearly two-thirds of them (64%) considered drive-to-store solutions as essential and had implemented them by leveraging their existing IT infrastructure (many retailers were in this cluster): however, only 18% of them saw drive-to-web solutions as essential. 'Pessimists' (35% of total) were insensitive to their customers' omnichannel needs and to the moves of competitors in that direction. They did not see interweaving solutions as relevant to loyalty. Last but not least, 10% of respondents belonged to the 'omnichannel' cluster. These brands already had in place several interweaving solutions, driven by customer demand and delivered by their mastering of the existing IT infrastructure. Significantly, these firms were successful in tracking customers across channels by means of digital loyalty cards and customer IDs. A year later, in 2018, the number of firms that rated drive-to-web as essential to loyalty management had risen from 20% to 45%, driven mainly by FMCG brands.

TABLE 8.1 Web/mobile-to-store interweaving solutions

Interweaving solutions	Advantages
Wish list: collection of desired products saved by customers to their user account	Enables consumers to remember desired products and find them in the store
Click & collect: associates an online order with the in-store collection of products	Enables consumers to combine some advantages of online shopping with the convenience of collecting the item in a chosen location (in-store or at a chosen point of collection)
Persistent shopping basket: retains products in a customer's shopping cart beyond one visit in order to pick up where they left off when they return	When logged in, persistent shopping carts follow a user across devices. Saving user sessions in any fashion improves their shopping experience by providing continuity and reduces cart abandonment
Store locator: service to find on a website or mobile app the closest physical store or a specific store	Helps a consumer find a physical store and/or get driving directions. Encourages website visitors or application users to patronize physical stores in order to convert them into clients
Promotion associated with an online purchase: provides the customer money-off coupons only valid in store after an online or mobile visit	Improves purchases from a mix of customers and introduces the physical store to online customers
Local search engine optimization (SEO): provides results that are relevant to a searcher based on location	Generates qualified traffic to physical stores from location-based search
Click & reserve: allows pre-booking products online without paying for them (≠ *in-store pick-up*)	Enables looking at, touching, smelling and even trying the product before deciding to buy (or not) the product. Secures product availability when coming to the store. Enables customers to benefit from the sales assistant's advice
Stock availability: checks the in-store product availability	Enables consumers to check the in-store product availability before arrival at the store. Saves consumers from fruitless shopping trips and encourages them to go to the store in order to look at, touch, smell and try the product
Online appointment: allows an appointment to be made with a sales manager for a personalized service	Assures consumers of a sales assistant's availability when they arrive at the physical store. Saves fruitless trips to stores and reduces waiting time
Mobile coupons based on geolocation: sends money-off coupons to a potential customer's mobile phone when they are close to the store	Attracts consumers in store, enables them to discover a retailer, multiple contacts with the brand, and enables them to live an in-store shopping experience

Source: adapted from Huré, Picot-Coupey and Michaud-Trévinal (2017).

In the 2018 survey we asked marketers to rank interweaving omnichannel solutions from 1 to 7 in terms of their potential for building loyalty. Figure 8.3 shows the results. The fact that the deployment of a customer ID/digital loyalty card across channels to track the customer across touchpoints had the highest rating (5.1) is testimony to the

TABLE 8.2 Store-to-web/mobile interweaving solutions

Interweaving solutions	Interest
Digitalized loyalty card/customer ID: synchronizes the customer account across touchpoints	Secures the purchases and enables consumers to benefit from personalized advice, thanks to an account history
Virtual catalogue: enables the visualization of all the brand's listed items, particularly those which are not available in the store but can be ordered	Brings in-store shoppers to the website during a shopping experience. Enables them to find the expected item. The virtual catalogue compensates the boundaries of a physical store in terms of assortment size
Promotion associated with a physical store purchase: provides customers money-off coupons only valid online after a visit to the physical store	Improves purchases from multichannel customers and introduces the website to off-line customers
Product tracking or ordering on mobile/tablet: enables customers to order the product from another touchpoint if out of stock; quickly locates the desired product in another (physical or digital) touchpoint	Enables access to stock, whatever the touchpoint, and emphasizes the value of other touchpoints
Persistent shopping basket: saves an in-store selection of products in order to find them again whatever the touchpoint	Enables the consumer to patronize multiple touchpoints sequentially or simultaneously without losing information

Source: adapted from Huré, Picot-Coupey and Michaud-Trévinal (2017)

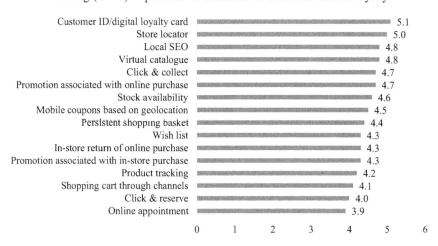

Rating (1 to 7) of potential of omnichannel solutions to build loyalty

Customer ID/digital loyalty card	5.1
Store locator	5.0
Local SEO	4.8
Virtual catalogue	4.8
Click & collect	4.7
Promotion associated with online purchase	4.7
Stock availability	4.6
Mobile coupons based on geolocation	4.5
Persistent shopping basket	4.4
Wish list	4.3
In-store return of online purchase	4.3
Promotion associated with in-store purchase	4.3
Product tracking	4.2
Shopping cart through channels	4.1
Click & reserve	4.0
Online appointment	3.9

FIGURE 8.3 Perceived potential of omnichannel solutions

growing awareness of the need to embrace omnichannel solutions to improve the customer experience and build loyalty. Store locators and local SEO emerge as the two most important drive-to-store services to offer online, while the most crucial drive-to-web feature is a virtual catalogue available in store.

We believe that loyalty management, CEM and omnichannel strategies will converge: they share the aim of making customers loyal by having them live positive, quality experiences seamlessly across touchpoints. To do so, they share the same steps to:

- build a brand presence at relevant touchpoints
- capture customer data at each touchpoint
- integrate touchpoint and CRM data
- derive customer insight and share it across the organization and with partners to inform strategic decision-making and add value to the customer journey.

With the majority of firms still in the CRM phase of loyalty management, and in the process of trying to understand how to evolve their marketing strategies in the direction of an omnichannel customer experience, there is the danger that they decide to start from scratch and thus ignore the wealth of tools and expertise they already possess in the form of their loyalty programme (and the customer insight it generates) and the skilled personnel that run it. Every day we see firms setting up working groups devoted to developing specific interweaving solutions (e.g. click & collect, involving IT, logistics, digital marketing, etc.) but only marginally involving people from CRM or loyalty programme management functions. This is a mistake for many reasons, not least of which is the fact that personnel responsible for managing a loyalty programme are likely to possess a cultural mindset oriented towards relationship, personalization and customer information management, which, as we discussed in Chapter 6, is regarded as a precondition for CEM to take root.

Across industries, the loyalty programme is in fact the most important touchpoint for systematically collecting individual customer data (Osservatorio Fedeltà, 2017). It is present in over 60% of firms. It connects different touchpoints: for example, in our 2019 international survey of the top 100 brands, 86% of programmes employed more than one type of media for customer interaction and 78% allowed for point collection both off and online, having solved, at least to a certain degree, the riddle of customer tracking across touchpoints. Omnichannel loyalty programmes enable firms to enrol new members across digital touchpoints before, during and after the in-store, physical interaction. At the same time, they allow members to freely move within an identified space where each activity before, during and after purchase has more value since it is more relevant or convenient (or simply possible) to perform for the member than it would be if they were outside such a space.

The loyalty programme is a valid platform to test improvements to the customer experience by adding value to it: once a customer is identified as a programme member, special services can be reserved to them and their journey tailored as appropriate. New services that solve pain points and enhance the customer experience are being introduced, tested and reserved for programme members by companies across a variety of industries. Hilton Honors and Marriott Rewards have done this with mobile check-in, room choice, door-unlocking functions and room service booking. Sephora's loyalty scheme members have access to click & reserve, online appointment booking and a make-up app called Virtual Artist which uses facial recognition to empower customers to 'try on' products anywhere. Indeed, in the clothing industry, all of the interweaving solutions discussed here have been launched in some guise and in many cases reserved to programme members only.

Thanks to developments in AI software, more will follow, such as image or voice searching of product catalogues and the advanced personalization of recommendations. Vendors of technologies for e-commerce, marketing automation, analytics and customer experience are looking at loyalty managers and loyalty programmes as a potential new market for their solutions. As their products are adopted, they will contribute to the evolution of loyalty management and expand the market for loyalty management products and services (LMPS).

The evolving market for LMPS

The market for loyalty management services is predicted to grow at a steady pace in the coming years. Estimated at between $1.68 and $1.99 billion in 2017, that figure is predicted to grow to $5.24–6.95 billion in 2023 according to some sources (see MarketsandMarkets, 2017; Sonawane, 2017; Orbis Research, 2018). In any case, a compound annual growth rate of about 20% is estimated (Hilbert, 2019). This is an attractive outlook for an industry that has been evolving quickly in the past 30 years, following the introduction of CRM, e-commerce, and new digital devices and touchpoints, in tandem with the shift of loyalty practices from loyalty programmes towards CEM. But it prompts a question: what is comprised under the name of 'Market for Loyalty Management'? And what will be there in the future?

Loyalty management requires organizations to plan, execute and orchestrate a variety of diverse activities: from designing the loyalty strategy, to translating it into a programme with rules and rewards (if a formalized loyalty programme), to managing the data flows and data analysis, devising CRM activities, managing communication campaigns across touchpoints, capturing individual customer feedback, and more. Elaborating on a classification suggested by Forrester (see Collins, 2017, p. 4), the business activities required for loyalty management can be classified in three broad groups:

- *Loyalty strategy.* To earn customer loyalty, companies need an approach that's rooted in customer understanding. Loyalty strategy development is defined as the research, planning, and design of loyalty strategies, initiatives and programmes. Specific capabilities include consumer market research, financial modelling, programme design, and loyalty measurement and analytics frameworks.

- *Loyalty management (strictly speaking).* To effectively track, recognize and reward loyal customers, companies need tools and technical expertise to manage the coordination of data, insights and business rules. Loyalty management strictly speaking is the back-end orchestration of loyalty initiatives and programmes. Specific capabilities include currency management, data management, business rules definition and management, integration, call centre management and rewards fulfilment.
- *Loyalty communication.* To deliver contextually relevant content to loyal customers, companies need flexible and integrated marketing tools. Loyalty communication is the execution of loyalty initiatives across channels. Specific capabilities include campaign management, content creation and consistent message delivery across channels.

Analyses of the loyalty management market are available for the US, North America, Germany and worldwide. The Italian loyalty management market might not be of specific interest to the international readership of this book, despite its size (the third-largest European economy and consumer goods market); however, we believe it is worthwhile to present some results from the study we conducted in 2018 on a sample of 250 suppliers of products and services for loyalty management, in which 196 valid questionnaires were analysed.

First, we put such findings in perspective with the responses from clients of loyalty management services vendors who participated in our 2018 survey, cited in the opening section of this chapter. Italian marketers, across industries, invested on average 42% of the loyalty management budget for the services and products of a variety of LMPS vendors. They employed on average six different types of LMPS vendors. We created a comprehensive list of 16 LMPS vendor categories, drawing from analyses by Forrester Research (see Collins, 2016) and Loyalty360 (see note 4) of the loyalty management services market and adding businesses who provide loyalty-related services in Italy, such as suppliers of rewards, premiums and gifts, that are not covered by international reports but play a major role in our country. We tested this list with our survey of vendors, who agreed it accurately represented the market. The different types of suppliers of LMPS are identified in Figure 8.4, where the percentage indicates the level of penetration among the surveyed clients.

As far as vendor responses are concerned, an interesting picture of the market emerged. The average company size was relatively small: 53% of vendors counted less than 20 employees, 28% between 21 and 100 employees and only 19% exceeded 100 employees. Ten years ago, 50% of the players in the market did not exist and 25% have entered the market only in the past five years: proof of the rapid evolution of loyalty management. Even where companies had been in the market for longer, on average they estimated to have been operating in the 'loyalty business' for no more than three years.

Some companies, such as consultancy services or communication agencies, indicated that loyalty management activities were only a marginal part of their offer. When asked to assess on a scale from 1 to 7 if loyalty management was their 'core business' as opposed to 'only one of the areas of application of our products

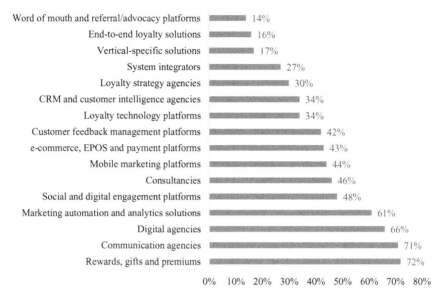

Note: EPOS – electronic point-of-sale

FIGURE 8.4 Types of LMPS supplier in Italy

and services', 22% selected the former, 36% the latter and the remainder settled for an intermediate position. This gives us a hint of the permeability of the market by new entrants. Companies were asked to state which of the above-mentioned three areas of loyalty management needs they catered for: 21% said they focused primarily on loyalty strategy, 55% on loyalty management strictly speaking and 24% on loyalty communication.

Although the surveyed companies complied with our request to identify themselves with one of the specific supplier types we listed, 70% stated that they feel they cover at least two types. Moreover, 40% said they provide DEM, loyalty programmes, coupons and rewards as part of their core offering. In other words, there was a high degree of overlap across the offerings of the various players. We conducted further research into this overlap. To link each of the three groups of loyalty management activities mentioned above (loyalty strategy, loyalty management and loyalty communication) with each of the 16 supplier types, three logistic regression models were run. In each model, the likelihood of belonging to one of the three broad areas was predicted with the different supplier types employed as independent variables. The three models revealed no issues in terms of multicollinearity. The analysis revealed that there are significant positive or negative associations between the choice of a supplier type and the likelihood of belonging to one of the three broad areas of loyalty management – the results are illustrated in Figure 8.5.

FIGURE 8.5 Groupings of supplier type by area of loyalty management

As we can see, loyalty management strictly speaking is the most crowded area. Half the players there have expanded into the less crowded areas of loyalty strategy and loyalty communication where, however, they are likely to face the established competition of, on the one hand, consultancies who tend to win jobs requiring the design of a loyalty strategy from scratch, and on the other, advertising agencies who may already have both credibility and a foot in the client company from delivering other communication activities. One thing emerges over all else: with so many loyalty management tasks being specialized today, cooperation and alliances are more necessary than ever. We believe the sheer variety of players in the LMPS market, where many new entrants have mastered advanced analytics and touchpoint management technologies, will contribute to the evolution of loyalty management.

In the 2018 survey, marketers declared that they would continue to devote the same percentage of their budget to LMPS and to a variety of vendors. Thus the outsourcing of rewards, communication and digital agency services will remain indispensable. At the same time, many will increase their use of marketing automation, analytics and social/digital engagement specialists – an indication that loyalty management is embracing diverse touchpoints and the use of insight. This is nicely captured in Figure 8.6, where the views of clients and vendors in the survey about which new technologies for loyalty management were of most interest are shown side by side. Vendors were asked which innovative loyalty solutions their customers were most interested in and the same question was asked to clients about their own companies.

As is evident, the vendors we surveyed in our study have higher levels of interest in new technologies for loyalty management than clients. This is perhaps unsurprising, and

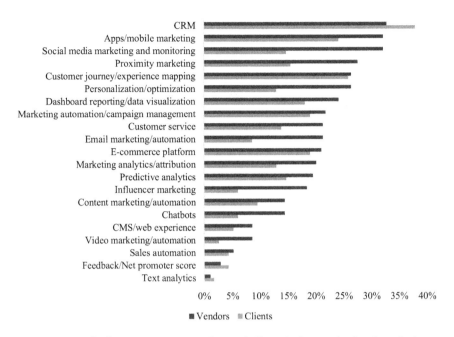

FIGURE 8.6 Level of interest among vendors and clients in innovative loyalty solutions

there can be little doubt that vendors will continue to be at the forefront of developing solutions to manage customer loyalty. It will be exciting to see what unfolds in the years ahead. We, at least, believe it will be to the benefit of the customer.

References

Collins, E. (2016) *The Forrester Wave™: Customer Loyalty Solutions for Midsize Organizations, Q1 2016.* Forrester Research, 4 January. Available at: https://www.datacandy.com/wp-content/uploads/2016/02/Forester-Report-Loyalty.pdf (Accessed: 12 March 2019).

Collins, E. (2017) *Vendor Landscape: Customer Loyalty Solutions.* Forrester Research, 14 August. Available at: https://www.datacandy.com/wp-content/uploads/2017/08/RES58234.pdf (Accessed: 14 March 2019).

Hilbert, D. (2019) 'Loyalty management market to increase at CAGR of 21.13% by 2023 – key vendors and landscape, trends, challenges and projections'. *RIS Report*, 19 January. Available at: https://risreport.com/19/16/20/loyalty-management-market-to-increase-at-cagr-of-21-13-by-2023-key-vendors-and-landscape-trends-challenges-and-projections/ (Accessed: 21 January 2019).

Homburg, C., Jozić, D. and Kuehnl, C. (2017) 'Customer experience management: toward implementing an evolving marketing concept'. *Journal of the Academy of Marketing Science*, 45(3), pp. 377–401.

Huré, E., Picot-Coupey, K., and Michaud-Trévinal, A. (2017) 'Omni-channel retailing: exploring how retailers interweave touch points (No. hal-01743685)'. Unpublished paper, available online: https://hal.archives-ouvertes.fr/hal-01743685/ (Accessed: 20 March 2019).

Jain, R., Aagja, J. and Bagdare, S. (2017) 'Customer experience: a review and research agenda'. *Journal of Service Theory and Practice*, 27(3), pp. 642–662.

Jayachandran, S., Sharma, S., Kaufman, P. and Raman, P. (2005) 'The role of relational information processes and technology use in customer relationship management'. *Journal of Marketing*, 69(4), pp. 1771–1792.

MarketsandMarkets (2017) *Loyalty Management Market – Global Forecast to 2021*. January. Available (fee for full access) at: https://www.asdreports.com/market-research-rep ort-321174/loyalty-management-market-global-forecast (Accessed: 21 January 2019).

Orbis Research (2018) *2018–2023 Global Loyalty Management Market Report (Status and Outlook)*. 9 October. Available at: https://www.orbisresearch.com/reports/index/2018-2023-globa l-loyalty-management-market-report-status-and-outlook (Accessed: 14 March 2019).

Osservatorio Fedeltà UniPR (2012) *Il futuro della Brand Loyalty e Lo Scenario della Fidelizza- zione nel Retail, Sintesi Rapporto di Ricerca*. Available at: https://osservatoriofedelta.it/work space/uploads/estratto_risultati-generali.pdf (Accessed: 20 February 2019).

Osservatorio Fedeltà (2015) *Lo stato dell'arte del Loyalty Management e del CRM in Italia*. Available via: http://www.osservatoriofedelta.it (Accessed: 8 March 2019).

Osservatorio Fedeltà (2016) *La gestione dei touchpoint per la Customer Experience e la Loyalty*. Available via: http://www.osservatoriofedelta.it (Accessed: 8 March 2019).

Osservatorio Fedeltà (2017) *Il Customer Experience Management nelle aziende italiane*. Available via: http://www.osservatoriofedelta.it (Accessed: 8 March 2019).

Reinartz, W., Krafft, M. and Hoyer, W. D. (2004) 'The customer relationship management process: its measurement and impact on performance'. *Journal of Marketing Research*, 41(3), pp. 293–305.

Sonawane, K. (2017) *Loyalty Management Market by Type (Customer Retention, Customer Loy- alty, and Channel Loyalty), Organization Size (Large and Small & Mid-size), and Industry Vertical (BFSI, Retail, Travel & Hospitality, Manufacturing, IT & Telecom, Media & Enter- tainment, Healthcare, and Others) – Global Opportunity Analysis and Industry Forecast, 2016– 2023*. Allied Market Research, August. Available (fee for full access) at: https://www. alliedmarketresearch.com/loyalty-management-market (Accessed: 14 March 2019).

Verhoef, P. C., Kannan, P. K., and Inman, J. J. (2015) 'From multi-channel retailing to omni-channel retailing: introduction to the special issue on multi-channel retailing'. *Journal of Retailing*, 91(2), pp. 174–181.

9

GETTING LOYALTY RIGHT: BARILLA AND STARBUCKS

Cristina Ziliani

Barilla's loyalty strategy from 1978 to 2018: from premium promotions to digital collection schemes

The case we present here is an outstanding example of the strategic use of loyalty promotions to establish a brand and support its leadership over a period of 40 years.[1] Barilla began as a bakery shop founded in Parma in 1877 by Pietro Barilla. The company – now Barilla Group – is still privately owned, by the fourth generation of the family. With a turnover of €3.4 billion and 8,400 employees, it is now the world's leading pasta maker with 40–45% of the Italian market and 25% of the US market. It is also the leading seller of bakery products in Italy. After several acquisitions beginning in 1973, it now controls the Barilla, Mulino Bianco, Pavesi, Voiello, Alixir and Academia Barilla (Italy), Harrys (France), Wasabröd (Sweden), Misko (Greece), Filiz (Turkey), Yemina and Vesta (Mexico) brands. Through its acquisition of the Swedish company Wasa, it is the world's leading producer of flatbread, a Scandinavian staple. The Barilla Group has several production plants all over the world: in Italy, Greece, France, Germany, Norway, Russia, Sweden, Turkey, the US and Mexico. The company also operates mills in Italy, Greece, Sweden, Turkey and the US.

1   We wholeheartedly thank Elena Bernardelli, the global brand activation director at Barilla, who shared with us both her experience and company data during precious hours of discussion on the success drivers of Barilla's loyalty programmes. The history of Barilla presented here draws on various materials provided, some of which are publicly available on the company website: see www.barillagroup.com/sites/default/files/ MULINO%20BIANCO%20ENG.pptx_.pdf for 'The Mulino Bianco Story'. The data presented in this section, if not otherwise stated, has been made available to the Loyalty Observatory to support the writing of this case study. An earlier version of this section appears (in Italian) in Ziliani (2015), reproduced here with the permission of EGEA. Omissions and mistakes are the responsibility of the author alone.

Building brand loyalty: Coccio and Sorpresine

Confronted with a challenging social and economic environment in Italy in the 1970s, Barilla chose a product diversification strategy and identified bakery products as a strategic market. In 1975 it launched the Mulino Bianco (literally 'White Mill') brand of cookies, which became an instant success. The brand name and mill logo – chosen to underline the attention paid to the quality of the ingredients – responded to an emergent trend towards rediscovering values linked to nature and tradition. Three years later, in a bakery sector dominated by two strong leaders (Motta and Ferrero), Barilla introduced its first proof-of-purchase collection scheme. Under the scheme, customers collected 'wheat spikes' and 'wheat sheafs' by cutting out small images of them printed on the product packaging as proof of purchase. Upon mailing them to the company they received a premium – the much-celebrated *coccio*, a terracotta bowl for milk featuring the Mulino mill logo, inspired by the old Italian tradition of soaking bread in milk for breakfast or as a cheap dinner in a bowl, something that millions of Italians were doing and millions more recalled their grandparents doing – a memory about family and tradition. Between 1978 and 1986 Barilla distributed over 20 million *cocci* as premiums and eight million families collected 600 million points (Morosini, 1994).

The strategic goal behind the Coccio Collection was clear from the outset: the Mulino brand was to enter Italian households by means of collectable objects, strongly linked to the brand's values and communication codes, and also accessible to non-heavy users of the brand. It was to be made a daily, familiar presence in Italian households. Mulino Bianco was a young brand on the market at the time. It became a follower in the cookie category thanks to the collection itself, but category handlers were not brand loyal. They enjoyed switching between brands and thus further category share growth seemed difficult to achieve. The collection's main goal was to expand the number of handlers – families consuming the brand – as much as possible in order to quickly gain category share. To support the brand in its march towards category leadership, the collection was to leverage the vast product portfolio, composed of dozens of different types of biscuits, bread substitutes and snacks. As competition mounted, the collection's success stimulated Barilla to advance its thinking behind it in order to engage Italian families even more. It should be said that Barilla was not relying solely on promotions to this purpose but worked on several innovation fronts: for example, it introduced a packaging innovation that greatly impacted upon consumed volumes: Mulino Bianco was the first brand to introduce family packs of snacks, containing individually wrapped snacks in quantities of eight, ten or more. The competing brand Motta was late in introducing the same type of pack, possibly because it had traditionally focused on the consumption of its products in the bar or cafe rather than at home.

Barilla did not stop there. In 1983 it introduced another successful loyalty promotion, this time aimed at children – Sorpresine. Gifts (the Italian *sorpresine* literally means 'little surprises') started to appear inside snack packs, small premiums born out of a partnership with Graziella Carbone, a specialist in sales promotion. In each snack pack, a matchbox was inserted, with the Mulino Bianco image on it, containing small games and objects that, in the beginning, had the shape of the products themselves: erasers in the shape of Mulino Bianco's pastries and muffins, small items for school, miniature board and card games, stickers and so on. These were destined to become icons of the 1980s and 1990s and Sorpresine represented the continuing success of the original strategy to make the brand a fixture of daily family life in Italy. Between 1983 and 1992, the Coccio Collection and the Sorpresine gift scheme proceeded hand in hand, with equal success. Each Sorpresine premium was produced in at least a million pieces, and the most popular ones reached 15 million pieces. Some 650 different premiums were designed and produced over the eight years of the promotion. Thirty years later, those children collectors, now in their forties, have formed groups that meet to swap, share and celebrate their Mulino Bianco-woven childhood memories!

Barilla's two premium promotion programmes – a collection and a gift scheme – were different but followed the same spirit: any single marketing decision was to remind the customer of the brand, any time of the day. Everything was done in-house at Barilla: new ideas were generated and tested every day, without the support of professional agencies, based on the idea that only the people who live the brand every day can think of premiums that truly express its uniqueness to customers. In 1990 another important branding step was taken: the building of the Mulino itself, a real mill on the hills of Siena, which will become that same year the set for a new TV campaign dedicated to the Mulino family directed by Giuseppe Tornatore with music by his long-time collaborator, the Academy Award winner Ennio Morricone (De Maio and Viola, 2008).

From 1978 to 1995, collection schemes were a strategic part of the Mulino Bianco brand marketing mix. After Coccio, tableware was introduced in the 1980s: sugar bowls, cookie jars, jugs, teapots, plates and trays inspired by Coccio Collection and coordinated with and among it. Terracotta products were sourced with Italian manufacturers only. This was not the first time that a successful premium stimulated an entire industry – it happened in the US with 'depression glass', glass objects employed as rewards to stimulate repeat visits in movie theatres and other outlets (Guenzi, 2015). In the late 1980s, Mulino became embodied in daily objects in children bedrooms, meaning the brand could 'own' a different dimension of the daily experience: playtime. The new premiums were playful, magic versions of the 'mill', containers for games, pastels, incredible objects full of surprises. In the early 1990s, Mulino Bianco moved back to the kitchen, where it already owned the breakfast moment with its above-mentioned breakfast and teatime tableware. The new premiums were tablecloths, indispensable accessories for everyday family meals in every Italian household. Embroidered with a different, exclusive, Mulino-inspired patterns each year, the tablecloths appealed to mothers, who also did the shopping and chose the brands. To this day, all Italians (or, at least, this book's authors) have at least one relative still using one of these tablecloths.

In the early 1990s, each Mulino Bianco business unit had its own loyalty promotion. Collection schemes peaked between 1992 and 1995 when there were four active schemes running simultaneously: a cross-category one, in which tokens could be accumulated with purchases of any Mulino Bianco product, and three category-specific collection schemes using snacks, cookies and bread substitutes. A significant majority of Italian families (80%) were engaged with two of them – the cross-category collection and one category-specific collection. Customers were rewarded with 'boosters' (i.e. extra points) for 'variety' (sending in proofs of purchases of at least 25 different SKUs across the brand portfolio) and 'velocity' (completing the collection within the first six months of the launch of the yearly collection). In Barilla's marketing department, four to five people worked full-time on the cross-category collection alone.

In those years, half the premiums were shipped directly to households, and retailers distributed the other half. Modern chain stores were growing their market share in the traditional and fragmented grocery market of Italy and were only too happy to cooperate with Barilla to deliver premiums because this created traffic in-store. Leveraging a growing network of stores as delivery points made collection operations more efficient for Barilla. Other brands ran collection schemes in those years and employed retail chains to deliver premiums, but Barilla took up most of the time retailers dedicated to the activity. Not only were there four Mulino Bianco collection schemes to run, but another collection related to Barilla pasta and sauces was soon added. However, change was coming. Retail chains were starting to introduce their own card-based loyalty schemes and when, after several years not running them, Barilla reintroduced Mulino Bianco collection schemes in 2006, it quickly discovered that consumers and retailers had changed and were no longer willing to do what the brand wanted them to do.

Monitoring and measuring performance

A crucial part of running a successful loyalty promotion is measuring its performance. Barilla invested in a Nielsen consumer panel, and telephone interviews were conducted to monitor closely how its collection schemes were faring. Such an analytical focus was indispensable if the company was to track progress towards its goal of expanding the number of handling households, and later, in the goal of growing Mulino Bianco's share among handlers. The latter had to be expanded overall and for each product category.

In measuring growth in the number of handling households, Barilla monitored four variables in each collection. First, the number of participants every month was measured and compared with the collection schemes of previous years. At one point, over three million families were involved per scheme. Second, Mulino Bianco's share (measured in volume) in handlers among Italian families, in general and for specific product categories, was monitored over time and special attention paid to whether that share had risen or fallen after participants had joined a collection and how it compared with previous collection schemes. For some product categories, families who joined the collection increased their share by 20%. A third variable Barilla focused on was the number of different SKUs in the brand portfolio purchased by collection participants, and its trend over time. For example, participants purchased 100% more than the average number of different SKUs purchased. Finally, the ratio of burned and earned points per collection was also taken into account. Such data would allow Barilla to evaluate which products had benefited the most from the collection, especially in the case of SKUs that were not supported by TV advertising. A product that contributed 4% to earned points but 6% to burned points showed a positive 'collection effect'.

Barilla identified separate variables to measure the growth of Mulino Bianco's share among handlers and portfolio coverage: (a) participants in the cross-category collection alone, (b) participants in category-specific collection(s) alone, (c) participants in both types of collection. This made it possible to check for effects specific to product category, and whether each collection worked more towards the number of handling households, the share among handlers, or portfolio coverage. On a methodological point, it must be said that the measure is always 'clean' in the year any collection scheme is launched because the following year handlers comprise both those who carry on from the previous year (or years) and those who join in the current year. In Barilla's case, it was theoretically possible to run analyses with the consumer panel to separate the effects, but it required extra work, and more importantly, increased detail meant less significant data. Accurate monitoring, however, made it clear that participation in both the cross-category and specific collection schemes generated a significant increase in Mulino Bianco's share among handlers, which justified the effort – in terms of the financial and human resources involved – of the multiple 'collection architecture' Barilla had set in place.

Reward redemption was closely monitored too. Monthly reports of consumers' requests and reservations of premiums were produced and compared with previous collection schemes, as well as the concentration curve of reward options (the few premiums that generated the highest proportion of requests). Moreover, each reward's total requests were decomposed based on the collection that had generated them in order to evaluate if the premiums that had been devised for a specific target group of consumers had appealed to that group in reality. For example, if a Mulino Bianco portable radio had been designed as a premium for customers who regularly ate crackers and similar bread substitutes, it was later checked if that group had contributed more, in percentage, to the redemption of radios when compared with other customer segments.

A change of direction

In February 1996, Barilla discontinued its flagship collection programmes. It was a major change of direction made necessary by the new economic climate. The company leadership felt that a strong response was necessary on its part to the rise in retailers' own labels and the discounters, which seemed to be taking the Italian market by storm. The company had lost ground in terms of its value-for-money positioning and decided to regain it, closing the collection schemes and reinvesting funds in a new price positioning. A considerable number of products in the Mulino Bianco portfolio were reduced in price, and TV advertising and price promotion were employed to communicate the change to consumers. As well as scrapping its collection schemes, Barilla halted the Sorpresine gift scheme. In the following years, the company lost ground in every product category, especially in snacks, where the widespread appeal to children of gifts in snack packs had probably been underestimated by everyone except Ferrero, who had never abandoned this type of promotion for its own snacks. After just three years, in 1999, Barilla acknowledged this loss to Ferrero and revived the gifts-in-pack model by reintroducing the Sorpresine scheme. Another three years later, in 2002, it launched the Mulino Friends premium, also a gifts-in-pack scheme, which became an immediate hit – so much so that they are still in use today. The Friends are toys in the shape of actual Mulino Bianco products and have become 'heroes' in children's play stories. These products-turned-heroes follow the long-running Barilla tradition of embodying brand in its premium products and speaking to target customers through products themselves. However, it would be a decade before this collection model was reintroduced into the Mulino Bianco marketing mix.

In the years between, Barilla tried new tactics for the Mulino Bianco brand. It worked to engage consumers at the point of sale through in-store events, organized around various themes such as breakfast products, breads, 'holiday pantry', 'back to school', and so forth. Secondary displays were set up in stores and multiple purchases rewarded with direct premiums that were given away by store hostesses. In 2003 the 'collection spirit' was introduced in the events calendar by choosing premiums that were coordinated, complementary and shared a common theme. The complete set of Mulino Bianco direct premiums for the year were presented to customers during the first event in the store. They would receive one 'coordinated item' on their first visit and, if they came back to attend later events, could receive others in the set. Soon stamps, found inside the premiums themselves, were added to the scheme and a stamp booklet provided to customers attending the event. Such a store-based collection scheme was reliant on online media. Being impossible to run in every store, the scheme could only be active in selected retail outlets and offline media advertising would not reach consumers living in areas where no store was participating. The Mulino Bianco website was, therefore, a key tool.

This was, of course, not an *entirely* new direction. Seven years after dropping the more traditional collection schemes, Barilla's new initiative represented a kind of 'visit-driven' collection scheme. The 'collection' technique and the brand philosophy of consistency in values, codes and traditions had simply been extended to the new territory of in-store brand activation promotions.

Three years after the introduction of the in-store collection scheme, market research conducted in 2006 into the Mulino Bianco's brand equity revealed that bread was only a marginal part of it, with consumers thinking little or not at all about bread when mentally representing Mulino Bianco. This was a weakness for

Barilla, which was hoping to expand its share in what was a rapidly growing daily consumption category (due to innovations both in the industrial production of soft bread and in advertising). A new strategic goal was set: work on Mulino Bianco's brand equity to develop it in the direction of bread and not exclusively biscuits and cakes as it had been until then. To pursue this goal the collection model was reintroduced exclusively to support the bread category. Given the variety and synergy of different segments and products within the category, such as 'soft' and 'crunchy' products, it was hoped that the collection logic would work as well as it had for the cross-category collection of the previous decade.

Given that the Mulino Bianco brand had entered various soft bread segments (loaves, soft tacos, sandwich breads and so on), a second strategic objective was assigned to the new Bread Collection scheme: to push the growth of Mulino Bianco's share among handlers of the various soft bread segments in the category. Mulino Bianco was no longer a challenger and had no need to expand the number of handling households. Therefore, the collection could be aimed at a reduced number of heavy-user households – a marked contrast from the logic of the late 1970s when the collection approach was adopted for the first time by a young brand that needed all users in order to grow share.

The approach worked. During its first year, the Bread Collection impacted handlers' behaviour significantly, driving up volumes as well as the brand's share of category spend, and above all, expanding the number of different Mulino Bianco bread products purchased by handlers and thus subtracted from the sales of competing brands. Just as ten years before, the number of different SKUs purchased by the average handler family grew by 100%. The collection had the greatest effect on newly launched products, those with the lowest shares in the category, a beneficial effect on the total product portfolio that was first observed during the cross-category collection of the 1970s. The new digital collection schemes that Mulino Bianco has experimented with in recent years have the same objectives. It is the interface that is different – no more physical cutting and pasting but clicks and taps on a smartphone screen – not the goals. The real challenge, however, lies with changes that have taken place in demand and in household habits, not in promotional techniques or technology.

The new face of collecting

Things started to change in the 2000s. The consumers engaging with the Bread Collection in 2006 were different from the members of Barilla's collection schemes of the 1980s and 1990s. As Nielsen data confirms, the number of Italian families willing to engage in a collection scheme in the 1980s and 1990s was much higher. It was between two and three million during the early days of the Mulino Bianco collection schemes, while in 2006 the Bread Collection engaged 800,000 households. There might be two causes at play here: the collection structure and redemption rules and a more general change in the attitude of consumers. We've said already that in the early days of Mulino Bianco, point redemption thresholds were low in order to engage a substantial number of families and expand the number of handlers. In 2006 the goal of targeting heavy users only (the top two deciles of the concentration curve) led to the setting of higher, more challenging thresholds that necessarily reduced the number of participants among category users. Many started collecting points but then gave up when they did not reach targets. On average, 5% of brand users in the category also redeemed in the Bread Collection, as opposed to 30% for the cross-category collection of the 1990s.

The same Nielsen data, however, tells another story. It is the overall phenomenon of 'collectors' that was on a downward slope, not just for Barilla. People's attitude towards clipping, saving, pasting and mailing proofs of purchase had changed. Barilla's competitor Ferrero, which never ceased its use of collection schemes, experienced the same erosion of the number of collecting households. The same happened to the Granarolo and Parmalat (dairy products brands) collection schemes that had been introduced to the market following Mulino Bianco's success. Collectors had changed: they had become used to supermarket point collection schemes, which are easier and don't require brand preference changes, cover the whole grocery shopping, rather than specific brands, and need no cutting or pasting, just a convenient plastic card. Collecting supermarket points is easier and premiums often look similar between supermarket and brand collection schemes – Barilla itself had run a few collection schemes whose rewards were small premium brand electrical appliances for the kitchen. Consumers were happy with the new convenient way of getting something for free, without having to clip proofs from product packaging.

This raises an interesting question for marketers and academics. Today, with digital collection schemes and digital promotions in general, the interface has changed and the gestures associated with participating in promotions too. Will marketers substitute more traditional ways of enrolling and engaging consumers? Will customers self-segment based on their preferences and familiarity with technology? Will memory of the promotion, intention to buy, and actual purchase rate change, compared with plastic cards or stamp collecting? The only way to know is to experiment with the new. That is precisely what Barilla did, and not only with collection schemes. In fact, in 2009, Mulino Bianco launched Nel Mulino che Vorrei ('In the Mill of My Dreams') (www.nelmulinochevorrei.it), an online platform where people can interact with the brand and suggest ideas on the most varied aspects: new products, new packaging, new promotions, recipes and even social and environmental projects. Members can take part in surveys and can personalize product packages and premiums with their own names, photos and traits. Cherry croissants and Focaccelle are two successful new products that have been developed following members' suggestions. The community reached 50,000 members in 2016, largely due to online social networks, and since its inception has generated over 10,000 ideas, 690,000 comments and over 3.5 million votes on members' posts.

To mark Mulino Bianco's fortieth birthday, Barilla decided to launch a new and totally digital collection scheme in 2015 called Mulino in Festa ('Festive Mill').[2]

---

2   The text that follows is based on an earlier version written by Fulvio Furbatto and Ambra Pazzagli and has been updated by the author, who is solely responsible for any omissions or mistakes. For more about the scheme, see www.miomulino.it.

The project involved 208 million product packages and 57 SKUs for 38 products in the biscuits, snacks, cakes and bread categories. It aimed to reward both immediate purchase and repeat purchases through point collection and instant wins. Sell-out and a higher frequency of purchases were its target metrics. Above all, the scheme, which ran from April to November 2015, aimed to stimulate cross-category purchases to develop medium-user and heavy-user loyalty. The target group was composed of 12.5 million families who could win a prize with any purchased product and participate in a digital collection scheme whose reward threshold was set at 65 points.

In order to take part in the Mulino in Festa promotion, customers entered their receipt data online at the scheme website or via the Mio Mulino mobile app. After registering, they could take part in the daily instant win – entering up to five receipt codes every day – to win a supply of Mulino Bianco products. All users who took part in the instant win by entering at least one receipt code were eligible for the weekly draw for a prize of a weekend for two at the 'real mill' of Chiusdino, featured in the TV adverts.

Each receipt code entered entitled the customer to a point. Once a user had collected 65 points, she could claim a porcelain cookie jar and customized mugs with her name on them. The style of the jar adapted the design of the historical premium while appealing to contemporary tastes. Extra points could be collected by entering bonus codes which the user could win by taking part in activities related to the collection scheme—many of which took place in-store where promotion cards were handed out to consumers to stimulate engagement. One of the novelties of Mulino in Festa was the opportunity for each user to donate up to a maximum of ten points or to receive them as a donation. In this way, points that were not redeemed were not lost either because they could be used by another customer to reach the prize threshold.

Of course, other companies and brands in Italy have introduced digital collection schemes. However, Mulino in Festa has distinctive traits as a body of digital promotions for FMCG. Firstly, it allows for multichannel user involvement, via the website and app. Users can connect with the brand while on the move, check their points balance and read about the promotion rules, prizes and premiums. In-app features mean they can take photos of their receipts and receive push notifications and personalized communication, all of which helps sustain engagement and reduce defection. The second innovation is the use of optical character recognition technology to read the images from receipts uploaded by the users and identify data. The system stores each customer's uploads in a customer purchase history that can also be accessed by customer service teams, thus optimizing their operations and costs. Thirdly, the algorithm-based receipt validation system employs two different recognition systems to assign a risk index to each uploaded receipt. All users claiming a reward are ranked according to risk in order to block fraudulent claims and optimize customer service.

Another innovative feature is the MyFanCare customer care tool, which is totally integrated in the promotion so that all requests and communications to customer care from different touchpoints (email, Facebook, website contact form, phone call with customer service) are consolidated in a single platform where they are classified by topic based on a semantic analysis, receive a priority index and are put through to dedicated operators. Last, but not least, a boosting plan is built into the initiative to offer extra points and different benefits to members in order to reach cross-selling goals and upselling or other sales targets that emerge during the eight-month life span of the promotion. For example, members are offered extra points and incentives to buy cross-category products (generated from analyses of their individual purchase history during the promotion). They can also gain extra points by sharing the promotion with their friends.

Looking into the future

The Mulino Bianco case is an outstanding example of the strategic use of loyalty promotions to establish a brand and support its leadership over a sustained period of time, throughout the inevitable ebb and flow of market, economic and social change. What can companies take away from this success story? It seems that there are two things that are critical to the effectiveness of loyalty-building promotion: (a) clear and precise goals need to be defined beforehand, and (b) all elements of the promotion, down to the last detail, must be carefully and methodically designed so that they are consistent with the brand's values and image. Even if the future is full of sophisticated technologies that we cannot even begin to imagine today, we firmly believe that the success of promotional activities going forward will continue to be predicated on these two key factors.

My Starbucks Rewards: from store card to digital loyalty ecosystem

Founded in 1971, Starbucks is one of the largest coffee house chains in the world. As of January 2019, it has more than 29,800 stores, two-thirds of which are outside the US, in over 75 countries (Starbucks, 2019). Consolidated net revenues have reached $6.6 billion. In 2018 it counted 75 million customers in the US, of whom 16 million were active members of its My Starbucks Rewards (MSR) loyalty programme (Starbucks, 2018). Under this loyalty scheme, customers who enter a Starbucks branch to drink coffee can be rewarded for it. MSR is regarded by some as the most successful loyalty programme in America and certainly by the company itself as a major source of growth. Scott Maw, the executive vice president and chief financial officer, declares that 'over the last couple years, almost all of our same-store sales growth came from those customers that we have digital relationships with and those that are in our Starbucks Rewards program' (Starbucks, 2018, p. 2). According to the CEO Kevin Johnson, programme members and digitally registered customers amount to a total of 30 million people (Pymnts, 2019). Starbucks is regarded today as a great example of a company that has evolved its loyalty strategy by successfully embracing and developing new tools and opportunities as they became available.

How the programme worked until April 2016

Starbucks launched its loyalty programme in 2001: the Gold card-based scheme had a $25 annual membership fee and provided members with a 10% in-store discount on purchases all year round (Nitin, 2017). However, the company ditched the scheme as sales generated through it stagnated and in 2009 they launched MSR. It was free to enrol in MSR. Customers could load any amount of money on to a gift card and register the card to protect the balance and start collecting 'stars'. Every time a customer made a purchase at Starbucks, they earned one star. The more stars they earned, the bigger the rewards. Customers registering a Starbucks loyalty card were defaulted to the Welcome Level, which included a free birthday beverage (Palnitkar, 2017). Once customers earned five stars, they reached the Green Level. At the Green Level, members got free refills of brewed coffee or tea, free selected syrups and milk when they ordered a beverage off the menu, a free beverage when they bought whole bean coffee, and free trial offers. Customers who accumulated 30 stars over a 12-month period reached the Gold Level. Gold Level members received free refills of ice and brewed coffee and tea, a free drink for every 12 stars, free food and drink offers, a personalized Gold Card that recognizes them as preferred customers, and customized coupons.

It is worth comparing the initial fee-based Starbucks programme with the MSR launched in 2009. The company shifted away from hard benefits like the 10% discount toward a 'free' card approach that meant no fees for registration and non-monetary rewards: free refills, free drinks for birthdays, free drinks every 12 stars, and so on. This approach changed the customer mindset from thinking in terms of discounts and prices to extras and free gains. Starbucks' decision to reward customers purchasing coffee beans is another telltale detail. It intended to pamper real fans of the product, those customers who love the brew so much so that they take coffee beans home to grind. This way the Starbucks brand and its loyalty initiative entered customers' homes, a loyalty strategy that seeks to own new consumption moments different from the traditional in-store experience. The 'levels' structure stimulates customers to climb the ladder through repeat visits. And removing the fee – even adding the free birthday drink rewarding the simple act of registering for the scheme – played in favour of opening the scheme to a much wider membership base, comprising not only heavy spenders but also light spenders, who probably found the previous fee-based programme unappealing.

In April 2016 Starbucks changed the programme structure of MSR. We describe the changes below and explore the elements that have made the programme unique over the last few years.

Changes to the programme

In February 2016 the company announced that it was making changes to the MSR programme. The new programme went into effect on 12 April that year. Under the new structure, customers earn reward stars based on the amount of money they spend at Starbucks: two stars are earned for every dollar spent on any drink, food, or other item. The more customers spend, the more they earn.

There have also been changes made to the programme's levels and rewards rate. The Welcome Level has been eliminated and, as they sign up, customers are enrolled into the Green tier: to maintain this status, they need to earn at least one star per year. Green members still get a free drink on their birthday and free refills in store, and they can pay or order in advance through the app (see next section). The accumulated stars, however, are of real value only when the customer reaches Gold status. This requires 300 stars, in contrast to the 30 stars previously needed, and 300 stars every 12 months (or a spend of $150 per year) are needed to maintain the status. Gold members will need 125 additional stars for a free reward; previously, they needed only 12 (i.e. visits). It has been noted that members often pay for their friends to earn more stars and get closer to their free drink. New monthly 'double-star days' help Gold members get there faster. Considering that a $62.50 spend is required to earn 125 stars, and a free drink is worth $5, the approximate payback percentage for Gold members is 8% (Palnitkar, 2017). High spenders might like the programme, but rewards for low-spending customers are small.

Starbucks justified the change by saying that some customers had been splitting their orders, asking a cashier to ring up a coffee and muffin separately, to 'game' the system and gain rewards faster; that led to longer queues and customer inconvenience. The other, more substantial reason was that the company wanted more members for MSR: fewer than one in six of Starbucks' 75 million monthly visitors in February 2016 belonged to MSR and with members spending twice as much as non-members (Garcia, 2016a) it is easy to see the reason for the move. Starbucks executives also said the shift to a 'dollars spent' model from a 'number of visits' model was the most requested programme change by customers themselves. They cited the US airline industry undergoing a similar conversion, with carriers moving to reward dollars spent rather than miles flown.

The change angered some customers, who perceived that they needed to spend more money to achieve the same benefits they got before, and led to some noise about how the loyalty programme wasn't as generous (Snyder, 2016). Some members complained on Twitter, raising awareness of the change among the customer base. To reassure members, Starbucks cited faster in-store queues and argued that the majority of members would earn their stars as fast or even faster than before, due also to promotions and new opportunities both in and outside the store. However, they acknowledged that a 'small minority' would earn rewards at a slower pace (Kilgore, 2016) and admitted that after the change there had been a reduction in traffic. Citing YouGov data, Adweek reported that the company's brand perception slumped by 50% after the MSR change announcement (Kell, 2016).

Deutsche Bank had downgraded Starbucks shares to hold on 12 April over concerns that changes to the loyalty programme could have a negative impact on same-store sales, and share prices slumped (Garcia, 2016a). Analysts were also worried about competitors exploiting the situation to poach Starbucks customers:

Dunkin' Donuts was said to have plans to target them two days after the MSR programme changes to attract them to try its programme (Kilgore, 2016). However, a few months after the protests, Starbucks reported that the changes were prompting new customers to join the programme, citing 900,000 new members in the second quarter of 2016 (though changes were not effective in the first month). That's an 8% increase on the first quarter of the year, and a 16% increase on the second quarter of 2015. So, what made MSR successful?

The app

The success of MSR is often attributed to its mobile rewards app, launched in 2011. According to a survey conducted by The Manifest business news website in May 2018, almost 50% of US smartphone owners who regularly use restaurant loyalty apps use the Starbucks app (Panko, 2018) with the second most used app in the sector – Domino's – used by only 34%.

The app offers a range of features, such as checking MSR programme account information in real time, a store locator, and payment management. Users can set up the payment feature by linking their app to a credit card or PayPal account: they then load money onto the app to use it as a debit card. There is no need to go to the store to load funds, although the option is still available for customers who prefer to do so. The prepaid mechanism acts as a 'lock-in', nudging customers to choose a Starbucks store over competitors since they have already set aside funds for the purpose. They carry their phone with them all the time and as additional purchase occasions arise, they are never out of a means of payment. Moreover, the substitution of cash and credit card can play the trick of making customers feel as if their drinks are practically free.

From the perspective of the company, the prepaid system provides funds that can be reinvested and saves Starbucks fees and commissions that arise when customers pay by credit card. Indeed it has been estimated that Starbucks might pay as much as $0.25 in fees on the sale of a $2.75 cup of coffee (Wathen, 2017). Last but not least, as some customers never use up their credit – this is true of gift cards as well as app-based wallet systems like the MSR app feature – the company earns on the breakage (as unused funds are known in the business). According to a study by *The Wall Street Journal*, in the first quarter of 2016 Starbucks had $1.2 billion in deposits loaded onto plastic cards and the app combined (Ferro, 2016; Meola, 2016). This figure is larger than the amount held at many smaller regional banks or prepaid card firms, and it is almost double the $621 million it had in 2014 (Garcia, 2016b). On breakage income alone – that is, income resulting from lost or unused gift cards – Starbucks earned $39.3 million in 2015 (Ferro, 2016) and $60.5 million in 2016 (Wathen, 2017), or the equivalent to the estimated operating profit of 300 company-owned stores. Bowman (2016) estimates that, with $5 billion in card transactions every year, Starbucks would be able to earn $50 million in interest with a 1% interest rate (assuming it reinvests in high-grade corporate bonds, treasury notes, and certificates of deposit). Combined with the breakage income, that would mean about $90 million in revenue from the loyalty programme, or the equivalent of profit from about 700 company-owned stores, and all without taking into account the increased spending and frequency of MSR members.

In the early days the novelty of the app further contributed to the loyalty programme's success. When other customers in line see people using their mobile phones to pay, their curiosity is aroused and they may be encouraged to sign up. The app tracks purchase history, stars earned on each purchase, and card reloads. Additionally, it delivers special promotions to users and sends them messages previewing new products before they appear in stores. Geolocation tracking incentivizes users to visit the nearest branch. The Starbucks app has helped greatly to differentiate the programme from other standard card-only programmes in a market fast becoming crowded with loyalty efforts. In fact, the app's payment feature generated over seven million transactions a week in the first quarter of 2015 in the US, and in the first quarter of 2016 it was used by 11 million people, accounting for 15% of sales and 21% of transactions. That same year it outpaced all other payment apps, including PayPal and Apple Pay. In 2017 it was used by 23.4 million Americans, edging out both Apple (22 million) and Google (11.1 million), according to an eMarketer report that credits Starbucks with having stirred a renaissance in domestic mobile payments in the US (Kats, 2018).

Initially, critics were sceptical about Starbucks' new loyalty programme because they thought that it was too complicated for some customers and difficult for baristas to promote at the till. However, Starbucks effectively trained their baristas to talk customers into moving from card to app. Indeed staff play a crucial role in determining loyalty programme adoption and success: Starbucks leveraged this by introducing the 'digital tipping' enhancement to the app. This feature gives customers the option to tip the store staff just moments after paying at the till. Customers have a two-hour window to select a tip ranging from 50 cents to $2. Not only does the feature promote a dialogue between staff and customers, and a better service, but it expands the base of customers who actually tip, an activity that might be undermined by a lack of time or small change and distraction.

Another enhancement to the app is the Shake to Pay feature, which simplifies mobile payments. By simply shaking their smartphone, customers can bring the barcode of their Starbucks card front and centre at any time. This gesture, one which links our long-standing gestures in the physical world to new digital devices, not only makes app payment more convenient, but it can surprise the customer and make them feel empowered, and hence positively remember the app experience. The app also offers a Gift tab where users can select a theme – from Happy Birthday to Thank You – and send a digital Starbucks gift card to any email address with just a few taps on their smartphone, a clever feature that serves a customer need, capitalizes on impulse (you can do it anytime, on the go), and contributes to using the customer's preloaded funds, hence … generating a need to reload. A range of other features of the app enhance the customer experience and engagement. Whenever customers check the app, a brand-new, time-limited bonus offer is created and displayed to reward loyal customers with even more stars. This has the effect of making the programme feel fresh all the time (McEachern, 2017). Starbucks were also quick to utilize the power of social media. Anyone with a Twitter account linked to their Starbucks card can buy coffee with a $5 gift card for anyone else on Twitter by tweeting at the handle @tweetacoffee and including the handle of the person receiving the gift (Champagne and Iezzi, 2014).

In 2015 Starbucks added its Mobile Order & Pay order-ahead service. The mobile order-ahead service refers to a consumer-facing mobile payment platform that allows customers to order food remotely, pay for the items on their phone, and pick up their order at a specific restaurant location, without once having to speak to a Starbucks employee (Meola, 2016). Within three months of launching, customers were placing up to seven million orders per week via this service. Competing quick-service restaurants have been quick to adopt mobile order-ahead services to enhance sales, strengthen customer loyalty, and secure traffic in store. By tapping into each customer purchase history, the Mobile Order & Pay feature encourages cross-selling by suggesting additional items available in store to add to the current order. Taco Bell sees 30% higher average order values on mobile compared to in store, while Starbucks' Mobile Order & Pay represented 10% of total transactions at high-volume stores as early as 2016 (Meola, 2016). In 2018 the company decided to open up Mobile Order & Pay beyond MSR members to any Starbucks customer. This would encourage acquisition to the programme indirectly, as users of the service, who give their mobile phone number and email address to gain access to it, are contacted directly via digital marketing and are then exposed to the benefits of the programme (Starbucks, 2018).

Soon after launching the Mobile Order & Pay service, and probably to give it more traction from the start, Starbucks announced that they were going to experiment with different types of delivery service: one that would involve its own employees and also a model that included a third-party service. Members of the loyalty programme would be able to request delivery through Mobile Order & Pay. Such a service if rolled out nationwide, it was envisioned, might alter competition and market shares, as time-strapped consumers would switch to Starbucks to take advantage of the delivery service. This raised the bar for the whole quick-service-restaurant industry (Samuely, 2016). Since the early trials of 2016, Starbucks has consolidated a partnership with Postmates and launched a new partnership with Uber Eats in 2019 that will make the delivery service available from 2,000 Starbucks stores in the US (Mogg, 2019). Consumers can place an order for Starbucks products with the Uber Eats app, track the order and expect delivery within 30 minutes. Special packaging has been developed to maintain the drinks at the right temperature. The move will acquire new customers to Starbucks among the Uber Eats user base and help expand Starbucks' share of existing customers' wallets since its products will reach customers out of store and fill new spots in their daily habits. With more Starbucks products available through more than one delivery service in the same city, the company will need to look into price consistency and price perception issues, but, at the end of 2018, 12% of Starbucks' total US sales came through its Mobile Order & Pay feature (Pymnts, 2019). Such early success suggests that, if managed well, this feature is here to stay.

The Gold Card

It is not just the app that points to the success of Starbucks' loyalty programme. When a member gains 30 stars in a 12-month period he or she achieves Gold Level status, which entitles them to a personalized Gold Card. According to McEachern (2017), the Gold Card is the true motivator to achieve Gold Level status since it provides the opportunity to feel exclusive and important. He argues that, differently from customers of other coffee chains, Starbucks customers feel a sense of pride and of being of a higher class when drinking Starbucks coffee compared to other coffee. For that reason, they love sharing images of what they are drinking on social media sites like Instagram and Twitter, and this 'show off' trait is what makes the Gold Card so effective.

However, according to the online platform Mobile Commerce Daily, more than 50% of MSR members were Gold Level customers in 2015 (McEachern, 2017) – hardly an elite status. There is the danger that, if customers start perceiving the card as a commodity, it might lose its differentiating power. From an operational viewpoint, moreover, it has been noted that Starbucks treats the Gold Card as a new card that must be registered in order to be associated with the customer rewards account. This might lead to duplications in the programme database, lost data and incorrect tracking of the customer purchase history.

From CEM to CRM

The use of customer data for customer relationship management (CRM) may be a recent phenomenon at Starbucks but it is one that is escalating. Scott Maw recently declared that Starbucks only started looking into the MSR programme data in 2016 (Starbucks, 2019). The company is committed to leveraging customer data to develop personalization strategies in the future, not just for members but for all customers with whom they have a digital relationship, a total of 30 million in the US. Starbucks Dash offers customers rewards for visiting a branch multiple times over a certain time period. A Dash incentivizes customers to start a predictable visit routine, awarding them more stars the more times they visit. The app keeps track of how often a member has visited and encourages them to move the video game-like progress bar towards earning their special reward. Bonus Star Combinations work the same way, and require that customers buy (usually) three different items within a certain number of days. Point offers and online games have been used to drive traffic to the stores specifically during afternoons, which are slow times of the day for the chain. Other bonuses reward behaviour that Starbucks wants to promote such as Mobile Order & Pay (50 bonus stars on first mobile order), or trying new products just introduced in the store (e.g. 30 bonus stars for the new breakfast sandwich) (Boezi, 2018). Data on customers whose frequency is higher than 90 days is used to reactivate them: lapsed customers receive Bonus Star Combinations for a set of items they have previously bought – to get their attention and enhance offer attractiveness – and such efforts have paid off (Starbucks, 2018).

Expanding the programme: from partnerships to digital ecosystem

Over time, loyalty programmes strive to expand earning options for their customers and, at the same time, attempt to recruit new members to the programme. Starbucks first expanded the scope of its loyalty programme when it introduced points for purchases outside of its retail locations. Starbucks coffee beans, tea and ready-to-enjoy drinks can be bought online and in other retail stores. By placing 'star codes' on participating product packs, Starbucks made it possible for customers to earn extra stars while grocery shopping at their local supermarket. For supermarkets, listing Starbucks products means cashing in on the brand popularity as the star codes are an added stimulus for brand-loyal customers to purchase in the categories where the supermarket has enlisted Starbucks products.

In 2015 a multi-year agreement with ride-sharing company Lyft was announced. The deal allows Lyft users who connect their Lyft account with the MSR account to collect MSR stars for each ride taken. First-time Lyft riders also earn enough stars for a free beverage by linking their accounts and taking a ride within a specified period of time. All Lyft drivers can automatically become Gold members (Harris, 2015; Oragui, 2018). Around the same time, the company revealed that MSR members would soon be able to read select daily news articles from the *New York Times* for free in the Starbucks mobile app. This move goes in the direction of adding value to programme membership without using discounts and by promoting more frequent use of the app. Meanwhile, the *New York Times* gained the opportunity of reaching new audiences while giving away a reasonable amount of content – 15 articles per day (Shah, 2016).

Just as a coffee and a newspaper go well together, Starbucks and music go back a long way. Music can be said to be at the centre of the 'third-place experience' [3] that Starbucks has been successfully building for 40 years. In 1994 a dedicated team began selecting original CDs spanning a variety of musical genres to sell and play Starbucks branches. Seasonal CDs have celebrated Valentine's Day, summer holidays and Christmas, but Starbucks has also become a champion of emerging artists, introducing their music to the public early in their careers (Miller, 2015). As the music industry and consumer habits evolved with the digital revolution, Starbucks began offering Wi-Fi in store in 2002 and in 2007 partnered with Apple to provide free access to iTunes Music (Alba, 2015).

In March 2015 Starbucks ceased sales of CDs in store and announced a new strategy. It partnered with Spotify, the music-streaming service, to use Spotify's mobile app to let music playlists be curated and shared between MSR members, baristas and 60 million Spotify subscribers. The Starbucks app allows users to identify songs being played in store, then download and save those they like to a playlist on Spotify's app. Starbucks employees receive a Spotify Premium subscription so they can help shape in-store music programming using tools provided by Spotify. These partner-

---

3   The 'third place' refers to Starbucks' focus on providing customers with a third option of where to feel comfortable beyond the home and the workplace.

influenced playlists are accessible on Spotify via the Starbucks app; thus customers can stream Starbucks music anywhere and anytime from their mobile device and continue enjoying the music of choice even after leaving the store. Moreover, Spotify users can obtain stars in the MSR programme (Samuely, 2016).

This was the first time that Starbucks loyalty programme stars could be accessed by a third party for the benefit of MSR members and Spotify users. The collaboration goes well beyond providing a substitute for a delisted category in store (music CDs) and offers fresh acquisition opportunities to the loyalty programme (Spotify's 60 million subscribers). The fact that Starbucks probably earned a fee from Spotify, which was seeking new subscribers in the US, is only one of many reasons for the strategy. The move adds a service that appeals to the profile of Starbucks' target audience (music lovers and digital users). It counteracts the risk that new digital services could keep customers away from stores (such as order-ahead) by introducing a service that brings them back. An existing but largely dormant digital asset of the company is put to value creation: 20 years of playlists that may be valuable to specific customer segments are made available. Just as when Amazon took the decision to cease reviewing books in-house and open its platform to customer reviews, Starbucks has embraced crowdsourcing for product choices (in this case, music). Involving customers in the co-creation of their store experience creates engagement. Furthermore, it leverages music's connection to human emotions, and the role of positive emotions in purchase and repatronage intentions and behaviour. Moreover, by linking data between the two apps, Starbucks gains insight on their customers' online and social habits. From there, other digital content can be added to what could become a vast digital content platform of the flavour of an Amazon Prime. New revenue streams may open up as Starbucks takes to selling to third parties its audience and targeting capabilities, digital payment expertise, payment services and more.

In 2018 the company announced the launch of the Starbucks Rewards prepaid Visa card, a co-branded credit card in partnership with Chase, the US consumer and commercial banking business of J.P. Morgan. Customers using the card earn stars with every purchase both in Starbucks stores and anywhere in the world that Visa is accepted. Cardholders automatically receive Gold status in the MSR programme. They receive a physical card within seven to ten days of their application, but a digital card is immediately loaded in their Starbucks app so that they can start earning stars right away. Since one star is earned for every dollar that is digitally loaded to the Starbucks app using the Starbucks Rewards Visa Card, the new credit card encourages mobile payment with the Starbuck app (J.P. Morgan, 2018).

With all these developments inevitably comes risks. As Starbucks adds partners to programme and payment options to expand the reach of star earning and burning and to monetize programme loyalty, it may face the risk of diluting programme equity due to excessive stretching or devaluating the 'star' value. Something similar has happened to airlines: fees from partners using air miles for their loyalty programmes are a major source of income for many airlines, but this has led to excessive 'minting' and the consequent devaluation of the 'currency'. If this happens, Starbucks will possibly need to find ways to have customers 'burn' some of the growing stock of distributed stars, as they burden the profit and loss statement of the company.[4] As this book goes to press there are rumours of changes to the programme in this direction (Petreycik, 2019).

A yet more subtle risk is that of fostering loyalty to the app as a means of payment, especially if it becomes an open wallet and is used to pay outside Starbucks too, rather than primarily to Starbucks itself. A third risk is that innovation outpaces capacity. When so many players are engaged (think of delivery apps, partner apps, payment intermediaries, social media, etc. – the Starbucks app connects with all of them and possibly more in the future) sustaining expectations and service quality may be a daunting task. Service failures and data breach challenges will inevitably multiply, if only due to the escalating number of users.

So much for the US. As this book goes to press, Starbucks is pursuing growth and learning opportunities in what is currently the most advanced market as far as digital ecosystems is concerned: China. In 2018 the company struck a deal with Alibaba that will see the unification of the Starbucks app and those belonging to the Alibaba ecosystem, such as Taobao, Tmall and Alipay. The aim is to provide customers with a unified digital experience, which includes services such as Starbucks Delivers, embedding the 'Say it with Starbucks' social gifting feature in the WeChat service, a digital reward programme and merchandise available from Starbucks' flagship store on Tmall (WARC, 2018).

Chinese consumers will experience a more seamless experience when ordering coffee, and Starbucks will be able to track sales and online searches more effectively since they will now come from a single source. Given that commerce in China is social, and the Alibaba 88 Membership loyalty programme is all about referrals (see Chapter 1), Starbucks expects to acquire large numbers of new members to MSR. As part of the partnership, Starbucks coffee will be available on Alibaba's Ele.me on-demand delivery platform and fulfilled from 2,000 stores across 30 cities in China (WARC, 2018). Just as we have seen with Amazon and Alibaba, opening up their once closed loyalty programmes to provide a better experience and gain insight, and secure customer loyalty going forward, seems to be the way ahead for Starbucks too. With the advancement of interconnected sophisticated digital ecosystems, the plastic loyalty may well soon be a distant memory.

References

Barilla case study

De Maio, C. and Viola, F. (2008) *Italia 2. Viaggio nel paese che abbiamo inventato*. Rome: Minimum Fax.

Guenzi, A. (2015) 'Le origini americane delle operazioni a premio'. In Ziliani, C. (ed.), *Promotion Revolution*, Milan: EGEA, pp. 251–279.

---

4   In fact, to manage loyalty programmes, monetary reserves must be built to face consumers' requests to claim their points, just as if these were company debits.

Morosini, I. (1994) 'Virtù dell'oggetto promozionale'. In Ivardi Ganapini, A. and Gonizzi, G. (eds), *Barilla: Cento anni di pubblicità e comunicazione*, Milan: Silvana, pp. 302–315.

Ziliani, C. (2015) *Promotion Revolution: Nuove strategie e nuovi protagonisti della promozione 2.0.* Milan: EGEA.

Starbucks case study

Alba, D. (2015) 'Starbucks' grande plan: selling coffee via apps'. *Wired*, 3 November. Available at: https://www.wired.com/2015/11/no-one-is-killing-it-with-retail-store-apps-like-starbucks/ (Accessed: 25 February 2019).

Boezi, M. (2018) 'Starbucks Rewards: an evolution in data-driven marketing'. *Control Mouse Media*, 8 August. Available at: https://controlmousemedia.com/starbucks-rewards-data-driven-marketing/ (Accessed: 24 February 2019).

Bowman, J. (2016) '20 million reasons why Starbucks' Rewards program is so powerful'. *The Motley Fool*, 11 June. Available at: https://www.fool.com/investing/2016/06/11/20-million-reasons-why-starbucks-rewards-program-i.aspx (Accessed: 25 February 2019).

Champagne, C. and Iezzi, T. (2014) 'Dunkin' Donuts and Starbucks: a tale of two coffee marketing giants'. *Fast Company*, 21 August. Available at: https://www.fastcompany.com/3034572/dunkin-donuts-and-starbucks-a-tale-of-two-coffee-marketing-giants (Accessed: 24 February 2019).

Ferro, S. (2016) 'Starbucks cards hold so much money the company could be a midsize bank'. *Huffington Post*, 16 June. Available at: https://www.huffingtonpost.com/entry/starbucks-gift-cards-12-billion_us_5762fab0e4b0df4d586f975b (Accessed: 24 February 2019).

Garcia, T. (2016a) 'Starbucks loyalty program wins gold stars from most but not all analysts'. *Marketwatch*, 22 April. Available at: https://www.marketwatch.com/story/starbucks-loyalty-program-wins-gold-stars-from-most-but-not-all-analysts-2016-04-22 (Accessed: 24 February 2019).

Garcia, T. (2016b) 'Starbucks has more customer money on cards than many banks have in deposits'. *Marketwatch*, 9 June. Available at: https://www.marketwatch.com/story/starbucks-has-more-customer-money-on-cards-than-many-banks-have-in-deposits-2016-06-09 (Accessed: 24 February 2019).

Harris, R. (2015) 'Why Starbucks is winning at loyalty'. *Marketing Mag*, 28 July. Available at: http://marketingmag.ca/brands/why-starbucks-is-winning-at-loyalty-152974 (Accessed: 25 February 2019).

J.P. Morgan (2018) 'Starbucks and Chase launch Starbucks Rewards[TM] Visa® Card'. Chase Media Center (press release), 1 February. Available at: https://media.chase.com/news/chase-launches-starbucks-rewards-card (Accessed: 25 February 2019).

Kats, R. (2018) 'The mobile payments series: US'. *eMarketer*, 9 November. Available at: https://www.emarketer.com/content/the-mobile-payments-series-the-us (Accessed: 15 March 2019).

Kell, J. (2016) 'How a loyalty program change hurt the Starbucks brand'. *Fortune*, 7 March. Available at: http://fortune.com/2016/03/07/how-a-loyalty-program-change-hurt-the-starbucks-brand/ (Accessed: 15 March 2019).

Kilgore, T. (2016) 'Starbucks' new loyalty program greeted with a stock selloff'. *Marketwatch*, 12 April. Available at: https://www.marketwatch.com/story/starbucks-new-loyalty-program-greeted-with-a-stock-selloff-2016-04-12 (Accessed: 24 February 2019).

McEachern, A. (2017) 'Loyalty case study: Starbucks Rewards'. *Smile.io*, 24 July. Available online at: https://blog.smile.io/loyalty-case-study-starbucks-rewards (Accessed: 24 February 2019).

Meola, A. (2016) 'Starbucks' loyalty program now holds more money than some banks'. *Business Insider*, 13 June. Available at: https://www.businessinsider.com/starbucks-loyalty-program-now-holds-more-money-than-some-banks-2016-6?IR=T (Accessed: 24 February 2019).

Miller, C. (2015) 'Longtime iTunes partner Starbucks goes big with Spotify'. *9to5mac.com*, 18 May. Available at: https://9to5mac.com/2015/05/18/spotify-starbucks-partnership/ (Accessed: 25 February 2019).

Mogg, T. (2019) 'Starbucks coffee delivery lands in 6 more cities via Uber Eats'. *Digital Trends*, 22 January. Available at: https://www.digitaltrends.com/home/starbucks-expands-coffee-delivery-to-6-more-cites-via-uber-eats/ (Accessed: 25 February 2019).

Nitin (2017) 'The science behind Starbucks' massively successful customer loyalty program'. *Zeta Global*, 31 March. Available at: https://zetaglobal.com/blog-posts/starbucks-reward-customer-loyalty-program-study/ (Accessed: 24 February 2019).

Oragui, D. (2018) 'The success of Starbucks App: a case study'. *The Manifest*, 12 June. Available at: https://medium.com/@the_manifest/the-success-of-starbucks-app-a-case-study-f0af6709004d (Accessed: 25 February 2019).

Palnitkar, S. (2017) 'Loyalty Rewards case study: new Starbucks Rewards program'. *Zinrelo*, 12 April. Available at: https://zinrelo.com/loyalty-rewards-case-study-new-starbucks-rewards-program.html (Accessed: 24 February 2019).

Panko, R. (2018) 'How customers use food delivery and restaurant loyalty apps'. *The Manifest*, 15 May. Available online at: https://themanifest.com/app-development/how-customers-use-food-delivery-and-restaurant-loyalty-apps (Accessed: 24 February 2019).

Petreycik, K. (2019) 'Starbucks to make some major changes to its rewards program'. *Foodandwine.com*, 5 March. Available online: https://www.foodandwine.com/starbucks-rewards-program-2019 (Accessed: 15 March 2019).

Pymnts (2019) 'Starbucks hits 16.3m mobile users, eyes expanded delivery'. *Pymnts.com*, 25 January. Available at: https://www.pymnts.com/earnings/2019/starbucks-mobile-order-delivery-loyalty/ (Accessed: 24 February 2019).

Samuely, A. (2016) 'Starbucks whips up mobile ordering with delivery options'. *Retail Dive*, n.d. Available at: https://www.retaildive.com/ex/mobilecommercedaily/starbucks-whips-up-mobile-ordering-with-future-delivery-options (Accessed: 24 February 2019).

Shah, K. (2016) 'Loyalty lessons from Starbucks' New York Times Rewards'. *Clutch*, 26 August. Available at: https://www.clutch.com/blog/loyalty/loyalty-lessons-from-starbucks-new-york-times-rewards/ (Accessed: 25 February 2019).

Snyder, B. (2016) 'Customers are furious with Starbucks' new rewards program'. *Fortune*, 23 February. Available online: http://fortune.com/2016/02/23/starbucks-rewards-program-changes/ (Accessed: 15 March 2019).

Starbucks (2018) 'Starbucks at the J.P. Morgan gaming lodging restaurant and leisure management access forum'. 9 March. Available via: https://investor.starbucks.com/events-and-presentations/current-and-past-events/event-details/2018/Starbucks-at-the-JP-Morgan-Gaming-Lodging-Restaurant-and-Leisure-Management-Access-Forum/default.aspx (Accessed: 24 February 2019).

Starbucks (2019) 'Starbucks reports Q1 fiscal 2019 results'. Press release, 24 January. Available at: https://investor.starbucks.com/press-releases/financial-releases/press-release-details/2019/Starbucks-Reports-Q1-Fiscal-2019-Results/default.aspx (Accessed: 24 February 2019).

WARC (2018) 'Starbucks launches its first virtual store in China'. Sourced from Starbucks and *Wall Street Journal*, 17 December. Available at: https://www.warc.com/newsandopinion/news/starbucks_launches_its_first_virtual_store_in_china/41463 (Accessed: 25 February 2019).

Wathen, J. (2017) 'These 3 companies earned $99 million from unused gift cards last year'. *The Motley Fool*, 15 July. Available at: https://www.fool.com/investing/2017/07/15/these-3-companies-earned-99-million-from-unused-gi.aspx (Accessed: 25 February 2019).

10

FUTURE CHALLENGES

Marco Ieva

Touchpoints and journeys

The rise of new technologies such as artificial intelligence (AI) has resulted in an overwhelming proliferation of touchpoints, that is, new points of contact between consumers and companies. Virtual assistants such as Alexa, Google Assistant, Siri and Cortana, computer-generated influencers such as Miquela Sousa, and chatbots that deliver customer service interactions are just some examples of new touchpoints that are increasingly present in the everyday life of consumers. Virtual assistants support consumers via voice recognition in accomplishing a growing variety of tasks at each stage of the journey towards purchase. Computer-generated influencers are digitally created agents that resemble humans and are controlled by specialized agencies. They publish posts and photos on their Instagram accounts to promote brands. Chatbots are currently the fastest growing among these new touchpoints: it is software that is designed to, via voice or text recognition, converse with humans, respond to consumer requests and perform specific actions. Examples include Walmart's Jetblack, discussed in Chapter 4.

These new touchpoints bring several challenges to brands. Let's think of a customer interacting through voice recognition with a virtual assistant to search for a new product. It is easy to understand that the search results retrieved through voice by a virtual assistant cannot be as extensive as they would be through a Web search: few brands will be mentioned by the virtual assistant and thus be in the initial consideration set of the consumer. Investment in such a touchpoint needs then to be tested for its effectiveness … getting 'near' is worth nothing. When it comes to search results, it's being first or being invisible. As we discussed in Chapter 4, early research has shown that for a brand, being in a customer's previous purchase or search set is essential to coming out top of the list. In other words, loyalty is crucial to visibility.

A second challenge is that marketing budgets are often fixed: money must therefore be reallocated across a wider variety of touchpoints, with different thresholds of visibility and effectiveness. Research is needed to measure the impact on the customer experience – and loyalty – of various combinations of touchpoints. Third-party touchpoints will increasingly represent an opportunity to avoid harming a brand. Some studies have shown that if companies struggle to improve the customer experience at a given touchpoint (the results of which can lead to customer dissatisfaction or service failure), it is better to outsource the management of that touchpoint. By letting a third party manage it, it will be branded differently and not specifically associated with the company brand (Kranzbühler, Kleijnen and Verlegh, in press). In other words, brands should focus on those touchpoints where they can excel, and give up trying to brand all possible touchpoints.

Another challenge for brands is to identify which new touchpoints are a fad and which might gain a wider consumer reach and thus be relevant. For instance, while new social networks and apps such as Telegram and new types of computer-generated influencers are attracting the attention of brands, there is rising criticism against fake social media interactions such as fake followers, likes and comments. This criticism is undermining the credibility of influences and social media marketing. Fake social media likes and interactions have now become a commodity. In some shopping outlets in Russia there are vending machines that target consumers and sell a hundred likes of their post on their favourite social network for less than a dollar. However, online touchpoints are still expected to gain much more investment and relevance. eMarketer has forecasted that in 2019, in the United States, the spending in digital advertising will be higher, for the first time, than the spending in traditional advertising (Ha, 2019).

Adding a new touchpoint does not necessarily mean introducing an innovative entrant to the market such as virtual assistants or computer-generated influencers. Some companies are introducing 'old' types of touchpoints that are nevertheless new to them. There is a long list of examples of online pure players who have started to add physical touchpoints to their offering. Amazon has not only launched its 4-star store, as we discussed in Chapter 1, but it has also created its own delivery fleet to increase control over product deliveries and to increase its recognition in the physical world (Kuehnl, Jozic and Homburg, in press). These changes are creating new customer journeys and it is understandably difficult for brands to design and exert control over their customers' journeys. Kuehnl, Jozic and Homburg (in press) have showed that companies should devote more effort into designing how consumers interact with multiple brand-owned touchpoints, rather than focusing on developing and improving a single touchpoint only. According to their study, focusing on combinations of touchpoints positively influences long-term customer loyalty.

Measuring and managing the customer experience

In this work we argue that loyalty management has morphed into CEM. Hence, academics and practitioners need to devise and test tools to measure customer experience across a variety of situations: in the store, online and across channels. Given the complexity of customer experience (demonstrated by Chapter 6), it is important to understand that there is no silver bullet when measuring it. The only metrics developed to date are self-reported measures collected through consumer surveys. Surveys always posit the challenging trade-off between the amount of information that can be collected and the reliability of that information. Long surveys can provide very important insights on every single aspect of the customer experience, but they can also leave the company with inaccurate, misleading or simply dishonest answers provided by consumers in a hurry or keen to get rid of the interviewer or there just to gain a monetary reward.

Consumer surveys should be complemented by other methods. What would be welcome is a systematic review and comparison of the available measures of customer experience. This would allow companies to understand how such measures are correlated among each other and which may be the most effective to use. Combining survey-based metrics with insights collected through qualitative methods, such as focus groups and in-depth interviews, or through more advanced quantitative methods, such as text mining on social media or emotional tracking, could also increase the robustness of the current metrics. Moreover, one should remember that adopting a customer experience perspective means accepting its subjective nature and, as such, its dependence on customers' attitudes, characteristics and memory. The work of Flacandji and Krey (in press) points to the importance of assessing a customer's memory of their experience instead of assessing the customer experience itself. They found that the likelihood that the customer would repeat a past experience largely depended on the memory associated with that experience (see also Kahneman, 2011). This again is an area of research very much in its infancy. We may have a great deal more to learn.

New data and technologies

The number of connected devices in use worldwide in 2018 was over 17 billion, with Internet-of-Things devices (which excludes smartphones, tablets, laptops and fixed-line phones) reaching seven billion (Lueth, 2018). If we were to calculate the amount of data that each device is both sending and receiving, we might grasp an idea of how much information, in different types and contexts, is produced every second. While loyalty cards are still an important source of information – in Italy they are the single major source of recurrent information on individual customers – companies can gather information from a growing variety of sources: 4G and 5G bandwidth, wireless points, mobile apps, advertising platforms, website analytics platforms, data management platforms, social networks, sensors, kiosks, Bluetooth connection, facial recognition tools embodied in the store, mobile location-based services, and so on. The key challenge for companies is selecting the relevant information depending on business goals and merging this huge amount of information to enrich each individual profile, with the final goal to drive customer loyalty through better informed and targeted marketing strategies and actions. This is a tough challenge for bricks-and-mortar companies that are undertaking digital transformation and are not ready for combining different information sources in order to achieve a unique view of the customer across all different touchpoints.

We showed in Chapter 8 that only a fraction of organizations declare themselves ready in this respect. The unique view of the customer represents, without any doubt, a valuable and necessary starting point to develop a loyalty strategy that is focused on who the customer is and how he interacts with the various touchpoints of the company. For this reason, it is very important that all the marketing tools employed to develop a relationship with each customer (e.g. loyalty programmes, promotions, CRM platforms, etc.) are designed with the key principles of linking customer information across touchpoints and being interconnected with all the other sources of information available within the company. Our experience shows, however, that companies often underestimate cultural and organizational obstacles that need to be removed if data is to be turned into actionable insight. Information-sharing across hierarchical levels and the incorporation of customer insight into strategic decision-making processes do not happen overnight and do not happen if the company does not change its processes. This is the reason why academics place so much emphasis on the cultural drivers of CEM. Our own research has consistently shown that companies that excel at loyalty management, be it loyalty programmes, CRM or even omnichannel, have successfully intervened to shape their organizational structure and values accordingly.

We think companies would do well to keep track of developments in blockchain and distributed ledger technology. It could theoretically be employed to increase the security and efficiency of points-management systems and reduce related costs, including those related to fraud. It might not be ripe yet, but it is an infrastructural innovation that will one day, maybe in a very different form from what we have now, be the basis of loyalty management systems, especially open ones that involve partners. The application of AI methods could also leverage customer information collected across different sources to improve the way companies communicate and recommend products and services to their customers. Beyond marketing automation, which is able to provide pre-created messages to specific audiences depending on certain rules, AI software can design, in real time, specific messages based on the available information.

The role of the marketer is also undergoing a significant change. This has become quite evident in the digital environment. Right now, most digital marketers tend to rely on Google for taking bidding decisions. Google algorithms are given the task of deciding which bids should be issued in search or display advertising (automated bidding) and which touchpoints should deserve higher investment thanks to data-driven attribution modelling. We could also imagine a (maybe distant) future where the marketer, both in the offline and online channels, is no longer in charge of designing strategies and touchpoints to achieve customer loyalty. His task will be only to decide which business goals are of primary importance and he will leave the design of the company strategy and touchpoints to the algorithms.

Ways to innovate loyalty programmes

In Chapter 5 we highlighted the most pressing issues loyalty programmes face that should be addressed by further academic research. In this section we will simply share some thoughts on their future. In a context where customers are triggered by a wide variety of stimuli across different channels, creating loyalty programmes that recognize and engage customers across offline, Web, mobile and social channels is indeed a challenge. To this aim, companies have the option of developing partnerships with other players that could provide reach and relevance to such programmes whilst at the same time guaranteeing a consistent customer journey and adequate data protection levels. In other words, the requirements for partnerships within loyalty programmes and coalitions, which historically have not always been thoroughly scrutinized and have often been on the basis of convenience and business opportunity, will need to be taken to a higher level of planning, measurement and monitoring.

As barriers to integrating diverse partners into loyalty ecosystems dissolve, brand consistency will become more and more crucial: do companies make sense together under the same 'roof'? It is a question that coalitions have been challenged with for decades, but it will become more and more pressing as loyalty ecosystems emerge. How connected they are may determine their success. We need to better understand how customers view such partnerships, what their rational, emotional and unconscious responses to consumer loyalty programmes based on this ecosystem model are. And such research needs to focus not only on their short-term reactions but on what can be built over a longer period too.

New threats to customer privacy

Marketers, academics and analysts might, quite rightly, think we are living in exciting times. The outstanding availability of data, information, technologies, algorithms and statistical tools has changed things and we are living in a very different world today to just two decades ago. But we are also experiencing a growing lack of privacy in our everyday lives. Privacy as an academic concept dates back to 1890 at least, when Brandeis and Warren formulated it as the right to be left alone. More recently, it has been defined as the right to control the access to the self (Altman, 1975), that is, the extent to which an individual can control who is accessing his personal information and how.

It is safe to assume that this personal control over personal information is in genuine danger. One only need think of the Cambridge Analytica scandal which broke in early 2018 when it was revealed that the political consulting firm had harvested the personal data of 87 million Facebook profiles without their consent and sold it to various political organizations who used it to influence major political events including Donald Trump's presidential campaign and the UK's EU referendum, both in 2016. While the vast amount of personal information made available by social media and mobile devices provides opportunities for criminal activities, even legal activities related to the selling and purchasing of data are somewhat alarming. A recent report in the *New York Times* found that over 70 companies receive anonymous, precise location data from mobile applications (for instance, local news and weather apps) that are permitted, by the users themselves, to track their location (Valentino-DeVries et al., 2018). It is reported that these companies are able to track up to 200 million mobile devices (this only in the United States).

The Cambridge Analytica–Facebook scandal has been deemed by some as a watershed moment in the public understanding of personal data. Quite apart from Facebook's stock price, it led to calls for tighter regulation of tech companies' use of data. Regulatory changes around consumer privacy had been already well under way in Europe. Initially proposed in January 2012 and adopted by the European Parliament in April 2016, the General Data Protection Regulation (GDPR) entered into force in EU member states on 25 May 2018. This regulation was designed to modernize data protection rules dating back to the 1990s and strengthen the protection of personal information of individuals. It requires companies to always ask the consumer, in an intelligible and easily accessible form, for their consent to process his or her data and executes heavy penalties to organizations that fail to comply with it. The net effects of GDPR, according to Davies (2018), has been that the use of third-party cookies has decreased and contextual targeting has increased due to issues around using third-party targeting data. Moreover, fines have been issued, for example in France where Google was fined for $50 million for failing to obtain explicit consent (Roberts, 2019). Facebook, too, was fined for sharing data with third parties during the Cambridge Analytica scandal.

What is evident is that consumer privacy is changing largely due to the impact of technology and law, with regulations and legislation frequently having to be updated in order to keep pace with rapid technological change. New trends in data privacy may impact upon loyalty management in at least three ways. First of all, one of the key benefits of loyalty programmes to companies is their capacity to collect information at an individual customer level. A customer who perceives this as a threat to his privacy may withdraw his consent to share information with that company and the latter loses potentially valuable insight. Data has value, it has tangible economic value, and the process of extracting and using it is defined by the Gartner Glossary as data monetization (Gartner, n.d.). In a cross-industry survey of companies conducted by McKinsey (Gottlieb and Rifai, 2017), the majority of respondents agreed that the primary goal of their data-and-analytics activities is to generate new revenue. They regarded data monetization as a valuable means of growth. Its capacity, however, depends on consumer willingness to share private information. Hence, the key driver remains the consumer.

Second, firms that regard data privacy as an authentic top priority will, according to Martin and Murphy (2017), experience positive performance, including higher customer loyalty. Leveraging data privacy, then, could be a key strength since it has the potential to achieve trust and loyalty from customers. With pressure from all sides to share personal data, consumers are increasingly relying on a brand's reputation for being a privacy advocate in deciding whether or not to share their data with them. For this reason, we think that a brand's 'privacy equity' should be developed and safeguarded.

Third, companies that collect customer information are all potentially at risk of a data breach. No company in the world is completely invulnerable to hackers stealing and releasing customers' personal information. It has been argued that data breaches should be considered as a type of service failure (Malhotra and Kubowicz Malhotra, 2011). A data breach can be devastating to a company's reputation and severely damaging to customer trust and loyalty. It is clear to us that companies must have in place the very best resources and software to prevent data breaches, as well as sound procedures to ensure the recovery of data and mitigation of harm caused to customer trust. There is a vast body of literature on the effects of service failures and service recovery: companies and academics should revisit it in the light of the increased probability of having to manage data breaches and related recovery policies going forward.

Some closing thoughts on customer loyalty

In 2017, Marc Benioff, the CEO of Salesforce.com, declared, 'Loyalty is dead' (Swinscoe, 2018). Such a stark declaration, made by the head of a company that makes profits on systems that allow the retention and development of customer relationships, might sound astonishing. In fact, he was referring to the idea of loyalty as a reward programme, as a tool, as an IT system. What we have tried to accomplish in this book is illustrate that customer loyalty is a long-term business objective that is very much alive and kicking. Tools and tactics – some of them dating back more than a century – may well be 'dead', but only if we ignore the endless opportunities to revive and enrich them with the new features at our disposal.

While new approaches have emerged in response to the changing customer journey, the final aim of marketers is, and has always been, fostering long-term customer loyalty. The context has changed. Consumers undertake different journeys, encounter dozens of touchpoints from different companies every day, are subscribed to many different loyalty programmes, newsletters, websites and social networks. Given this, one might be tempted to pronounce customer loyalty over, to say that consumers do not really develop feelings of loyalty towards brands, to say that younger new generations no longer trust brands and companies. However, if we think about our everyday life, we realize that the way we act and speak is shaped, at least partially, by loyalty: we have our favourite type of coffee every morning (sometimes the barista knows it without us even asking), we still tend to eat our favourite meal, we still develop, to different extents, loyalty towards our favourite series and actors, towards our partner, towards the company we work for. In other words, we need loyalty for a good, rich, enjoyable life. Even in the current complex environment, there is more room than ever for fostering and developing customer relationships based on nurturing their loyalty. We hope that with this book we have contributed something, however modest, to our readers' understanding of this fascinating subject. It's not the finished article, more work needs to be done, but what is clear to us is that loyalty management is here to stay.

References

Altman, I. (1975) *The Environment and Social Behavior: Privacy, Personal Space, Territory, and Crowding*. Monterey, CA: Brooks/Cole Publishing Company.

Brandeis, L. and Warren, S. (1890) 'The right to privacy'. *Harvard Law Review*, 4(5), pp. 193–220.

Davies, J. (2018) 'The impact of GDPR, in 5 charts'. *Digiday UK*, 24 August. Available online at: https://digiday.com/media/impact-gdpr-5-charts/ (Accessed: 18 March 2019).

Flacandji, M. and Krey, N. (in press) 'Remembering shopping experiences: the shopping experience memory scale'. *Journal of Business Research.*

Gartner (n.d.) 'IT Glossary – Data Monetization'. Available at https://www.gartner.com/it-glossary/data-monetization (Accessed: 18 March 2019).

Gottlieb, J. and Rifai, K. (2017) 'Fueling growth through data monetization'. *McKinsey*, December. Available online at: https://www.mckinsey.com/business-functions/mckinsey-analytics/our-insights/fueling-growth-through-data-monetization (Accessed: 18 March 2019).

Ha, A. (2019) 'eMarketer predicts digital ads will overtake traditional spending in 2019'. *Techcrunch*, 20 February. Available online at: https://techcrunch.com/2019/02/20/emarketer-digital-ad-forecast/ (Accessed: 16 March 2019).

Kahneman, D. (2011). *Thinking Fast and Slow*. New York: Farrar Straus Giroux.

Kranzbühler, A. M., Kleijnen, M. H. and Verlegh, P. W. (in press) 'Outsourcing the pain, keeping the pleasure: effects of outsourced touchpoints in the customer journey'. *Journal of the Academy of Marketing Science.*

Kuehnl, C., Jozic, D. and Homburg, C. (in press) 'Effective customer journey design: consumers' conception, measurement, and consequences'. *Journal of the Academy of Marketing Science.*

Lueth, K. L. (2018) 'State of the IoT 2018: number of IoT devices now at 7B – market accelerating'. *IoT Analytics*, 8 August. Available online at: https://iot-analytics.com/state-of-the-iot-update-q1-q2-2018-number-of-iot-devices-now-7b/ (Accessed: 16 March 2019).

Malhotra, A. and Kubowicz Malhotra, C. (2011) 'Evaluating customer information breaches as service failures: an event study approach'. *Journal of Service Research*, 14(1), pp. 44–59.

Martin, K. D. and Murphy, P. E. (2017) 'The role of data privacy in marketing'. *Journal of the Academy of Marketing Science*, 45(2), pp. 135–155.

Roberts, M. (2019) 'Impact of the GDPR after almost a year'. *Update Blog*, 3 March. Available online at: https://im4thupdates.blogspot.com/2019/03/impact-of.html (Accessed: 16 March 2019).

Swinscoe, A. (2018) 'Loyalty is dead, long live loyalty!' *Forbes*, 14 October. Available online at: https://www.forbes.com/sites/adrianswinscoe/2018/10/14/loyalty-is-dead-long-live-loyalty/ (Accessed: 16 March 2019).

Valentino-DeVries, J., Singer, N., Keller, M. H. and Krolik, A. (2018) 'Your apps know where you were last night, and they're not keeping it secret'. *New York Times*, 10 December. Available online at: https://www.nytimes.com/interactive/2018/12/10/business/location-data-privacy-apps.html (Accessed: 16 March 2019).

INDEX

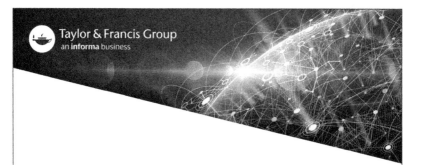